Making
CONNECTIONS
Skills and Strategies for Academic Reading

2

Second Edition

Jo McEntire | Jessica Williams

CAMBRIDGE
UNIVERSITY PRESS

University Printing House, Cambridge CB2 8BS, United Kingdom

One Liberty Plaza, 20th Floor, New York, NY 10006, USA

477 Williamstown Road, Port Melbourne, VIC 3207, Australia

314–321, 3rd Floor, Plot 3, Splendor Forum, Jasola District Centre, New Delhi – 110025, India

103 Penang Road, #05-06/07, Visioncrest Commercial, Singapore 238467

Cambridge University Press is part of the University of Cambridge.

It furthers the University's mission by disseminating knowledge in the pursuit of education, learning and research at the highest international levels of excellence.

www.cambridge.org
Information on this title: www.cambridge.org/9781108657822

First published 2008
Second edition 2013

20 19 18 17 16 15 14 13 12 11 10

Printed in Italy by Rotolito S.p.A.

A catalogue record for this publication is available from the British Library.

ISBN 978-1-108-65782-2 Student's Book with Integrated Digital Learning
ISBN 978-1-107-65062-6 Teacher's Manual

Cambridge University Press has no responsibility for the persistence or accuracy of URLs for external or third-party internet websites referred to in this publication, and does not guarantee that any content on such websites is, or will remain, accurate or appropriate.

TABLE OF CONTENTS

SCOPE AND SEQUENCE

Making CONNECTIONS

MAKING CONNECTIONS 2 is an intermediate academic reading and vocabulary skills book. It is intended for students who need to improve their strategic reading skills and build their academic vocabulary.

Understanding Vocabulary in Context

Good readers look for context clues to help them figure out the meanings of new and unfamiliar vocabulary. Context clues are the words, parts of words, and sentences that are near or around the unfamiliar word. They can help you guess what an unfamiliar word means. This is an important skill to develop because you don't have to keep stopping to look up unfamiliar words in the dictionary. You can then read more quickly, which makes it easier to remember and understand what you are reading.

Examples & Explanations

The **media** – organizations such as newspapers and television, which provide news and information – are changing quickly because of new technology.

Definition: Writers often define the meanings of important words immediately after writing them. They may introduce the definition by a dash (–), by the word *or*, or by placing the definition between commas right after the word. They may also use the verbs *be* or *mean*: *X is . . .* or *X means . . .*

Symbols can express important messages. For example, the heart often expresses the meaning of love.

Exemplification: Sometimes writers don't give exact definitions. Instead, they give examples that show the meaning of the word. Often, they will introduce the examples with signal words such as *for instance* or *such as.*

The teacher thought about **eliminating** question 4 of the final test. In the end, however, he decided to keep it.

Contrast: Sometimes you can figure out a word because the writer gives a contrast or an opposite meaning. Here the writer says that the teacher thought he might *eliminate* one of the test questions. The word *however* signals a contrast with the next phrase *he decided to keep it.* Therefore, *to eliminate* means the opposite of *to keep*; it means "to remove."

A big news story in May 2011 was the **devastation** that was caused by the Japanese earthquake and tsunami.

General knowledge: You can understand an unfamiliar word by knowing something about the general topic. In this case, you may know that the 2011 earthquake and tsunami caused terrible destruction, so *devastation* means "terrible destruction."

> Each unit begins with an in-depth study of key skills and strategies for reading academic texts, helping students to learn how and when to use them.

> Students learn strategies for approaching academic texts and skills for consciously applying the strategies.

The Language of Vocabulary in Context

Writers often use *context clue signals* – words or phrases that tell the reader that a context clue is coming. Here is a list of signals that can help you find clues in a reading and figure out the meaning of unfamiliar vocabulary.

CONTEXT CLUE SIGNALS		
DEFINITION	**EXEMPLIFICATION**	**CONTRAST**
X, or	*for example*	*but*
X is	*for instance*	*however*
X, that is,	*such as*	*in contrast*
X means		*on the other hand*
X is defined as		*unlike*
X is also called		*whereas*
X is also known as		

Strategies

These strategies will help you understand vocabulary in context while you read.

- When you read an unfamiliar word, don't stop. Continue to the end of the sentence that contains the word, and read the next sentence.
- If you don't understand the general meaning and feel you are getting lost, return to the unfamiliar word.
- Search for signal words and phrases that introduce context clues. There may be signals of definition, exemplification, or contrast. Use the clues to guess the meaning.

Skill Practice 1

As you read the following sentences, think about the type of context clue that can help you figure out the meaning of the word in **bold**. Circle the type of clue. If you can use more than one type of clue, circle all that apply. Then, if any context clues helped you, highlight them. The first one has been done for you.

1 When Marcus entered the classroom, he felt calm. However, as soon as he turned over the test paper, he began to feel **agitated**.
   a definition
   b exemplification
   ⓒ contrast
   d general knowledge

2 Journalists must be **versatile**. For instance, they must be good at writing, listening to people, speaking, working quickly, and doing research.
   a definition
   b exemplification
   c contrast
   d general knowledge

FEATURES

- Critical thinking skills
- Real-time practice of skills and strategies
- Study of the Academic Word List
- Audio files of all readings available online

(Before You Read)

Connecting to the Topic

Discuss the following questions with a partner.

1 How do you get your local news? Your national news? Your international news?
2 Do your parents get the news the same way you do? How about your grandparents and great-grandparents?
3 How did your parents, grandparents, or great-grandparents get the news when they were your age?

Previewing and Predicting

Good readers quickly look over a reading before they begin to read it in depth. This is known as *previewing*. Previewing helps you better understand a reading because it gives you a general idea of what to expect in the reading. One way to do this is to read the title and look at any illustrations and graphic material (pictures, photos, charts, tables, or graphs). Previewing will help you predict what a text will be about.

A **Read the title of Reading 1, and look at the photos on pages 7–8. What do you think this reading will be about? Choose the best way to complete the sentence below.**

I think this reading will be about _____
a the history of news.
b news on the Internet.
c famous people in the news.
d the role of the telegraph in the news.

B **Compare your answers with a partner's.**

While You Read

As you read, stop at the end of each sentence that contains words in bold. Then follow the instructions in the box in the margin.

6 ● UNIT 1

Predicting the content of a text is critical for reading college books, and students practice this skill extensively before beginning each reading.

Each unit contains 4 readings, providing students with multiple opportunities to practice applying the skills and strategies.

Students learn how to use the skills and strategies by applying them to each text while they read it.

READING 1

◄)) The News Media in the Past

1   The news is not new. Humans have always wanted to know what is happening in the world. Prior to newspapers and television, that is, before the news media of today, people wanted to hear information about events and other people. They wanted to hear local news as well as reports from places far away. A long time ago, information traveled by **word of mouth**. Villagers asked travelers questions about what was happening in other villages. Villagers also used to gather around and listen to men known as *town criers*. These men shouted out news from the town square. This human appetite for news has not changed; however, how people learn about the news has changed dramatically.

2   Before the invention of printing, people wrote newspapers by hand. For example, over 2,000 years ago, the Chinese government employed educated people to write the news. At about the same time, Julius Caesar, the leader of the powerful Roman Empire, put a daily newspaper on the walls of government buildings and public baths. Because most people were **illiterate** in both China and Rome, the governments also paid people to read the news aloud. This meant that ordinary people who could not read could also hear the news.

3   After the invention of the printing press in about 1440, it became possible to print the news. Printed news came out first in brief one-page reports. These early news reports were not very accurate. Writers often invented stories in order to interest readers. German newspapers, for instance, reported stories about the crimes of Count Dracula. Local people were terrified by

WHILE YOU READ **1**
Use context clues in the next two sentences to figure out the definition of *by word of mouth*. Highlight the clues.

WHILE YOU READ **2**
Use context clues in the next sentence to figure out the definition of *illiterate*. Highlight it.

There's always been an interest in learning the latest news.

"Reading is an interactive process, in which readers use their knowledge of language, text organization, and the world to understand what they read."

"Reading is goal-oriented and strategic; good academic readers know when to use the right reading skills."

Skill Review

In Skills and Strategies 1, you learned that writers often use signal words and phrases that introduce clues to the meaning of words that you may not know. These may be signals of definition, exemplification, contrast, or general knowledge. Recognizing these signals is an important reading skill.

A Look back in Reading 1, and find and highlight the words in the left-hand column of the chart below. Search for signal words and phrases that introduce context clues. Identify the type of context clue for each word, and put a check (✓) in the correct column below. The first one has been done for you.

WORD OR PHRASE	DEFINITION	EXEMPLIFI-CATION	CONTRAST	GENERAL KNOWLEDGE
prior to (adv) Par. 1	✓			
invention (n) Par. 3				
brief (adj) Par. 3				
spanned (v) Par. 5				
functioning (v) Par. 5				

B Use the type of context clues you chose in step A to figure out the meaning of each word in **bold** below. If you need help, go back and reread the clues in the sentences that contain the words. Then circle the correct meaning.

1 **prior to:**
a after
b while
c before
d at the same time

2 **invention:**
a a newly designed machine
b a printing press
c an old machine
d printed news

3 **brief:**
a long
b complicated
c short
d difficult

4 **spanned:**
a started
b connected
c reported
d worked

5 **functioning:**
a working properly
b not working properly
c costing a lot
d not costing a lot

10 ● UNIT 1

Students continually review the skills and strategies, helping them build up a valuable set of tools for reading academic texts.

Vocabulary Development

Definitions

Find the words in Reading 2 that complete the following definitions. When a verb completes the definition, use the base form, although the verb in the reading may not be in the base form.

1 To se
2 Whe
3 _____
4 Smal
5 The
6 Send (n) P
7 _____
8 A/Ar
9 Whe
10 _____

Word Fan

Word meanin you le you to

A The from Re are fro and lear

B Choo words fr followin verb ten Use the noun fo

1 The s static

2 Movi and l

18 ● UNIT 1

---

3 Young people today sometimes do not like the _____ of their community. They prefer new ideas and activities.

4 There has been a recent _____ in the number of people using a smart phone to send e-mail.

5 Many countries celebrate Independence Day. On this day, children often dress in the _____ colors of their country.

6 The media often have a strong _____ on public opinion.

7 Technology has made a/an _____ change in the way we communicate. Our great-grandparents would be very surprised by the many different ways that people today connect with one another.

8 I can _____ my banking information from anywhere in the world.

9 Today's cars can _____ quickly. Some can reach 100 kilometers (62 miles) per hour in just a few seconds.

10 The technological development that has had the most _____ for online media in the last 10 years has been the smart phone.

Academic Word List

The following are Academic Word List words from Readings 1 and 2 of this unit. Use these words to complete the sentences. (For more on the Academic Word List, see page 257.)

accessible (adj)	dramatically (adv)	global (adj)	negative (adj)	traditional (adj)
access to (n)	focuses on (v)	impact (n)	publish (v)	transmitted (v)

1 The report only contained _____ things; it didn't include all the good things.

2 The radio had an important _____ on the way people got their news.

3 The village in the mountains was not _____ by car.

4 The number of people who get their news online has increased _____ since 2000.

5 This is a/an _____ business. It has offices on five continents.

6 She wore the _____ dress of her country to the party.

7 The news often _____ wars and disasters instead of happy things.

8 Newspapers often _____ photos of celebrities without permission.

9 Information is _____ almost instantly by millions of miles of underground cables.

10 When I was traveling, I did not have _____ the Internet, so I bought newspapers to keep up with the news.

Students expand their vocabularies by studying key words from each reading and academic words from each unit.

THE APPROACH

The *Making Connections* series offers a skills-based approach to academic reading instruction. Throughout each book, students are introduced to a variety of academic reading and vocabulary-building skills, which they then apply to high-interest, thematically-related readings.

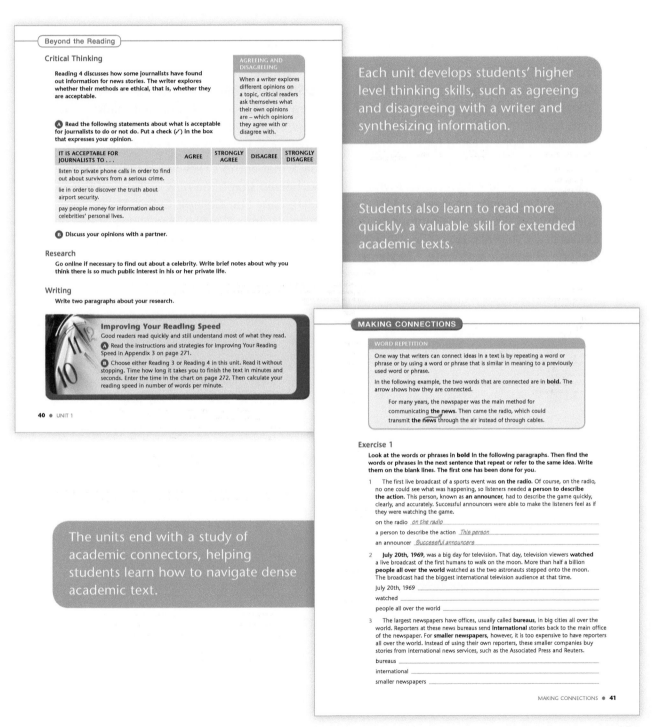

Beyond the Reading

Critical Thinking

Reading 4 discusses how some journalists have found out information for news stories. The writer explores whether their methods are ethical, that is, whether they are acceptable.

AGREEING AND DISAGREEING

When a writer explores different opinions on a topic, critical readers ask themselves what their own opinions are – which opinions they agree with or disagree with.

Ⓐ Read the following statements about what is acceptable for journalists to do or not do. Put a check (✓) in the box that expresses your opinion.

IT IS ACCEPTABLE FOR JOURNALISTS TO . . .	AGREE	STRONGLY AGREE	DISAGREE	STRONGLY DISAGREE
listen to private phone calls in order to find out about survivors from a serious crime.				
lie in order to discover the truth about airport security.				
pay people money for information about celebrities' personal lives.				

Ⓑ Discuss your opinions with a partner.

Research

Go online if necessary to find out about a celebrity. Write brief notes about why you think there is so much public interest in his or her private life.

Writing

Write two paragraphs about your research.

Improving Your Reading Speed

Good readers read quickly and still understand most of what they read.

Ⓐ Read the instructions and strategies for improving Your Reading Speed in Appendix 3 on page 271.

Ⓑ Choose either Reading 3 or Reading 4 in this unit. Read it without stopping. Time how long it takes you to finish the text in minutes and seconds. Enter the time in the chart on page 272. Then calculate your reading speed in number of words per minute.

40 ● UNIT 1

Each unit develops students' higher level thinking skills, such as agreeing and disagreeing with a writer and synthesizing information.

Students also learn to read more quickly, a valuable skill for extended academic texts.

The units end with a study of academic connectors, helping students learn how to navigate dense academic text.

MAKING CONNECTIONS

WORD REPETITION

One way that writers can connect ideas in a text is by repeating a word or phrase or by using a word or phrase that is similar in meaning to a previously used word or phrase.

In the following example, the two words that are connected are in **bold**. The arrow shows how they are connected.

For many years, the newspaper was the main method for communicating **the news**. Then came the radio, which could transmit **the news** through the air instead of through cables.

Exercise 1

Look at the words or phrases in **bold** in the following paragraphs. Then find the words or phrases in the next sentence that repeat or refer to the same idea. Write them on the blank lines. The first one has been done for you.

1 The first live broadcast of a sports event was **on the radio**. Of course, on the radio, no one could see what was happening, so listeners needed **a person to describe the action**. This person, known as **an announcer**, had to describe the game quickly, clearly, and accurately. Successful announcers were able to make the listeners feel as if they were watching the game.

on the radio *on the radio*

a person to describe the action *This person*

an announcer *Successful announcers*

2 **July 20th, 1969**, was a big day for television. That day, television viewers **watched** a live broadcast of the first humans to walk on the moon. More than half a billion **people all over the world** watched as the two astronauts stepped onto the moon. The broadcast had the biggest international television audience at that time.

July 20th, 1969 _____

watched _____

people all over the world _____

3 The largest newspapers have offices, usually called **bureaus**, in big cities all over the world. Reporters at these news bureaus send **international** stories back to the main office of the newspaper. For **smaller newspapers**, however, it is too expensive to have reporters all over the world. Instead of using their own reporters, these smaller companies buy stories from international news services, such as the Associated Press and Reuters.

bureaus _____

international _____

smaller newspapers _____

MAKING CONNECTIONS ● **41**

Acknowledgments

Many people have helped shape this second edition of *Making Connections 2*. We are grateful to all of the supportive and professional staff of Cambridge University Press for the opportunity to create this new edition. There are many others who did so much to make this project successful, including Page Designs International – Don Williams, the page designer; and especially Bernard Seal, our project manager, who has provided guidance and wisdom for all of the *Making Connections* books.

Thanks to Poyee Oster, photo researcher; Mandie Drucker, fact-checker and copyeditor; Patricia Egan, proofreader; and as always, Karen Shimoda, freelance development editor, whose dedication and attention to detail know few limits. And, as in the first edition, we want to acknowledge the contribution of Ken Pakenham, the author of the first *Making Connections* book created for the series.

Finally, textbooks are only as good as the feedback that authors receive on them. Many thanks to the following reviewers whose insights helped shape the new editions of the entire *Making Connections* series: Macarena Aguilar, Lone Star College-CyFair, Texas; Susan Boland, Tidewater Community College, Virginia; Inna Cannon, San Diego State University, California; Holly Cin, University of Houston, Texas; Stacie Miller, Community College of Baltimore County, Maryland.

1

THE NEWS MEDIA

SKILLS AND STRATEGIES

- Understanding Vocabulary in Context
- Finding Main Ideas

Understanding Vocabulary in Context

Good readers look for context clues to help them figure out the meanings of new and unfamiliar vocabulary. Context clues are the words, parts of words, and sentences that are near or around the unfamiliar word. They can help you guess what an unfamiliar word means. This is an important skill to develop because you don't have to keep stopping to look up unfamiliar words in the dictionary. You can then read more quickly, which makes it easier to remember and understand what you are reading.

Examples & Explanations

The **media** – organizations such as newspapers and television, which provide news and information – are changing quickly because of new technology.

Definition: Writers often define the meanings of important words immediately after writing them. They may introduce the definition by a dash (–), by the word *or*, or by placing the definition between commas right after the word. They may also use the verbs *be* or *mean*: *X is . . .* or *X means . . .*

Symbols can express important messages. For example, the heart often expresses the meaning of love.

Exemplification: Sometimes writers don't give exact definitions. Instead, they give examples that show the meaning of the word. Often, they will introduce the examples with signal words such as *for instance* or *such as*.

The teacher thought about **eliminating** question 4 of the final test. In the end, however, he decided to keep it.

Contrast: Sometimes you can figure out a word because the writer gives a contrast or an opposite meaning. Here the writer says that the teacher thought he might *eliminate* one of the test questions. The word *however* signals a contrast with the next phrase *he decided to keep it*. Therefore, *to eliminate* means the opposite of *to keep*; it means "to remove."

A big news story in March 2011 was the **devastation** that was caused by the Japanese earthquake and tsunami.

General knowledge: You can understand an unfamiliar word by knowing something about the general topic. In this case, you may know that the 2011 earthquake and tsunami caused terrible destruction, so *devastation* means "terrible destruction."

The Language of Vocabulary in Context

Writers often use *context clue signals* – words or phrases that tell the reader that a context clue is coming. Here is a list of signals that can help you find clues in a reading and figure out the meaning of unfamiliar vocabulary.

CONTEXT CLUE SIGNALS		
DEFINITION	**EXEMPLIFICATION**	**CONTRAST**
X, or	for example	but
X is	for instance	however
X, that is,	such as	in contrast
X means		on the other hand
X is defined as		unlike
X is also called		whereas
X is also known as		

Strategies

These strategies will help you understand vocabulary in context while you read.

- When you read an unfamiliar word, don't stop. Continue to the end of the sentence that contains the word, and read the next sentence.
- If you don't understand the general meaning and feel you are getting lost, return to the unfamiliar word.
- Search for signal words and phrases that introduce context clues. There may be signals of definition, exemplification, or contrast. Use the clues to guess the meaning.

Skill Practice 1

As you read the following sentences, think about the type of context clue that can help you figure out the meaning of the word in bold. Circle the type of clue. If you can use more than one type of clue, circle all that apply. Then, if any context clues helped you, highlight them. The first one has been done for you.

1 When Marcus entered the classroom, he felt calm. However, as soon as he turned over the test paper, he began to feel **agitated**.
   a definition   c contrast
   b exemplification   d general knowledge

2 Journalists must be **versatile**. For instance, they must be good at writing, listening to people, speaking, working quickly, and doing research.
   a definition   c contrast
   b exemplification   d general knowledge

3 When James worked in the office, his job was **sedentary**. In contrast, when he became a reporter, he was almost always away from his desk.

a definition

b exemplification

c contrast

d general knowledge

4 Most people prefer **portable** music players, such as the iPod.

a definition

b exemplification

c contrast

d general knowledge

5 The police **estimated** that over 10,000 people came to hear the speaker. They weren't exactly sure of the number because there were too many people to count.

a definition

b exemplification

c contrast

d general knowledge

6 The national report said that most of the **illiterate** citizens, those who cannot read or write, live outside of the main cities.

a definition

b exemplification

c contrast

d general knowledge

Skill Practice 2

Read the sentences in Skill Practice 1 again. Using the type of context clues you chose for each sentence, figure out the meaning of each word in bold. Circle the correct meaning. The first one has been done for you.

1 When Marcus entered the classroom, he felt calm. However, as soon as he turned over the test paper, he began to feel **agitated**.

(a) very nervous

b angry

c peaceful

d confused

2 Journalists must be **versatile**. For instance, they must be good at writing, listening to people, speaking, working quickly, and doing research.

a able to do one thing

b able to do lots of different things

c able to communicate well

d better at one skill than another

3 When James worked in the office, his job was **sedentary**. In contrast, when he became a reporter, he was almost always away from his desk.

a well paid

b moving around a lot

c sitting a lot

d exciting

4 Most people prefer **portable** music players, such as the iPod.

a advanced

b easy to take anywhere

c inexpensive

d not difficult to use

5 The police **estimated** that over 10,000 people came to hear the speaker. They weren't exactly sure of the number because there were too many people to count.

a counted very exactly

b didn't know

c made a careful guess

d hoped

6 The national report said that most of the **illiterate** citizens, those who cannot read or write, live outside of the main cities.

  a unable to read or write   c uneducated
  b poor   d not very good in school

Skill Practice 3

The following sentences contain words in bold that you may not know. Look for context clues and use strategies to figure out the meaning of these words. Write the meanings on the blank lines. The first one has been done for you.

1 From 1930 to 1945, the number of immigrants coming to the United States **declined**. During this time, it was more difficult to get a job, and once World War II started, it was more difficult to travel. However, as soon as the war ended, immigration increased again.

   became smaller _____

2 Many people believe that energy from the sun and wind – **alternative** sources of energy – are better choices than energy from oil and gas.

   _____

3 There have been many **informative** news stories recently about why our world is getting warmer and what people can do to stop it. These stories have made people think about how to use less energy.

   _____

4 As newspapers became cheaper, more **consumers** began to buy them. And as more people began to buy and read them, newspapers became even cheaper.

   _____

5 The newspaper decided not to print the picture of the plane crash. In the picture, you could see passengers who were dead and badly hurt. They decided the pictures were too **horrifying**.

   _____

6 The chocolates were so delicious that she could not **resist** them. She ate so many pieces that she began to feel sick.

   _____

7 There were many **positive** things about the building project, but there were also many parts of it that the manager did not like.

   _____

Connecting to the Topic

Discuss the following questions with a partner.

1 How do you get your local news? Your national news? Your international news?

2 Do your parents get the news the same way you do? How about your grandparents and great-grandparents?

3 How did your parents, grandparents, or great-grandparents get the news when they were your age?

Previewing and Predicting

Good readers quickly look over a reading before they begin to read it in depth. This is known as *previewing*. Previewing helps you better understand a reading because it gives you a general idea of what to expect in the reading. One way to do this is to read the title and look at any illustrations and graphic material (pictures, photos, charts, tables, or graphs). Previewing will help you predict what a text will be about.

A **Read the title of Reading 1, and look at the photos on pages 7–8. What do you think this reading will be about? Choose the best way to complete the sentence below.**

I think this reading will be about _____

a the history of news.
b news on the Internet.
c famous people in the news.
d the role of the telegraph in the news.

B **Compare your answers with a partner's.**

While You Read

As you read, stop at the end of each sentence that contains words in bold. Then follow the instructions in the box in the margin.

The News Media in the Past

1   The news is not new. Humans have always wanted to know what is happening in the world. Prior to newspapers and television, that is, before the news media of today, people wanted to hear information about events and other people. They wanted to hear local news as well as reports from places far away. A long time ago, information traveled **by word of mouth**. Villagers asked travelers questions about what was happening in other villages. Villagers also used to gather around and listen to men known as *town criers*. These men shouted out news from the town square. This human appetite for news has not changed; however, how people learn about the news has changed dramatically.

WHILE YOU READ 1

Use context clues in the next two sentences to figure out the definition of *by word of mouth*. Highlight the clues.

2   Before the invention of printing, people wrote newspapers by hand. For example, over 2,000 years ago, the Chinese government employed educated people to write the news. At about the same time, Julius Caesar, the leader of the powerful Roman Empire, put a daily newspaper on the walls of government buildings and public baths. Because most people were **illiterate** in both China and Rome, the governments also paid people to read the news aloud. This meant that ordinary people who could not read could also hear the news.

WHILE YOU READ 2

Use context clues in the next sentence to figure out the definition of *illiterate*. Highlight it.

3   After the invention of the printing press in about 1440, it became possible to print the news. Printed news came out first in brief one-page reports. These early news reports were not very accurate. Writers often invented stories in order to interest readers. German newspapers, for instance, reported stories about the crimes of Count Dracula. Local people were terrified by

There's always been an interest in learning the latest news.

these reports, and often did not know that most of the information was false. The first real newspapers began to appear in England and France in the early 1600s. In 1690, the first newspaper in the United States started in Boston, and by 1752, Canada had its first newspaper. More newspapers appeared in North America in the early 1800s. However, few people read them because most people could not afford to buy a newspaper. The average cost of a newspaper in the United States was six cents, which was a lot of money for most people in those days. In addition, most people at that time were still illiterate.

4   By the 1840s, however, life in Europe and North America was changing very quickly, and newspapers were changing, too. New industries needed more educated workers, so there were many more schools. As a result, more people learned to read. Moreover, new technology reduced the price of paper and printing, so newspapers were much cheaper. Finally, in the United States, large numbers of immigrants were arriving. They were eager to find out about their new land and to learn English, and newspapers helped them do both. The *New York Sun*, for example, cost only one cent. It focused on entertaining stories about both famous and ordinary people. The *New York Sun* soon became popular with the public, and more and more people began to read it – especially immigrants, who learned a lot of English by reading newspapers like the *Sun*.

5   The development of the telegraph was the next important change in how news traveled. By the 1850s, 23,000 miles of telegraph wires spanned the United States from one coast to another. This meant that local and national news could travel almost instantly from city to city. Then, in the 1860s, engineers built telegraph **cables,** or large wires, under the oceans. Newspapers could report international news very quickly. However, early telegraph cables often did not work well. When Abraham Lincoln, president of the United States, was assassinated on April 16, 1865, the Atlantic Ocean cable was not working. It took 12 days for news of his death to get to England by ship. However, by the 1880s, international telegraph was functioning well. A good example of this happened in August 1883, when a volcano on the Indonesian island of Krakatoa erupted. A telegraph operator on the island sent out news of this natural disaster. Four hours later, a U.S. newspaper printed the news story about Krakatoa. This was the first time news from a different country was published the same day it happened.

With the development of the telegraph, news moved faster.

WHILE YOU READ ❸

Use context clues to figure out the definition of *cables*. Highlight it.

Main Idea Check

The main idea of a reading is what the whole reading is about.

Which sentence gives the main idea of Reading 1?

a Throughout history, humans have needed to understand the news.
b The telegraph was an invention that changed how people got the news.
c Methods for communicating the news are much better today than in the past.
d Technology has changed the way news is communicated.

A Closer Look

Look back at Reading 1 to answer the following questions.

1 There is more interest in the news today than there was in the past. **True or False?**

2 Why does the writer include the example about Julius Caesar in paragraph 2?
   a It shows that the news was more important in the past than today.
   b It shows that Julius Caesar was an intelligent leader.
   c It shows that news wasn't important to the Roman people.
   d It gives information about an early use of written news.

3 According to paragraph 3, why didn't most people buy newspapers in the early 1800s?
   a Most people were immigrants and couldn't speak English.
   b Readers at that time did not want to read stories about love and crime.
   c Newspapers were too expensive for most people.
   d There were only a few newspapers at that time.

4 According to paragraph 4, why did newspapers become more popular in the United States in the 1840s? Circle all that apply.
   a They became cheaper.
   b They had good stories that people enjoyed reading.
   c They helped immigrants to learn English.
   d More people could read.
   e They gave immigrants news about their home countries.

5 The news of the eruption of Krakatoa appeared in U.S. newspapers the day after it happened. **True or False?**

6 Look through the reading for the dates listed below. Then match each date with the event that happened at that time.

   1690   Krakatoa erupted.
   1752   Telegraph cables under the oceans were introduced.
   1840s   The first U.S. newspaper started in Boston.
   1860s   Newspapers became cheaper and more popular.
   1883   The first newspaper in Canada started.

Skill Review

In Skills and Strategies 1, you learned that writers often use signal words and phrases that introduce clues to the meaning of words that you may not know. These may be signals of definition, exemplification, contrast, or general knowledge. Recognizing these signals is an important reading skill.

A Look back in Reading 1, and find and highlight the words in the left-hand column of the chart below. Search for signal words and phrases that introduce context clues. Identify the type of context clue for each word, and put a check (✓) in the correct column below. The first one has been done for you.

WORD OR PHRASE	DEFINITION	EXEMPLIFI-CATION	CONTRAST	GENERAL KNOWLEDGE
prior to (*adv*) Par. 1	✓			
invention (*n*) Par. 3				
brief (*adj*) Par. 3				
spanned (*v*) Par. 5				
functioning (*v*) Par. 5				

B Use the type of context clues you chose in step **A** to figure out the meaning of each word in **bold** below. If you need help, go back and reread the clues in or around the sentences that contain the words. Then circle the correct meaning of the words.

1 **prior to:**
   a after
   b while
   c before
   d at the same time

2 **invention:**
   a a newly designed machine
   b a printing press
   c an old machine
   d printed news

3 **brief:**
   a long
   b complicated
   c short
   d difficult

4 **spanned:**
   a started
   b connected
   c reported
   d worked

5 **functioning:**
   a working properly
   b not working properly
   c costing a lot
   d not costing a lot

Definitions

Find the words in Reading 1 that complete the following definitions. When a verb completes the definition, use the base form, although the verb in the reading may not be in the base form.

1 A/An _____ person or thing is from a place near to where you live. (adj) Par. 1

2 People who live in a small town are called _____. (n pl) Par. 1

3 To get together in a large group in one place is to _____. (v) Par. 1

4 Acts that are against the law are _____. (n pl) Par. 3

5 If you are _____, you are really frightened. (adj) Par. 3

6 When you have enough money to buy something, you can _____ it. (v) Par. 3

7 People who come to live in a new country are _____. (n) Par. 4

8 If a person really wants to do something, he or she is _____ to do it. (adj) Par. 4

9 Thin pieces of metal that carry electricity or other signals are called _____. (n pl) Par. 5

10 A/An _____ is a mountain that throws fire and hot rocks from a hole in its top. (n) Par. 5

Words in Context

Complete the sentences with words or phrases from Reading 1 in the box below.

appetite	average	erupt	natural disasters
assassinated	dramatically	focused on	publish

1 The news story _____ the differences between the two international leaders.

2 It is important to prepare for _____. It is possible that one will happen near us at some time in the future.

3 The government did not want the newspapers to _____ the story. They were worried that people would be unhappy with the government after reading it.

4 As people in the Philippines watched smoke coming from the volcano, they knew it was about to _____.

5 The _____ cost of a cup of coffee has not increased very much over the past two years.

6 When President Kennedy was _____ in 1963, news of his death shocked the world.

7 People have always enjoyed stories about the rich and famous, but our _____ for them appears to be growing.

8 The total number of smokers in Canada has decreased _____ since the 1990s.

Critical Thinking

In Reading 1, the writer discusses the purposes of the news.

EXPLORING OPINIONS

Critical readers form their own opinions about important topics in a text.

A Which purposes of the news do you think are the most important? Fill out the chart below. Rank each purpose from *1–4*, with *1* being the most important.

PURPOSE OF THE NEWS	RANK
Inform people about what is happening in the world.	
Warn people that an important event is going to happen, for example a bad storm.	
Entertain people.	
Help people form opinions about the world and world events.	

B Compare your chart with your classmates' charts. Then discuss which of the following organizations you think should deliver the news, and how the news might be different for each of these organizations.

- The government
- A company that wants to make money
- A company that does not make any money
- A school or university

Research

Think of a major event that happened in your country's history. For example, it could be a natural disaster, a serious crime, or a war. Go online to research the event, and take brief notes. Find answers to the following questions.

- When and where did it happen?
- Who was involved in the event?
- How did people first hear about the event – in the newspapers, on the radio, or on television?

Writing

Write two paragraphs. The first paragraph will describe the event you chose to research. The second paragraph will describe how people found out about the event.

Connecting to the Topic

Discuss the following questions with a partner.

1 In the past, the public had to wait for a news report to find out what was happening in the world. What do you do when you need to find out about events that have just happened in the last few hours?

2 Do you think that there are any differences in how the news is reported in newspapers, on television, or on the Internet? Explain your answer?

Prevewing and Predicting

You will understand a text more easily if you get an idea of its content before you start reading. One way to do this is to read the first sentence of each paragraph and think of a question it might answer. Reading the first sentence can give you ideas about what the writer will develop and explain in that paragraph.

A **Read the first sentence of each paragraph in Reading 2, and think of a question you expect the paragraph to answer. Then choose the question below that is most like your question. Write the number of the paragraph (1–5) next to that question. The first paragraph has been done for you.**

PARAGRAPH	QUESTION
	How did early television change the news?
	What changes made the radio more convenient?
1	What was the next development in the news after newspapers?
	What are the newest changes in the media?
	How has television news changed the world?

B **Compare your answers with a partner's. You and your partner can also think about other questions each paragraph might answer.**

While You Read

As you read, stop at the end of each sentence that contains words in bold. Then follow the instructions in the box in the margins.

🔊 The History of Electronic Media

1   For many years, the newspaper was the main method for communicating news. Then came the radio, which could transmit the news through the air instead of through cables. The radio quickly became very popular. It had a huge impact on the news because people could now listen to **live events**. They could listen to the events at the same time as they were happening, although they were happening far away. In 1924, listeners in England heard the first live international sports event – a cricket match. It came to them from halfway around the world – from Sydney, Australia. Later, during World War II, families everywhere listened to the news from Europe. They could hear the sounds of war. Radio news made events seem closer and more real.

2   New technology also made the radio more convenient. The first radios were bulky and expensive, and they used electricity. In the 1950s, there

was a new kind of radio – the transistor radio. Transistor radios were small and cheap. They also used batteries, so they were portable. These changes made the radio news **accessible** to a larger number of listeners. Even poor people or people who lived far away from any city could now easily listen to a radio. Today, transistor radios are still the most popular form of communication in the world, especially in poorer countries. In fact, there are almost seven billion of them in use today.

3   Starting in the 1950s, television brought events into people's homes. For the first time, people could see the news as well as hear it. Because

> **WHILE YOU READ ❶**
> Read ahead and find a phrase in this paragraph that defines the adjective *live*. Highlight the phrase.

A family gathers around the radio to listen to an early live news broadcast.

> **WHILE YOU READ ❷**
> Read ahead and find a clue that signals the definition of *accessible*. Highlight the clue.

it is so real, television can have a very significant influence on people's ideas and opinions. It has often provided news and information that have led to far-reaching changes in society – changes that have affected people's lives around the world. For example, the Vietnam War was the first war that people could watch on television. Every night on the news, families watched American soldiers and Vietnamese citizens die. As a result, public opinion turned against the war. Finally, this negative news on television every night forced politicians to end the war.

4 Television news has become an even more powerful influence around the world since it began broadcasting news **around the clock**. In 1980, the television network CNN started to broadcast global news 24 hours a day, 7 days a week. In 1991, its impact increased when it brought the Gulf War live from Baghdad into people's homes. Live, around-the-clock news is not limited to CNN anymore; there are many other news networks all over the world. For example, in 1996, Al Jazeera television began to bring news and discussion of world events to the Arabic-speaking world. It frequently shows stories that are not available on Western television, and its news broadcasts have had a strong impact on people's views, or opinions, especially in the Middle East. For example, its non-stop reporting of the 2011 revolutions in Tunisia and Egypt had a powerful influence on events in those countries. People who were trying to change the government in these countries watched Al Jazeera to find out where people were gathering on the streets in order to call for political change.

5 The pace of change in the media is accelerating. Television is still important, but today traditional newspapers and television are not the sole way to get the news. Digital media have provided other ways to find news. Much of today's news is digital, and it is accessible and convenient. The **digital media** began with the Internet on computers, but it is now available from other delivery systems, such as smart phones, tablets, and MP3 players. People can choose the time, the place, and the delivery system. The media, and how it is delivered, will continue to change as technology changes.

WHILE YOU READ ③

Read ahead and find a phrase in the next sentence that defines *around the clock*. Highlight the phrase.

WHILE YOU READ ④

Read ahead to find examples of where to get *digital media*. Highlight the examples.

Digital media lets people get the news at any time.

Main Idea Check

> The main idea of a reading is what the whole reading is about.

Which sentence gives the main idea of Reading 2?

a Television and radio are not as important today as they were in the past.
b The news is now available 24 hours a day from all over the world.
c The invention of television and radio led to important changes in the news.
ⓓ Changes in technology have led to changes in the way the news is communicated.

A Closer Look

Look back at Reading 2 to answer the following questions.

1 According to paragraph 1, what was new and different about radio news? Circle all that apply.

ⓐ It reported events as they happened.
b It was cheaper than newspapers.
ⓒ It quickly reported news from far away.
ⓓ It broadcast sounds of live events.
e It was more popular than other kinds of news.

2 Transistor radios were more convenient than older radios. **True or False?**

3 Why does the writer use the example of the Vietnam War in paragraph 3?

a It shows that television was important for politicians.
b It shows that people could see the news on television.
ⓒ It shows that the television news had a powerful influence on people's opinions.
d It shows that war is terrible.

4 According to paragraph 4, how did CNN change television news?

a It was the beginning of digital news media.
ⓑ It provided news 24 hours a day.
c It broadcast news in Arabic for the first time.
d It turned people against the Gulf War.

5 Television networks, such as CNN and Al Jazeera, usually broadcast the same stories. **True or False?**

6 Paragraph 5 talks about six delivery systems for getting the news. It calls two of them "traditional" and four of them "digital." Complete the chart by putting the six types of news delivery systems into the correct columns.

TRADITIONAL	DIGITAL
~~TRITALK~~ *News Papers*	*internet on computer* ① *smart Phone* ② *tablets* ③ *MP3 Players.* ④

Skill Review

> In Skills and Strategies 1, you learned that writers often provide clues to the meaning of words that you may not know. Finding these clues is an important reading skill.

A The following words are from Reading 2. Find the words in the reading. Look for clues to help you figure out the meanings. Then match each word with its definition by writing the correct letter on the blank line.

___ 1 bulky (*adj*) Par. 2

___ 2 far-reaching (*adj*) Par. 3

___ 3 forced (*v*) Par. 3

___ 4 views (*n*) Par. 4

___ 5 revolution (*n*) Par. 4

___ 6 sole (*adj*) Par. 5

a opinions or ways of looking at something

b large, difficult to carry

c the only

d made someone do something they did not want to do

e a sudden and great change, especially the violent change of a system of government

f having a big influence over a wide area

B Choose the correct word from the list above to complete the following sentences.

1 For several years, CNN was the ____*sole*____ television news network broadcasting around the clock. However, other networks like Al Jazeera now broadcast 24/7.

2 The Internet has had _____effects on how people get the news. Through the Internet, people can get their news whenever they want.

3 The first personal computers were very ___*bulky*___. Today, however, laptops are light and easy to carry.

4 The war ___*forced*___ many people to leave their country

5 People changed their ___*views*___ on women getting jobs after World War I. They realized that women were needed in the workplace.

6 The French ___*revolution*___ began in 1789 when the French people decided they did not want the king to control the country.

Definitions

Find the words in Reading 2 that complete the following definitions. When a verb completes the definition, use the base form, although the verb in the reading may not be in the base form.

1 To send something electronically is to _____ it. (v) Par. 1

2 When something is seen or heard as it is happening, it is _____. (adj) Par. 1

3 _____ means easy to use and helpful. (adj) Par. 2

4 Small objects that produce power are called _____. (n pl) Par. 2

5 The word _____ describes things that are bad or without hope. (adj) Par. 3

6 Sending out pictures and sound on the radio or television is called _____. (n) Par. 4

7 _____ means relating to the whole world. (adj) Par. 4

8 A/An _____ is something that causes a strong effect or change. (n) Par. 4

9 When something is _____, it is able to be used. (adj) Par. 4

10 _____ is the speed at which something happens. (n) Par. 5

Word Families

Word families are different *parts of speech*, or word forms, that have similar meanings. Some parts of speech are *verbs*, *nouns*, *adjectives*, and *adverbs*. When you learn a word, learn the other words in its word family, too. This will help you to increase your vocabulary.

A **The words in bold in the chart are from Reading 2. The words next to them are from the same word family. Study and learn these words.**

NOUN	VERB	ADJECTIVE
acceleration	**accelerate**	—
access	access	**accessible**
influence	influence	influential
significance	—	**significant**
tradition	—	**traditional**

B **Choose the correct form of the words from the chart to complete the following sentences. Use the correct verb tenses and subject-verb agreement. Use the correct singular and plural noun forms.**

1 The school has good public _____ because it is near buses and subway stations. It's easy for students to get there.

2 Movie stars are very _____. Many young people copy their fashions and behavior.

3 Young people today sometimes do not like the _____ of their community. They prefer new ideas and activities.

4 There has been a recent _____ in the number of people using a smart phone to send e-mail.

5 Many countries celebrate Independence Day. On this day, children often dress in the _____ colors of their country.

6 The media often have a strong _____ on public opinion.

7 Technology has made a/an _____ change in the way we communicate. Our great-grandparents would be very surprised by the many different ways that people today connect with one another.

8 I can _____ my banking information from anywhere in the world.

9 Today's cars can _____ quickly. Some can reach 100 kilometers (62 miles) per hour in just a few seconds.

10 The technological development that has had the most _____ for online media in the last 10 years has been the smart phone.

Academic Word List

The following are Academic Word List words from Readings 1 and 2 of this unit. Use these words to complete the sentences. (For more on the Academic Word List, see page 257.)

accessible (adj)	dramatically (adv)	global (adj)	negative (adj)	traditional (adj)
access to (n)	focuses on (v)	impact (n)	publish (v)	transmitted (v)

1 The report only contained _____ things; it didn't include all the good things.

2 The radio had an important _____ on the way people got their news.

3 The village in the mountains was not _____ by car.

4 The number of people who get their news online has increased _____ since 2000.

5 This is a/an _____ business. It has offices on five continents.

6 She wore the _____ dress of her country to the party.

7 The news often _____ wars and disasters instead of happy things

8 Newspapers often _____ photos of celebrities without permission.

9 Information is _____ almost instantly by millions of miles of underground cables.

10 When I was traveling, I did not have _____ the Internet, so I bought newspapers to keep up with the news.

Critical Thinking

Reading 2 raises several important points that the writer
does not fully explain. For example, paragraph 2 claims that
transistor radios are still popular today, especially in poorer
countries. The writer does not explain why this is true.

A Discuss the following questions with a partner.

1 Why do you think people in poorer countries still use radios
today in order to get their news?

2 There are many twenty-four-hour news networks around the world today. Why do you
think these networks are so popular?

3 The writer states that Al Jazeera television reports news that is often not available on
western networks. Why do you think western television shows different news stories
than Al Jazeera?

4 The final paragraph suggests that the media will continue to change. In what ways do
you think it will change in the future?

B Share your answers with your class.

Research

Read a front-page story in a newspaper and then find the same story on a news
website, such as CNN.com. Take notes about the details of the story. Then find
answers to the following questions.

● Which way did you prefer to get your news – from the newspaper or the website?

● Why did you prefer this way?

Writing

Write two paragraphs. The first paragraph will describe the story. The second
paragraph will describe how you got the information and which way you preferred
to read about this story. Make sure you explain your reasons.

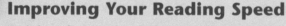

Improving Your Reading Speed

Good readers read quickly and still understand most of what they read.

A Read the instructions and strategies for Improving Your Reading
Speed in Appendix 3 on page 271.

B Choose either Reading 1 or Reading 2 in this unit. Read it without
stopping. Time how long it takes you to finish the text in minutes and
seconds. Enter the time in the chart on page 272. Then calculate your
reading speed in number of words per minute.

Finding Main Ideas

Finding main ideas is a very important reading skill. In academic courses, the instructor will often ask you to say what a reading is about. In other words, the instructor wants you to find and explain the main ideas of the reading. Each paragraph has a main idea. Sometimes the main idea is expressed in one sentence, which is often at the beginning of the paragraph. Sometimes, the main idea is at the end of the paragraph. Sometimes, however, the main idea is not clearly stated in a single sentence, so the reader must figure out the main idea by reading the whole paragraph.

Examples & Explanations

There are many different kinds of news stories; however, they generally share several characteristics. As reporters look for news stories, they look for recent events that are interesting or are important to their readers. They also usually report more local events than events in countries that are far away. Personal stories are popular because readers can relate them to their own lives. This explains the number of stories about famous people. Another important characteristic of a news story is that it is usually negative. Therefore, stories about natural or human disasters appear more frequently than stories about human successes. These characteristics can be found in most newspaper stories.

A main idea has two parts: a topic and a claim. Therefore, good readers ask two questions to find the main idea as they read a paragraph.

- What is the *topic*? (What is the general subject of the paragraph?)
- What *claim* does the writer make about the topic? (What does the writer want to say to the reader about the general subject?)

In this paragraph, the topic is *news stories*.

The writer claims that they *generally share several characteristics*.

Therefore, the main idea of this paragraph is:
News stories generally share several characteristics

Strategies

These strategies will help you find the main idea in a reading.

- As you read, keep asking yourself: *What is the topic? What claims does the writer make about the topic?*
- Pay special attention to the first sentence, which often contains both the topic and the claim.
- Also pay attention to the last sentence of the paragraph. Writers often restate the main idea, especially in longer paragraphs.

Skill Practice 1

Use the strategies you just read about to identify the topic of the following paragraphs. Read the four possible choices. Circle the choice you think best describes the topic. Discuss your answers with a partner.

1   The first modern newspapers began in Europe in the seventeenth century. The *French Gazette*, which appeared in 1631, and the *London Gazette*, which was first published in 1665, are examples of early newspapers. These early newspapers focused more on international news than local news. French newspapers often wrote about England while English newspapers often complained about the French. Newspapers focused on other countries because they were not allowed to write about national or local events. The governments did not want the public to know what was happening in their own country.

Topic:

a Early European newspapers
b International news
c The *French Gazette*
d Seventeenth-century governments

2   Twitter is an online service that allows people to send short messages to large numbers of people very quickly. These messages are known as *tweets*. Twitter began as a way to help a small group of people quickly share ideas. However, it soon became an important way for people to share news. People share news about sports, for example. When Japan scored a goal in the 2010 soccer World Cup, viewers wrote 2,940 tweets per second within 30 seconds after the goal. It is also used for serious news. For example, in 2009, people in Iran used Twitter to describe what was happening after the elections. This was important because it was difficult to find this news in traditional media.

Topic:

a An online service
b Twitter
c The history of Twitter
d Twitter and sports

3   The news is one of the best ways for language learners to improve their English. English learners can go online to read newspapers, listen to the radio, and watch television. However, it is often difficult to understand this information in English. Vocabulary can be challenging, and news announcers speak very quickly. So many media organizations have extra help for English learners. For example, the BBC provides online news for English learners. This news is easier to understand and has exercises to help students learn more. The *New York Times* and CNN also provide news for second language learners. These online sites help English learners across the world improve their English.

Topic:

a The news and language learning
b The BBC
c Reading newspapers online
d The news

4   In September 2011, parents in the Mexican city of Veracruz were terrified to hear that a group of gunmen had attacked a local school. The parents rushed to the school in such a panic that there were over 24 car accidents. The emergency phone system stopped working because so many people called the police. However, when parents finally reached the school, all was quiet. There were no gunmen. Police quickly arrested the two men who had sent out these completely untrue tweets. This example shows that Twitter can be very useful in transmitting news quickly, but that the news may not always be accurate.

Topic:

a Veracruz

b Emergency services

c Twitter

d Accuracy in the news

Skill Practice 2

Read the paragraphs in Skill Practice 1 again. Review your topic choice for each paragraph. This time, decide what the writer wants to say about the topic. What is the writer's claim? Circle the best choice.

1 **Claim:**

   a Early newspapers were first published in Europe.

   b Early newspapers included the *French Gazette* and the *England Gazette*.

   c The first newspapers began in the seventeenth century.

   d Early newspapers focused on international news.

2 **Claim:**

   a Twitter sends messages very quickly.

   b Twitter started to help small groups share ideas.

   c Twitter helps people learn about news.

   d Twitter is very popular.

3 **Claim:**

   a Online news is difficult to understand.

   b The news can help language learners improve their English.

   c BBC, CNN, and the *New York Times* are examples of online news sites.

   d English language learners need to practice by reading.

4 **Claim:**

   a Gunmen attacked a Mexican school.

   b Twitter is a good way to transmit information.

   c Twitter can be used to send out untrue news.

   d Police arrested the men who sent out the tweets.

Skill Practice 3

Read the following three paragraphs about a famous reporter and newspaper owner, Joseph Pulitzer. For paragraphs 1 and 2, choose the sentence that gives the main idea (the topic and claim) of each paragraph. For paragraph 3, work with a partner to write the main idea on the blank line.

1   Joseph Pulitzer was a man who faced many problems. He was born in Hungary, but he left his country and traveled to the United States. He went to St. Louis, Missouri, where many German-speaking immigrants lived. His English was poor, so he got a job as a reporter at a German newspaper. He worked hard to learn English and earn money. In 1878, he bought a newspaper company that was losing money, but Pulitzer quickly turned it into one of America's most popular and successful newspapers. Joseph Pulitzer soon became very wealthy and powerful.

Main idea:

a Pulitzer worked very hard.
b Pulitzer was a popular journalist.
c Pulitzer had a difficult life, but he was still successful.
d Pulitzer bought a newspaper company because he could not find a job.

2   Pulitzer went to New York and bought another newspaper. The newspaper, the *New York World*, became successful because he knew what people wanted to read about. New York at this time was full of new immigrants who were eager to learn about the city and to learn English. They also wanted entertainment, and Pulitzer understood this. He wrote in simple, clear English and printed a lot of pictures. His newspaper was full of stories about love, crime, and rich, powerful people. Soon, it became the city's top newspaper.

Main idea:

a Pulitzer used simple sentences so people could understand his newspaper easily.
b Pulitzer's newspaper was important for immigrants who wanted to learn English.
c Pulitzer's newspaper had stories about love and crime.
d Pulitzer succeeded because he understood what people wanted to read.

3   Joseph Pulitzer believed journalism was a very important profession. He wanted it to be a respected profession like law or medicine. He became a philanthropist and gave money to Columbia University to start a school of journalism. Today, he is most well known for starting the Pulitzer Prize. Each year, journalists and photographers win prizes for the best stories and photographs.

Main idea:

Joseph wanted to be a Professional Journalist like other field.

Connecting to the Topic

Discuss the following questions with a partner.

1 What kind of person should report the news? What training should they get?

2 How do we know if news is true?

3 Can ordinary people – people like you or your friends – report the news?

4 What would you do if you were the only person who saw something important happen – something important enough to be in the news? Explain your answer.

Previewing and Predicting

> Reading the first sentence of each paragraph is a quick way to predict what a text will be about.

A **Quickly read the first sentence of each paragraph in Reading 3. Decide what the topic of the paragraph will be. Then read the following topics. Write the number of the paragraph (1–7) next to the topic that best describes it. The first paragraph has been done for you.**

PARAGRAPH	TOPIC
2	It will explain how news was reported in the past before citizen journalism.
4	It will give a detailed example of one online news site.
1	It will describe changes in the news media today.
7	It will describe recent changes in the news business.
6	It will describe problems of citizen journalism.
5	It will explain how traditional journalists and citizen journalists can work together.
3	It will explain how traditional journalists are losing control over the news.

B **Compare your answers with a partner's.**

While You Read

As you read, stop at the end of each sentence that contains words in bold. Then follow the instructions in the box in the margin.

◀) Citizen Journalism

1   The news media today is in one of the most significant periods of change in its history. Change is not new to the news. The telegraph in the 1840s, cheap paper and huge numbers of immigrants in the 1880s, the radio in the 1920s, and television in the 1950s all transformed news reporting. However, the biggest change has taken place in digital media. In digital media, well-trained journalists with a lot of experience are not the only people reporting the news. Free, convenient technology means that almost anyone with a computer or smart phone can report news online. These people are known as *citizen journalists*, or **bloggers**.

2   Before citizen journalism, experienced journalists controlled the news. They researched a story, wrote an article, and showed it to their editors. The editors decided whether the story was worthwhile. If they decided it was not very interesting, they rejected it. If they thought it was interesting, they would check the story and make sure it was well written. Then the story appeared in a newspaper or on television. Journalists expected the public to believe the story and not to question it. In most cases, reporters and editors decided what news to publish and what news to **ignore**.

3   Today, traditional journalists no longer have this control over the news. Citizen journalists have the same technology as traditional reporters and can easily publish news. This news can reach millions of people through the Internet on websites and blogs – another name for online journals. Millions of people have created their own blogs and use them to write about many things, including the news. They invite readers to answer them by adding, or **posting**, comments to the blog. One amazing thing about blog postings is their speed. Bloggers often post news before the traditional media report it. For instance, when Hurricane Katrina hit New Orleans, bloggers posted video and text of the devastation before many of the major news organizations. Blogs can also provide very specific and personal information that is not available from traditional news media. After the tsunami in Southeast Asia, bloggers were the first to tell the world what was happening. Blogs were able to provide information to friends and families who were waiting for news of survivors of the disaster.

4   One large online news site is the South Korean OhmyNews website. This website, which was founded in 2000 by Oh Yeon-ho, publishes hundreds of stories every day. Millions of readers visit this site. In 2003, 25,000 citizen journalists were writing stories for OhmyNews. Four years later, more than 40,000 were reporting. These citizen journalists are not professional journalists; they are office workers, salespeople, farmers, and doctors. As Oh Yeon-ho explains, "With OhmyNews, we wanted to say goodbye to twentieth-century journalism. . . . Our main concept is every citizen can be a reporter."

5   Sometimes traditional media also depend on citizen journalists. In November 2008, a group of gunmen attacked the Indian city of Mumbai.

WHILE YOU READ ❶

Look back for the definition of *bloggers*. Highlight it.

WHILE YOU READ ❷

What is the claim in paragraph 2? Highlight it.

WHILE YOU READ ❸

Look in the sentence for the definition of *posting*. Highlight it.

They attacked several buildings, including a police station, restaurant, hospital, and a well-known hotel, the Taj Mahal Palace and Tower Hotel. The gunfight lasted for hours, and over 150 people were killed. Traditional news media found it difficult to report on the fast-moving events. However, within minutes, citizen journalists from all over the city began reporting using online services such as Twitter and YouTube.

The Taj Mahal Palace and Tower Hotel

People uploaded photos and even transmitted video from inside the burning Taj Hotel. News networks including CNN used these pictures and information in their broadcasts. At one point, citizen journalists were posting seven messages every five seconds on Twitter. One of these journalists was Arun Shanbhag, who was near the hotel when it was attacked. He described what was happening and uploaded many photos. "I felt I had a responsibility to share my views with outside world," he later explained. These examples show the power of citizen **journalism**.

6   Citizen journalism is powerful, but it also has problems. One problem is accuracy. Anyone can post a story, so how do readers know what is true? For example, in 2008, someone posted on CNN iReport that Steve Jobs, the CEO of Apple, had suffered a heart attack. This was not true, but it resulted in the company quickly losing 10 percent of its value. After just 20 minutes, CNN deleted the post. Another issue is what kind of information citizen journalists should publish. For example, traditional media decided not to broadcast videos of the execution of the Iraqi leader Saddam Hussein; however, someone posted a video of his death on the Internet just minutes after the execution. Five years later, when Muammar Gaddafi, the former leader of Libya, was killed, traditional media decided they would post videos of his death. They believed they had to do this because bloggers would post these videos anyway. It is clear that traditional media no longer have absolute control of the news.

7   Online news sites have also forced the traditional media to change the way they do business. Traditional media make money mainly through advertising. However, since more people get their news online, fewer people are buying newspapers or watching the news. Advertisers have therefore begun to buy more online advertising and spend less on advertising in traditional media. This has caused the traditional news media to lose money. One solution has been to move to the Internet. Most large news organizations now have websites. For example, CNN has a very successful website with an audience of more than 20 million people per month. The growth in digital media and citizen journalism has resulted in many changes in the business and reporting of the news.

WHILE YOU READ ④
What is the topic of paragraph 5? Highlight it.

Main Idea Check

Here are the main ideas of paragraphs 2–7 in Reading 3. Match each paragraph to its main idea. Write the number of the paragraph on the blank line.

_____ A Before the Internet, reporters and editors controlled the news.

_____ B One popular news site shows that people are very interested in reading and participating in citizen journalism.

_____ C Traditional media do not control news on the Internet.

_____ D Because newspapers and television stations are losing money to online sites, they are opening their own online news sites.

_____ E There are two main problems with citizen journalism.

_____ F Sometimes citizen journalists report the news for traditional media.

A Closer Look

Look back at Reading 3 to answer the following questions.

1 Only trained and experienced journalists have the skills to report news stories online. **True or False?**

2 Choose a word to complete the following definition: A / An _____ is an ordinary person who posts news online.

  a blog

  b traditional journalist

  c editor

  d citizen journalist

3 Although blogs are not written by trained reporters, they have an important role in communicating information. **True or False?**

4 What reason does Oh Yeon-ho give in paragraph 4 to explain why he started OhmyNews?

  a He believed that traditional journalism would be better online.

  b He wanted to stop being a journalist.

  c He thought traditional journalism was not interesting.

  d He believed that ordinary people should write the news.

5 Why does the writer use the example of the Mumbai attacks in paragraph 5?

  a It shows that reporting is sometimes very dangerous.

  b It shows that citizen journalists can sometimes report news more easily than traditional journalists.

  c It explains why people were killed in these attacks.

  d It shows that traditional journalists cannot report on serious news stories such as the Mumbai attack.

6 According to paragraphs 3–6, which examples show that digital technology makes the delivery of news very fast? Circle all that apply.

  a Reports from the Southeast Asian tsunami
  b OhmyNews
  c Saddam Hussein's execution
  d Reports of problems caused by Hurricane Katrina
  e The Mumbai attack

7 Citizen journalism may be inaccurate because untrained people are publishing news very quickly and usually without an editor. **True or False?**

8 According to paragraph 7, why are newspapers losing business to online news sites?
  a More people now find their news online, so fewer people are buying newspapers.
  b Citizen journalists do not make a lot of money.
  c Many people want to write their own news.
  d Traditional news organizations have started their own online sites.

Skill Review

In Skills and Strategies 2, you learned that writers express the main idea in different places in a paragraph. Identifying the main idea in each paragraph is an important reading skill.

A Look over Reading 3 again, and review the Main Idea Check. Where did you find the main idea of each of the six paragraphs? Put a check (✓) in the correct columns to show where you found the main idea of each paragraph.

PARAGRAPH NUMBER	FIRST SENTENCE	SECOND SENTENCE	LAST SENTENCE	WHOLE PARAGRAPH
2				
3				
4				
5				
6				
7				

B Compare your answers with a partner's.

Definitions

Find the words in Reading 3 that complete the following definitions. When a verb completes the definition, use the base form, although the verb in the reading may not be in the base form.

1 To _Transform_ means to change a lot. (v) Par. 1

2 When you _research_ something, you find information about it. (v) Par. 2

3 People who check news stories are called _editors_. (n pl) Par. 2

4 If something is _worthwhile_, it is important or useful enough to do. (adj) Par. 2

5 If you pay no attention to something, you _ignore it_ it. (v) Par. 2

6 Destruction in a large area is known as _devastation_. (n) Par. 3

7 _survivors_ are people who live after experiencing a dangerous situation. (n pl) Par. 3

8 To _attack_ is to try to hurt or destroy something with violence. (v) Par. 5

9 To continue over a period of time means the same as to _last_. (v) Par. 5

10 An answer to a problem is a/an _solution_. (n) Par. 7

Words in Context

Ⓐ Use context clues to match the first part of each sentence to its correct second part and to understand the meaning of the words in bold.

1 People protested in the streets after
    a **uploaded** it to her website.

2 Some parts of story were incorrect, so the editor
    b everyone can be a reporter. This **concept** is quite new.

3 After she finished writing the story, the reporter
    c **control** the media. For example, newspapers cannot say bad things about the president.

4 When the president finished speaking,
    d the **former** president for all his hard work.

5 The most important aspect of citizen journalism is that
    e many people in the **audience** wanted to ask him questions.

6 When the company Apple first started, it was not worth much, but
    f the **execution** of the president. They were very angry.

7 In some counties, the government tries to
    g its **value** has increased sharply in the last 10 years.

8 The president of the company thanked
    h **rejected** the idea of publishing it.

Ⓑ Compare your answers with a partner's. Discuss what clues helped you match the parts of the sentences and helped you understand what the words in bold mean.

Critical Thinking

In Reading 3, you learned that sometimes citizen journalists report information that is not accurate. How can we evaluate information in order to separate the accurate from the inaccurate news?

> **EVALUATING INFORMATION**
>
> Critical thinkers look at information carefully and decide if it is accurate.

A Make a list of questions that could help you decide if a piece of news is likely to be accurate or not. One example is done for you.

- *Is the information current, or recent? Or is it old and out of date?*
- _____
- _____
- _____

B With a partner, discuss your list of questions. Then discuss the accuracy of Internet news sites that you have used in the past. Which sites seem most accurate to you? Which sites do not?

Research

Log on to blogsearch, google.com, or a similar website to help you find a blog about a subject that interests you. For example, you could search for news about your country, a favorite sport, or a famous person.

Writing

Post online comments to one of the blog entries that interest you. For example, you could add more information about the subject, or you could express your opinion. (Most blogs require you to give your e-mail address. If you do not want to do this, write your comments on paper.) Share your blog entry or written comments with a partner.

Connecting to the Topic

Read the definition of *ethical*, and then discuss the following question with a partner.

> **ethical** *(adj)* relating to beliefs of what is right and what is wrong

What is *un*ethical behavior for a reporter? In other words, what behavior is unacceptable for a reporter?

a Pretending to be someone else in order to find out information for a story
b Writing facts and information that are not true
c Printing or saying negative things about a person if those things are true
d Secretly putting microphones in people's homes to hear what they say, and then reporting their conversations
e Taking photos of people in public without asking them, and then printing the photos in a newspaper

Previewing and Predicting

> The first paragraph often introduces the main idea of a whole reading. It can also provide important background information that will help you understand the context of the reading. Therefore, reading the first paragraph is often a good way to preview a reading and predict its content.

Ⓐ Read the first paragraph in Reading 4, and choose one of the following as the main idea of the whole reading.

a Reporters are under a lot of pressure to find good news stories.
b Reporters sometimes break the law in order to get a news story.
c Pressure to get a good news story sometimes tempts reporters to behave unethically.

Ⓑ Compare your answer with a partner's.

While You Read

As you read, stop at the end of each sentence that contains words in bold. Then follow the instructions in the box in the margin.

Ethical Reporting

1   Reporters have always been under pressure to find a good story. This pressure may sometimes tempt them to do things that are not ethical. Perhaps their story will be better if they change the facts a little. Perhaps they will even need to break the law to get a better story. What can reporters do in order to get their story? Can they break the law? Can they lie? Can they write about people's personal lives? How far can reporters go to find a story? These are important questions in the topic of ethical reporting.

2   One way reporters try to find a story is by **going undercover**. When reporters go undercover, they don't tell people they are reporters. They pretend to be someone else so they can go to places where reporters cannot usually go. Even in the early days of newspaper reporting, journalists went undercover for a good story. In 1887, for example, an American reporter called Nellie Bly pretended to be mentally ill in order to enter a mental health hospital. The nurses and doctors thought she was a real patient. She pretended to be mentally ill so she could write a story about the terrible conditions in the hospital. Nellie Bly is an early example of undercover reporting, and her story led to significant changes in how patients are treated in mental hospitals.

3   In recent years, there have been many examples of reporters going undercover to get a good story. A British reporter, Ryan Parry, went undercover to show that security at Buckingham Palace in London was not very good. He used fake documents to get a job at the palace. His job let him walk freely around the palace. In another case in England, a journalist used fake papers to get a job at London's Heathrow Airport. He used hidden cameras and microphones to record his story about weak airport security. Airport police arrested him but only after he had gone inside several planes. These undercover journalists reported important stories that had an impact on national security.

4   Undercover reporters don't only focus on issues of national security. In South Korea, reporters went undercover to find out about illegal activities. They watched as people on ships were throwing dangerous chemicals into the sea off South Korea's shore. These poisonous chemicals were then passed on to people through the fish they ate. In the United States, a group of television reporters did an undercover story about a supermarket. One of the reporters used fake documents to get a job in the meat department. He found out that the supermarket was selling old meat and fish that were unsafe to eat. They showed all of this on their television program. Thousands of Americans watched and were shocked at what they saw. As a result of the story, the supermarket had to make improvements in its meat and fish **department**.

5   In most countries, it is illegal to use fake documents. So reporters who use fake documents are breaking the law. This raises a number of ethical

WHILE YOU READ 1

Read ahead and use context clues to help you figure out the definition of *going under cover*. Then highlight the definition.

WHILE YOU READ 2

What is the topic of paragraph 4? Highlight it.

questions. Is it acceptable for reporters to break the law if the story benefits society? Should those reporters get into trouble? The reporters who got jobs at Buckingham Palace and Heathrow Airport published stories that led to better security. The South Korean news story led to laws against throwing poisonous chemicals into the sea. The U.S. television report showed dangerous conditions in the supermarket. In each of these cases, although the reporters broke the law, their stories helped the public. Some people say this is good journalism because it helps society. Other people disagree and think it is always wrong to break the law.

6   Although people disagree about whether journalists can break the law to get a good story, everyone agrees that journalists must always tell the truth. Unfortunately, there have been a few cases of reporters who wanted a story so much that they lied about it. Janet Cooke, a reporter at *The Washington Post*, published a story about an eight-year-old boy in Washington, D.C., who was a drug addict. The story, "Jimmy's World," shocked people all over the United States. The police even tried to find Jimmy in order to help him, but Cooke refused to tell the police where he lived. A few months later, Cooke won a Pulitzer Prize for the story. By this time, however, her editor was uncertain that the story was true. Cooke finally confessed that the story was a lie and that there was no Jimmy. She resigned, and *The Washington Post* gave back the **Pulitzer Prize**.

7   After Janet Cooke's resignation, *The Washington Post* continued as a successful newspaper. In England, however, reporters from one the oldest newspapers in that country behaved so badly that the newspaper itself had to shut down. The *News of the World* was first published in 1843. It was the cheapest newspaper in England and quickly became very popular. It focused on crime and celebrities. The *News of the World* reporters were under great pressure to get interesting stories more quickly than any other

WHILE YOU READ ③

What is the claim of paragraph 6? Highlight it.

The *News of the World* shut down after its reporters broke the law.

newspaper, even if it meant breaking the law. In 2007, British police discovered that these reporters had hacked into people's phones. Listening to private phone calls is illegal. However, journalists had hacked into hundreds of private calls, including those of celebrities, politicians, sports stars, and victims of serious crimes. On July 7, 2011, the behavior of these reporters forced the owner to close the paper after 168 years of business.

8 Ethical reporting also raises questions about reporters and the privacy of the people in their stories. The public has a huge appetite for news about the rich and famous, so reporters are under pressure to write stories about these celebrities. To make stories interesting, reporters try to find out very personal information about the lives of these people. Although celebrities do not like it when reporters write about their personal lives, the law says reporters can print any information if it is true. Therefore, the media are full of these stories. This news may not be important, **but the public wants to read about it.**

9 Sometimes reporters also take photographs of the rich and famous. These reporters are called *paparazzi*. They make celebrities' lives very difficult because they follow them wherever they go. Sometimes the paparazzi take pictures that the celebrities would not like. For example, they may take photographs that make the celebrities look fat or ugly. Famous movie and television stars complain that they have no privacy. Although people love to see these photographs, many people also believe that the paparazzi do not always act responsibly. Some people, for example, think that the actions of the paparazzi led to Princess Diana's death in 1997. Paparazzi on motorbikes were following the princess's car through Paris streets. The driver was going very fast in order to escape the paparazzi. He lost control and crashed, killing the princess and her friend. After the accident, police discovered the driver had been drinking. Nevertheless, many people still think the accident was the fault of the paparazzi.

WHILE YOU READ 4

Where is the main idea of paragraph 7?
a) First sentence
b) Second sentence
c) Last sentence

WHILE YOU READ 5

Look back in the last sentence for a definition of *paparazzi*. Highlight it.

Paparazzi follow celebrities everywhere.

10 The news is a product, just like bread, cars, or computers. News organizations want people to watch or read their stories – on television, in the newspaper, or online. That is how they make money. With so many people looking for news, it is not surprising that reporters are under a lot of pressure to find sensational news stories that everyone wants to read. Occasionally, reporters go too far and act unethically. Usually, however, reporters are responsible and tell the truth. Today, most major news organizations have rules to make sure that their reporters act ethically and that their stories are true.

Main Idea Check

Match the main ideas below to five of the paragraphs in Reading 4. Write the number of the paragraph on the blank line.

_____ A Reporters go undercover to report problems with national security.

_____ B Reporters go undercover to report on health and food safety.

_____ C The paparazzi do not always act responsibly.

_____ D Writing the truth is the most important part of reporting.

_____ E Reporters write about the rich and famous because the public likes it.

A Closer Look

Look back at Reading 4 to answer the following questions.

1 Why does the writer use the example of the reporter at Buckingham Palace in paragraph 3? Circle all that apply.

a It shows that security at the palace was very weak.

b It is a good example of undercover reporting.

c It shows that undercover reporting is a crime.

d It shows that a reporter's story can result in important changes.

e It shows that job applicants sometimes lie.

2 According to paragraphs 2 and 3, why do reporters go undercover?

a They can get better stories.

b They know undercover reporting is not ethical.

c They know they will not get into trouble.

d They think it is easy to go undercover.

3 Using fake documents is against the law in most countries. **True or False?**

4 Some people believe that reporters should not get into trouble when they go undercover if the stories benefit society. **True or False?**

5 Reread paragraph 6 about the Janet Cooke story. As you read, number the events in time order. Begin with the first thing that happened. Then write the correct number for each event on the blank lines.

_____ Cooke won a Pulitzer Prize.

_____ Cooke finally told everyone that her story was not true.

_____ Cooke wanted to write a sensational news story.

_____ People all over the United States read Cooke's story.

_____ The newspaper returned Cooke's Pulitzer Prize.

_____ Cooke wrote a story about a young boy who lived in a world of drugs.

6 A reporter can legally report anything as long as it is true. **True or False?**

7 Which statement is *not* correct according to paragraph 9?

a) Paparazzi followed Princess Diana's car, which was going very fast.

b One of the paparazzi's motorbikes hit Princess Diana's car.

c Many people believe that the paparazzi were responsible for Diana's death.

d The driver of Princess Diana's car drank alcohol before he started driving.

8 The reading talks about the results of undercover reporting. Match the reporter to the result of each example of undercover reporting.

___ 1 Nellie Bly

___ 2 Ryan Perry

___ 3 A journalist at Heathrow Airport

___ 4 South Korean journalists

___ 5 Television reporters at a U.S. supermarket

a Improved security at the Palace

b Improvements to the handling of fish and meat

c Laws against throwing chemicals into the sea

d Improvements to patient care in mental hospitals

e More security at Britain's airport

Skill Review

> In Skills and Strategies 2, you learned that a main idea has two parts: a topic and a claim. Understanding the main idea of each paragraph will help you better understand the text.

The following is a list of topics for paragraphs 7–10 in Reading 4. Read the topic and put a check (✓) next to the statement that provides the best claim.

PARAGRAPH	TOPIC	✓	CLAIM 1	✓	CLAIM 2
7	Breaking the law		can have serious effects for a newspaper		sometimes helps reporters get news quickly
8	The public's appetite for stories about celebrities		leads to important news		leads to a lot of stories about famous people
9	The paparazzi		were responsible for Princess Diana's death		do not always behave responsibly
10	Reporters		are under a lot of pressure		make money by writing news stories

Definitions

Find the words in Reading 4 that complete the following definitions. When a verb completes the definition, use the base form, although the verb in the reading may not be in the base form.

1 The feeling of responsibility or worry is called ___responsed___ . (n) Par. 1

2 To ___Pretended___ means to act or behave as if something is true or real. (v) Par. 2

3 People who are ___mentally ill___ have psychological problems. (adj – 2 words) Par. 2

4 ___security___ means safety and protection. (n) Par. 3

5 If something is not real, it is ___fake___ . (adj) Par. 3

6 Official papers are called ___documents___ . (n pl) Par. 3

7 If something is ___illegal___ , it is against the law. (adj) Par. 4

8 When someone is ___shocked___ , they are very surprised, usually by bad news. (adj) Par. 4

9 A person who cannot stop using drugs is a/an ___addict___ . (n) Par. 6

10 Famous people are also called ___celebrities___ . (n pl) Par. 7

Words in Context

Complete the passages with words from Reading 4 in the box below.

arrested	complained	poisonous	resigned
benefit	confessed	privacy	sensational

1 There was a ___sensational___ news story on television yesterday. It showed that a
   _a
famous food company had sold cakes and cookies that contained ___poisonous___
   _b
chemicals that make people sick. The president of the company ___confessed___
   _c
that he had known about this but did nothing to stop it. He said he was very sorry,
and yesterday he ___resigned___ . Now there is a new president who says he has
   _d
stopped the sale of those cakes and cookies.

2 Yesterday the government passed a new law that will protect the ___privacy___
   _e
of Internet users. Many people had ___complained___ that companies were using and
   _f
selling their personal information. The new law will stop this from happening in the
future, which will ___benefit___ Internet users all over the world. Anyone who
   _g
breaks this law will be ___arrested___ and may have to pay a $100,000 fine.
   _h

Academic Word List

The following are Academic Word List words from Readings 3 and 4 of this unit. Use these words to complete the sentences. (For more on the Academic Word List, see page 257.)

benefits (v)	documents (n)	illegal (adj)	research (v)	survivors (n)
concept (n)	ignore (v)	rejected (v)	security (n)	transformed (v)

1 Travelers often have to take off their shoes as part of airport _____.

2 She kept her passport and other important _____ in a locked box.

3 Using a fake name to get a job is _____.

4 After the terrible airplane crash, the police looked for _____.

5 Citizen journalism _____ the public because it is often faster than traditional news.

6 Journalists often _____ their stories for a long time. They want to get as much information as possible.

7 The other students in the class _____ my ideas for the project.

8 The _____ of citizen journalism is quite new – only about 15 years old.

9 Teenagers often _____ their parents' advice and do what they want to do.

10 The Internet has _____ the way people get the news.

Critical Thinking

Reading 4 discusses how some journalists have found out information for news stories. The writer explores whether their methods are ethical, that is, whether they are acceptable.

A Read the following statements about what is acceptable for journalists to do or not do. Put a check (✓) in the box that expresses your opinion.

IT IS ACCEPTABLE FOR JOURNALISTS TO . . .	AGREE	STRONGLY AGREE	DISAGREE	STRONGLY DISAGREE
listen to private phone calls in order to find out about survivors from a serious crime.				
lie in order to discover the truth about airport security.				
pay people money for information about celebrities' personal lives.				

B Discuss your opinions with a partner.

Research

Go online if necessary to find out about a celebrity. Write brief notes about why you think there is so much public interest in his or her private life.

Writing

Write two paragraphs about your research.

Improving Your Reading Speed

Good readers read quickly and still understand most of what they read.

A Read the instructions and strategies for Improving Your Reading Speed in Appendix 3 on page 271.

B Choose either Reading 3 or Reading 4 in this unit. Read it without stopping. Time how long it takes you to finish the text in minutes and seconds. Enter the time in the chart on page 272. Then calculate your reading speed in number of words per minute.

WORD REPETITION

One way that writers can connect ideas in a text is by repeating a word or phrase or by using a word or phrase that is similar in meaning to a previously used word or phrase.

In the following example, the two words that are connected are in **bold**. The arrow shows how they are connected.

> For many years, the newspaper was the main method for communicating **the news**. Then came the radio, which could transmit **the news** through the air instead of through cables.

Exercise 1

Look at the words or phrases in bold in the following paragraphs. Then find the words or phrases in the next sentence that repeat or refer to the same idea. Write them on the blank lines. The first one has been done for you.

1   The first live broadcast of a sports event was **on the radio.** Of course, on the radio, no one could see what was happening, so listeners needed **a person to describe the action.** This person, known as **an announcer,** had to describe the game quickly, clearly, and accurately. Successful announcers were able to make the listeners feel as if they were watching the game.

on the radio *on the radio*

a person to describe the action *This person*

an announcer *Successful announcers*

2   **July 20th, 1969**, was a big day for television. That day, television viewers **watched** a live broadcast of the first humans to walk on the moon. More than half a billion **people all over the world** watched as the two astronauts stepped onto the moon. The broadcast had the biggest international television audience at that time.

July 20th, 1969 _____

watched _____

people all over the world _____

3   The largest newspapers have offices, usually called **bureaus**, in big cities all over the world. Reporters at these news bureaus send **international** stories back to the main office of the newspaper. For **smaller newspapers**, however, it is too expensive to have reporters all over the world. Instead of using their own reporters, these smaller companies buy stories from international news services, such as the Associated Press and Reuters.

bureaus _____

international _____

smaller newspapers _____

Exercise 2

Make a clear paragraph by putting sentences A, B, and C into the best order after the numbered sentence. Look for repeated or similar words to help you. Write the letters in the correct order on the blank lines.

1 Being a journalist can be very dangerous. ____ ____ ____

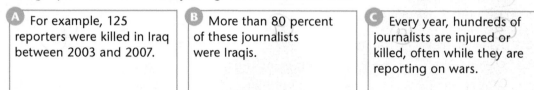

| **A** For example, 125 reporters were killed in Iraq between 2003 and 2007. | **B** More than 80 percent of these journalists were Iraqis. | **C** Every year, hundreds of journalists are injured or killed, often while they are reporting on wars. |

2 Photojournalism is a particular type of journalism. ____ ____ ____

| **A** Sometimes, however, they photograph events that are not planned, such as natural disasters and battles. | **B** Photojournalists record images of scheduled events like political speeches and demonstrations. | **C** Often, these unplanned photographs can be the most dramatic and powerful. |

3 In most parts of the world, journalists are free to report the news. ____ ____ ____

| **A** In these countries, the population often turns to the Internet, especially blogs, for the news. | **B** These blogs can play an important role in telling the people what is happening in their country. | **C** However, in some other parts of the world, governments prevent journalists from reporting the news. |

4 Important weddings often have very large television audiences. ____ ____ ____

| **A** Almost 2 billion people watched the funeral of Pope John Paul II on television in 2005. | **B** However, funerals sometimes have even larger audiences than weddings. | **C** The wedding of Prince Charles and Princess Diana in 1981 attracted 750 million viewers. |

5 One of the most famous early news broadcasts was of the Hindenburg disaster.

____ ____ ____

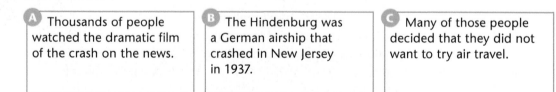

| **A** Thousands of people watched the dramatic film of the crash on the news. | **B** The Hindenburg was a German airship that crashed in New Jersey in 1937. | **C** Many of those people decided that they did not want to try air travel. |

2

EDUCATION

SKILLS AND STRATEGIES

- Using the Dictionary
- Finding Supporting Details

Using the Dictionary

As you learned in Skills and Strategies 1 on page 2, good readers use context clues to figure out the meanings of unfamiliar words while they are reading. However, you don't have to figure out the meaning of all unfamiliar words. You only need to figure out the key words that help you understand the main ideas of the reading. When you can't figure out the meaning of these words from context, then you will need to look them up in the dictionary. Dictionaries provide the pronunciation and meaning of a word as well as the part of speech, such as *noun*, *verb*, *adjective*, or *adverb*. Sometimes they give examples of the word in a sentence. All of this information can help you to understand what an unfamiliar word means and how to use it.

Examples & Explanations

elite /eɪˈliːt, ɪ-/ *n* those people or organizations considered to be the best or most powerful

The entry usually begins with grammatical information. It provides the pronunciation, and then the part of speech. The grammatical information gives you a clue to the meaning.

essential /ɪˈsen·tʃəl/ *adj* extremely important or necessary • *A knowledge of Spanish is essential for this job.*

The second part of the entry provides the definition.

determine /dɪˈtɜr·mən/ *v* to control or influence something directly; to decide • *We should be allowed to determine our own future.* • *Eye color is genetically determined.*

Finally, the entry may contain an example or examples of the word in a sentence. This helps you understand the meaning and can show you other words that often appear with it.

return /rɪˈtɜrn/ **1.** *v* to come or go back to a previous place, subject, activity, or condition • *He returned to New York last week.* **2.** *v* to put, send, or give something back to where it came from • *Emily returned the blouse because it didn't fit.*

Some words have more than one meaning. Dictionaries usually give the different meanings in separate numbered definitions. The example sentences can help you choose the correct numbered definition.

stick <THIN PIECE> /stɪk/ *n* a thin piece of wood • *The campers collected sticks to start a fire.* **stick** <ATTACH> /stɪk/ *v past* **stuck** /stʌk/ to attach or become attached • *Stick the tape to the back of the picture.* • *It was so hot that my clothes stuck to me.*

Some words have more than one part of speech. In some dictionaries, these appear in separate entries beginning with a synonym. The synonyms, the parts of speech, and the example sentences can all help you choose the correct entry.

Strategies

These strategies will help you use the dictionary effectively.

- When you read an unfamiliar word, decide if you can guess its meaning first by using the strategies you learned in Skills and Strategies 1 on page 3.

- If you cannot guess the meaning, continue to read the next two sentences. If you still do not understand, underline the word or make a note in the margin and keep reading.

- After you have finished reading, if there is a key word that you do not understand, check a *learner dictionary*. Learner dictionaries are easier to use than dictionaries for native speakers, and they contain information that is especially useful for language learners.

- If you have access to the Internet, another quick way to look up a word is in an online dictionary. For example, go to dictionary.cambridge.org, and type in your word.

- If the dictionary provides more than one meaning for a word, go back to the reading to see which meaning is the best choice.

- If there are entries in the dictionary for more than one part of speech, go back to the reading and look for clues that will help you choose the correct one. For example, if the word comes after *the*, *a*, or an adjective in the reading, it is probably a noun. If it has an ending, such as *-ed* or *-ing*, it is probably a verb or maybe an adjective.

Skill Practice 1

Read the following sentences. They each contain a word in bold that has more than one possible meaning. Then read the dictionary entries for the word. Look for clues to help you decide which definition matches the sentence. Circle the correct definition.

1 **Bright** students often get high scores on their examinations.
   a *(adj)*: full of light; shining
      The rooms were bright and cheerful.
   b *(adj)*: clever and quick to learn
      They were bright children and were always asking questions.

2 Many people believe that a university **degree** is important for success.
   a *(n)*: an amount or level
      This job requires a high degree of skill and experience.
   b *(n)*: a course of study or qualification at school or a university
      She left school without finishing her degree.

3 She hopes that the national university will **admit** her next year.
   a *(v)*: to allow someone to enter a place or institution
      The theater does not admit anyone until 15 minutes before the movie begins.
   b *(v)*: to agree that something is true, especially unwillingly
      He admitted that he had lied.

4 Although the United States still measures distance in feet and miles, the metric system has become the **standard** for most of the world.

   a (n): a pattern or model that is generally accepted
   The government has established a standard for international business contracts.

   b (n): a level of quality
   The standard of these products is very poor.

5 Religious organizations **run** several of the schools in the village.

   a (v): to move quickly on foot
   He ran quickly to get to school on time.

   b (v): to operate or be in control of something
   It is difficult to run a business without good workers.

Skill Practice 2

The following sentences contain words that can be used as more than one part of speech. The different parts of speech have different meanings. If you can figure out the part of speech, you can figure out which meaning is correct. Read each of the five sentences, and figure out the part of speech of the word in bold. Look for clues to help you figure out the part of speech. Then look at the dictionary entry for the part of speech you have chosen. Decide if the definition is correct. Circle the definition.

1 Only half of the students in the class were **present** for the test.

   a (n): gift; something that you receive on a special occasion
   My grandparents gave me a laptop as a present.

   b (adj): in a particular place
   The whole family was present for the holiday dinner.

2 They all **signed** the contracts in their lawyer's office.

   a (n): a notice that gives information, directions, or a warning
   There were no street signs, so we lost our way.

   b (v): to write your name, usually on a written or printed document
   Artists often sign their paintings in the bottom right corner.

3 I trust my best friend because she is always very **direct** and tells the truth.

   a (adj): honest
   I like her open and direct manner.

   b (v): to order someone to do something, especially officially
   The police officer directed the man to stop.

4 Educating all of the world's children is a great **challenge**.

   a (v): to invite someone to compete
   The boy challenged his neighbor to a fight.

   b (n): a difficult job that requires a lot of work
   Mathematics is a challenge for many students.

5 The soldiers **freed** all of the prisoners.
  a (v): to release or let go
    He tried to free his hands from the ropes.
  b (adj): without cost
    The tickets to the movie were free for all children under 10 years old.

Skill Practice 3

The following sentences contain words in bold that you may not know. For most of them, there are not enough context clues to guess the meaning. Use a dictionary to figure out the meaning of these words. All of these words have more than one meaning. Use the strategies you have just learned to decide which meaning is correct. Write the definition on the blank lines. The first one has been done for you. Check your answers with a partner.

1 Several airlines **suspended** flights between New York and London for a short time last month.

  stopped

2 The test results were used to **match** students' abilities with different school programs.

  accommodation to compare

3 In the last 10 years, most of the young people have **deserted** their villages.

  give up, leave

4 Many parents and experts argue that university admission tests are not **fair**.

  acceptable

5 My uncle was a **regular** customer at the Italian restaurant on the corner.

  normal

6 The report showed that the population had **shifted** from the farms to the city.

  changed

7 The students tried very hard to **master** the skills their teacher taught them.

  to come up, you knew

8 A good educational system is **critical** for a country's economy.

  very important

9 He was **positive** that he would get into the best school, so he was surprised when he did not.

  focal a little bit

10 There was a **faint** smell of flowers in the room.

  weak

Connecting to the Topic

Discuss the following questions with a partner.

1 How old were you when you first started school?

2 Do all children in your home country go to school?

3 How long do most of these children stay in school?

4 Does the government control the schools?

5 Are schools free, or do parents have to pay for their children's education?

Previewing and Predicting

> Reading a title and looking at illustrations and graphic material can help you predict what topics will be in a text.

A Read the title of Reading 1, and look at the photo on page 49 and the graph (Figure 2.1) on page 50. Then put a check (✓) next to the topics you think will be included in the reading.

_____ A Differences in education around the world

_____ B The writer's education

_____ C The value of education

_____ D How to teach mathematics

_____ E The connection between education and success

B Compare your answers with a partner's.

While You Read

As you read, stop at the end of each sentence that contains words in bold. Then follow the instructions in the box in the margin.

◀)) Education Around the World

1   When you think of school, you may think of a classroom like the one in the picture below, but not all classrooms are like this. One school may have dirt floors and no chalkboard; another may be in a modern building with computers. Education comes in many different forms and has a long history. In early times, schools were available only to the elite who could afford to pay for their education, but this changed at the **onset** of industrialization. When industrialization began, new industries needed more educated workers. In order to meet this need, the number of schools expanded, and education became accessible to more children. Today, most nations want all of their children to go to school. This is because educated citizens can take care of themselves, and they contribute to their nation's development.

WHILE YOU READ ❶

Highlight the words in the next sentence that help you figure out the meaning of *onset*.

2   Most countries divide education into three levels: primary, secondary, and higher, or university, education. Primary school begins when children are about five years old and lasts for six to nine years. It is usually free, and it is also generally compulsory. Primary instruction often includes reading, writing, mathematics, and history. In some parts of the world, children go to school even before they are five. For example, in Japan and the Czech Republic, many children under five go to preschool. These schools are growing in popularity, especially in Europe, North America, and Japan. This is because working parents cannot stay at home to care for their children. Parents also believe that preschools give their children an advantage when they begin primary school.

3   Secondary school lasts for three to six years. It begins when children are about 12 years old. Some countries, such as Germany and Hungary, place secondary schoolchildren in schools based on their scores on a national test. Children with high test scores go to secondary schools that emphasize academic subjects, such as math, science, and literature. Children with lower test scores go to schools that teach more practical and technical skills, such as computer technology, car repair, or hotel management. Recently, some nations have stopped separating their students in this way and now educate all children together.

4   **Not** all students have the opportunity to get a university education. There are several reasons for this. In some countries, the entrance test for universities is very difficult, and only a small number of students pass. In

WHILE YOU READ ❷

As you read, determine which sentences give the main idea of paragraph 4: a) the first and last or b) the first and second?

China, this test is called the *gaokao*, or "big test." Every high school student takes it at the same time and has only one chance to pass each year. In 2007, 10 million Chinese students took the exam, and around 40 percent failed. Elsewhere, there are not enough places in colleges and universities. For example, in 2007, only 18 percent of the 18-year-olds in Hong Kong were able to find a place in a local university. Finally, the cost may be very high, and some people cannot afford it. This is true in the United States, where the average cost of a four-year university degree is around $21,000 per year.

5   Governments play an important part in education. Most children around the world attend government schools. In general, government schools are free, although there may be **fees**, especially at the secondary level. Most of the funding for these schools comes from government taxes. In other words, citizens and businesses pay for education. A government also influences the curriculum. This influence varies, or changes, from one country to another. The government of Vietnam, for example, controls the curriculum and decides what should and what should not be taught.

6   Education provides benefits for both individuals and nations. Students who stay in school have a better chance of finding good jobs. For this reason, parents all over the world work hard to make sure their children get a good education. Many parents hope their children will study in a university. In the United States, for example, people with a university degree earn an average of 74 percent more than people without a university degree. (See Figure 2.1). They earn an average of a million dollars more in their lifetime. For nations, the impact of education on development is also **clear**. Countries with the highest rates of secondary school graduation usually also have the highest productivity. For individuals and their countries, education is essential for success.

WHILE YOU READ ❸

Which word in the sentence helps you figure out the meaning of *fees*?
a) Although
b) Especially

WHILE YOU READ ❹

Which definition of *clear* matches the meaning in the sentence?
a) To remove something that is causing a problem
b) Easy to understand

Figure 2.1 Average U.S. Salaries by Level of Education in 2010

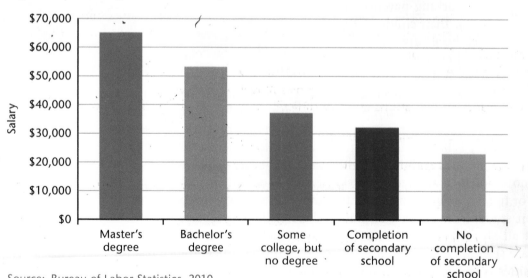

Source: Bureau of Labor Statistics, 2010

Main Idea Check

Here are the main ideas of each paragraph in Reading 1. Match each paragraph to its main idea. Write the number of the paragraph on the blank line.

_____ A The goals of primary education are similar in most countries.

_____ B In many countries, students may go to different secondary schools, depending on their abilities.

_____ C There are several reasons why some students do not have an opportunity to attend a university.

_____ D There have been many important changes in the history of education.

_____ E Education gives both individuals and nations an advantage.

_____ F Governments have a significant impact on schools.

A Closer Look

Look back at Reading 1 to answer the following questions.

1 Why did the number of schools increase as countries became more industrialized?
   a Parents understood that school gave their children an advantage.
   b Citizens were better educated.
   c Work became more complicated, so more educated workers were needed.
   d Governments had more taxes to fund schools.

2 According to the paragraph 2, why do parents send their children to preschool?
   a They believe it will give their children an advantage.
   b Preschool education is compulsory.
   c They do not agree with the curriculum in government schools.
   d Students who have gone to preschool do better on tests.

3 According to paragraph 4, in some countries, not everyone has an opportunity to get a university education. Which of the responses below is *not* given as a reason for this?
   a A university education can be too expensive for some people.
   b There are not enough places in the universities for everyone.
   c The government cannot pay for everyone's university education.
   d The entrance examinations are very difficult, and not everyone can pass them.

4 Most children go to schools run by the government. **True or False?**

5 Which statement is correct according to the reading?
   a Some primary schools focus on academic subjects, and some focus on technical subjects.
   b Test scores can determine the type of school a child attends.
   c Secondary students with low scores choose either an academic or a technical curriculum.
   d Secondary school lasts for six to nine years and is usually free.

6 According to Figure 2.1, in the United States, how much do people with a graduate's degree earn?

   a An average of three times as much as secondary school graduates

   b A million dollars in their lifetime

   c About $30,000 more than people with a secondary school education

   d Fifty percent more than people with a Bachelor's degree

Skill Review

> In Skills and Strategies 3, you learned that you sometimes need to use a dictionary to find the meanings of unfamiliar words. Learning to use the dictionary is a very important reading skill.

A The following sentences are from Reading 1. Each of the words in **bold** has more than one meaning. First, look for clues to help you figure out the part of speech of the word in **bold**. Then use a dictionary to find the definition that matches the part of speech you identified. Write the part of speech next to *a*, and write the definition on the blank line.

1 Most countries divide education into three **levels**: primary, secondary, and higher, or university, education.

   a (_____): _____ front or height rank _____

   b (_____): _____

2 In some countries, the entrance test for universities is very difficult, and only a small number of students **pass**.

   a (__verb__): _____ to move _____

   b (_____): _____

3 Every high school student takes the test at the same time, and has only one **chance** to pass.

   a (_noun_): _____ opportunity. _____

   b (_____): _____

4 Elsewhere, there are not enough **places** in colleges and universities, so it is not possible for all high school students to go on to college.

   a (_noun_): _____ space _____

   b (_____): _____ area _____

B Using your dictionary, find another meaning of the word in **bold**. What part of speech is it? Write the part of speech next to *b*, and write the second definition on the blank line.

Definitions

Find the words in Reading 1 that complete the following definitions. When a verb completes the definition, use the base form, although the verb in the reading may not be in the base form.

1 To _extended_ is to become larger in size or number. (v) Par. 1

2 _develops_ means the growth or the process of becoming more modern and advanced. (n) Par. 1

3 If something is _compulsory_, it is required. (adj) Par. 2

4 The numbers of correct answers on a test are called _high scores_. (n pl) Par. 3

5 To _emphasize_ means to show that something is important. (v) Par. 3

6 A/An _opportunity_ is the chance to do something you want to do. (n) Par. 4

7 If something is _elsewhere_, it is in another place or in other places. (adv) Par. 4

8 The _curriculum_ means all the courses taught in a school. (n) Par. 5

9 To _varies_ means to change in some way or to cause similar things to be different. (v) Par. 5

10 The rate at which a country makes things is called _Productivity_. (n) Par. 6

Words in Context

Complete the sentences with words or phrases from Reading 1 in the box below.

academic	contributes to	funding	industrialization
advantage	fees	individuals	meet the need

1 China has experienced a rapid rate of _____. Hundreds of factories have been built in the past 10 years.

2 The government must help businesses, but it is also important to protect the rights of _____.

3 Education has had to change in order to _____ for more skilled workers.

4 A high percentage of people with a university degree _____ a country's success.

5 The _____ was not enough, so the university had to ask for more money from the government.

6 Most parents believe that learning a second language is a/an _____ in today's global world.

7 The university offered several scholarships for students with a record of _____ excellence.

8 Many colleges charge extra _____ for services, such as using technology and playing sports.

Critical Thinking

Reading 1 discusses the benefits of education, both for an individual and for a country.

A Discuss these questions with a partner.

1 What is your level of education now? Have you finished high school?

2 What are your educational goals? What subjects are you studying or do you plan to study?

3 If you are in college, or plan to go to college, do you want to graduate with a bachelor's degree? A master's degree?

4 How will the subjects you choose and the degree you earn help you in the future?

5 What is your country doing to encourage students to go to university?

B Share your answers with your class.

Research

Research higher education in a country you know well. Find answers to the following questions.

- Is there a good choice of colleges and universities? Can students choose practical subjects as well as academic ones?
- How do students gain admission to universities?
- Are there enough university places for students?
- What is the average annual cost of university tuition?

Writing

Write two paragraphs. The first paragraph will describe higher education in the country you researched. Include information you learned from your research. The second paragraph will discuss your educational goals and explain how succeeding in these goals will benefit you and your country.

Connecting to the Topic

Discuss the following questions with a partner.

1 How do you feel when you take a test? Do you enjoy taking a test? Why or why not?

2 What kinds of tests or examinations have you taken in school?

3 What is the most stressful test you have ever taken? Explain your answer.

Previewing and Predicting

> Reading the first sentences of each paragraph is a quick way to predict what a text will be about.

A Quickly read the first two sentences of paragraphs 2–7 in Reading 2. Decide what the topic of the paragraph will be. Then read the following topics. Write the number of the paragraph (*2–7*) next to the topic that best describes it. The second paragraph has been done for you.

PARAGRAPH	TOPIC
	Tests after secondary school
	How tests can affect health
	Test pressure in university exams
	Test preparation programs
	Tests of national performance
2	The impact of test results on a student's future

B Compare your answers with a partner's.

While You Read

As you read, stop at the end of each sentence that contains words in bold. Follow the instructions in the box in the margin.

◀》 Testing in Education

1   Twelve-year-old Winston Lim of Singapore waits nervously for the results of an examination that will determine which secondary school he can attend. American Mark Saunders goes to class every Saturday to prepare for his university entrance examination. Like Winston and Mark, almost everyone in school takes tests. They are a regular part of education, and they often have a significant impact on people's lives. Tests measure how much people know or what they can do. Examinations are given at all levels of education, from primary school to university. In classrooms, teachers write the tests and give them to their classes. Other kinds of tests are standardized. They are usually written by testing experts. In some countries like Singapore, standardized testing begins very early. Every Singaporean takes a standardized test at the age of 11. Other countries, such as Italy, begin standardized testing after two or three years of secondary school.

2   The score on these standardized tests can often determine a student's educational future. This is because scores can determine what subjects students can study. Students who want to study math and science must have good math scores. Students who prefer an arts curriculum must have good scores on reading and writing tests. Those with low scores may not get into an academic program at all. Instead, they may begin training for their future job immediately. Parents and educators, however, are beginning to ask if this system works. They are beginning to ask two important questions: Do standardized tests really measure how well a student understands

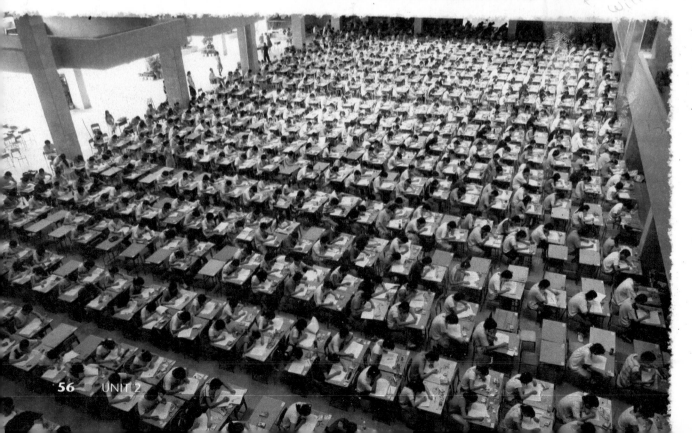

the subjects? This approach may be efficient, but should a student's future be determined by the results of a **test**?

3   Examinations in secondary school are just the beginning. Standardized tests are also used for university admission. Great Britain and many of its former **colonies**, including India, Tanzania, and Malaysia, use the A-level or a similar examination to help determine who will get into university. France, Switzerland, and some other countries in Europe use the International Baccalaureate examination. In the United States, most students take the SAT (Scholastic Achievement Test). Many parents and educators believe that these entrance tests have become too important. They argue that admission to a university should not depend on one examination. They say that it is important to include other factors, such as students' grades in school and students' interests outside of school. In fact, universities in many countries do consider other factors of a student's performance. However, a test is frequently the critical factor.

4   In many countries, the number of university places is limited, so there is very strong competition. Students are under great **pressure** to get a high score on their admission tests. A university education can make an enormous difference in the kind of job the students will get and how much money they will make. Many students spend hours, and even years, preparing for these exams. Occasionally, the pressure leads to **cheating** by both students and teachers. In 1992, 10,000 TOEFL scores in China were rejected because students had seen the exam questions before the day of the exam. In 2010, teachers and officials at schools in Australia were accused of helping their students cheat. They were able to obtain illegal copies of a university entrance examination and give it to their students. In 2011, in the United States, nearly 200 teachers in Atlanta helped students cheat on a national test.

5   The pressure is especially strong in South Korea and Japan, where hundreds of private schools prepare students for these examinations. These schools have become extremely profitable businesses. In Japan, for example, parents may pay an extra $10,000 a year for their children to attend a *juku*, or "cram school." Students who fail their college entrance examination may spend an extra year at special schools to prepare to take their exams again. In South Korea, 74 percent of all students who want to attend a university go to a cram school, or *hagwon*, at an average cost of $2,600 per student. For these students who want to

WHILE YOU READ 1

What is the main idea of paragraph 2? Highlight it.

WHILE YOU READ 2

What kind of context clue helps you figure out the meaning of *colonies*: (a) examples or (b) contrast? Highlight the clues.

WHILE YOU READ 3

What part of speech is *pressure*?
a) Noun
b) Verb
c) Adjective

WHILE YOU READ 4

Highlight the example of *cheating* that helps explain its meaning.

get into the best university, the day is not over when their school day ends. South Korean student Eunjin reports, "I am in school from 8:00 in the morning until 4:00. Then I go to a hagwon all evening. I don't get home until 1:00 in the morning, and I still have to do my homework."

6   This pressure on students can contribute to serious health problems. As a result, like many other countries, the South Korean government is trying to decrease the pressure on high school students. Here, a new law states that hagwons must close by 10:00 at night. Government employees check these private schools to make sure they close on time. There are also changes in university admissions tests. Universities now consider school grades and other student abilities as part of their admission policy. Lastly, the South Korean government is trying to improve elementary and secondary schools so that students will not need to go to cram schools after class. It is not certain if these changes will help. An increasing number of hagwons, for example, close by 10:00, but expect their students to work online after they return home. However, the government reported that spending on hagwons decreased by 3.5 percent in 2010, so it believes the new policy is beginning to work.

7   Tests are not just important for individual students. Nations also use tests to evaluate educational performance. Every three years, the Programme for International Student Assessment (PISA) tests 15-year-olds in industrialized nations. It measures knowledge of mathematics and science and reading and problem-solving ability. Countries can compare the performance of their students with the performance of students in other countries. In 2009, students from Shanghai, China were in first place; students from the United States were in 17th place. (See Table 2.1.) This is important information for governments. They may use this information to make changes in educational systems and **policies**.

WHILE YOU READ 5
What is the main idea of paragraph 7? Highlight it.

Table 2.1 Programme for International Student Assessment (PISA) Results for Fifteen-Year-Olds in 2009

RANK	MATHEMATICS	SCIENCE	READING
1	Shanghai – China	Shanghai – China	Shanghai – China
2	Singapore	Finland	Korea
3	Hong Kong	Hong Kong	Finland
4	Korea	Singapore	Hong Kong
5	Finland	Japan	Singapore
6	Liechtenstein	South Korea	Canada

Source: Organization for Economic Cooperation and Development

Main Idea Check

Here are the main ideas of paragraphs 2–7 in Reading 2. Match each paragraph to its main idea. Write the number of the paragraph on the blank line.

___ A Pressure to get into university can lead to cheating.

___ B Standardized tests are used for university admission.

___ C Tests can evaluate a country's performance.

___ D Students from South Korea and Japan often attend cram schools to prepare for university entrance exams.

___ E People are questioning whether standardized tests are the best way to determine a child's educational future.

___ F The South Korean government is trying to decrease the pressure on its students.

A Closer Look

Look back at Reading 2 to answer the following questions.

1 Standardized tests are written by classroom teachers. True or False?

2 According to paragraph 2, how are examinations in secondary school used? Circle all that apply.
   a To decide if students can get into the national university
   b To determine what subjects students can study
   c To decide if students will study an academic or more practical curriculum
   d To help meet the needs of growing industries
   e To give workers more training and skills

3 Some parents and educators think universities should consider more than the entrance examination. They should consider other factors. Reread paragraph 3. Which of the following factors were *not* listed?
   a Students' activities outside of school, for example, sports and music
   b Recommendations by their teachers
   c Their secondary school grades
   d Their work history

4 According to paragraph 4, both students and teachers have cheated on exams. True or False?

5 According to paragraph 5, why are hagwons so successful?
   a The government provides support for hagwons.
   b Parents want to show other parents that they have spent a lot of money on their children.
   c Parents are willing to do anything to help their children get into universities.
   d Everyone who attends hagwon classes gets into a university.

6 Competition to get into universities can create a lot of pressure. According to the reading, what are some of the consequences of this pressure? Circle all that apply.

a Some schools and students cheat to get good scores.

b Students may study for as long as a year to take the entrance examination again if they fail it the first time.

c Parents sometimes pay the university to accept their children.

d Parents pay a lot of money to send their children to special study programs after school.

e Students pay other students to take the test for them.

7 Which statements are correct according to Table 2.1? Circle all that apply.

a Hong Kong performed better than Finland in mathematics and reading.

b Singapore got the second highest mathematics score.

c Finland performed higher than Hong Kong in science and reading, but lower in mathematics.

d Compared to the other six countries, South Korean students performed well in reading and science.

Skill Review

In Skills and Strategies 2, you learned that writers express the main idea in different places in a paragraph. Identifying the main idea of each paragraph is an important reading skill.

A Look over Reading 2 again, and review the Main Idea Check. Where did you find the main idea of paragraphs 2–7? Put a check (✓) in the correct columns to show where you found the main idea of the paragraphs.

PARAGRAPH NUMBER	FIRST SENTENCE	SECOND SENTENCE	LAST SENTENCE	WHOLE PARAGRAPH
2		✓		
3		✓		
4		✓		
5	✓			
6	✓			
7	✓	✓		

B Compare your answers with a partner's.

Definitions

Find the words in Reading 2 that complete the following definitions. When a verb completes the definition, use the base form, although the verb in the reading may not be in the base form.

1 To _____*test*_____ means to evaluate or judge how much someone knows. (v) Par. 2

2 Countries that are ruled by another country are called _____*colonies*_____. (n pl) Par. 3

Factors → 3 _____*Examinitions*_____ are things that influence a result. (n pl) Par. 3

4 To spend time thinking about a decision is to _____*argue*_____ it. (v) Par. 3

5 If something is very large, or huge, it is _____*enormous*_____. (adj) Par. 4

6 _____*cheating*_____ means behaving in a dishonest way. (n) Par. 4

7 To _____*obtain*_____ something means to get it. (v) Par. 4

8 A business that makes a lot of money is _____*profitable*_____. (adj) Par. 5

9 To _____*evaluate*_____ two or more things is to think about how they are similar. (v) Par. 7 *compare*

10 A/An _____*Policies*_____ is a set of guidelines or rules. (n) Par. 7

Word Families

Ⓐ The words in bold in the chart are from Reading 2. The words next to them are from the same word family. Study and learn these words.

Ⓑ Choose the correct form of the words from the chart to complete the following sentences. Use the correct verb tenses and subject-verb agreement. Use the correct singular and plural noun forms.

NOUN	VERB	ADJECTIVE
argument	**argue**	—
competition	compete	competitive
efficiency	—	**efficient**
evaluation	**evaluate**	—
performance	perform	—

1 There is an enormous amount of _____*competition*_____ to get into the best universities.

2 A combination of students' test scores, teacher recommendations, and their _____*performance*_____ in secondary school determine whether they are admitted to the national university.

3 The government did a/an _____*evaluation*_____ of the admission tests for all of the universities in the country. They found that some of the tests were more difficult than others. *argument*

4 The students made a good _____*performance*_____ for wearing jeans to school. They said they would work better if they were comfortable.

5 Employers value creativity as well as _____efficiency_____. They want new ideas, but they also want workers who are well organized and do not waste time.

6 The committee _____evaluates_____ each application before they made a decision.

7 Some students _____perform_____ best when they are under pressure; others do better when they are relaxed.

8 Some parents _____argue_____ that there are too many tests in schools today.

*9 The new manager was very _____efficient_____. She completed her work quickly and accurately.

10 The children _____compete_____ for first prize in the race.

Academic Word List

The following are Academic Word List words from Readings 1 and 2 of this unit. Use these words to complete the sentences. (For more on the Academic Word List, see page 257.)

academic (*adj*)	emphasize (*v*)	evaluated (*v*)	factor (*n*)	obtained (*v*)
contribute to (*v*)	enormous (*adj*)	expand (*v*)	individual (*n*)	policy (*n*)

1 Although the school focused on _____ subjects, students were still able to take classes, such as art, dance, and sports.

2 Teachers often _____ the importance of asking questions.

3 There is a strict attendance _____ in this class: being absent five times results in failing.

4 Every _____ should be able to get into a university if she or he gets good test scores.

5 Taking a test can _____ feelings of nervousness and anxiety.

6 Cost is one _____ that explains why a declining number of high school students in England apply for university.

7 When Jack _____ his scores, he was happy to see that he had passed.

8 A college degree makes a/an _____ difference in how much money a person earns in a lifetime.

9 The teacher _____ Ahmed's writing and placed him in college-level English.

10 Hong Kong is trying to _____ access to local universities so that more students can study there instead of going overseas.

Critical Thinking

In Reading 2, the writer discusses the impact of testing on students' lives.

Discuss the following questions with a partner. Use your own ideas and opinions to explain your answers.

1 Do standardized tests really measure how well a student understands a subject?
2 Is it fair to use only the results of a test in order to determine a student's future?

> **EXPLORING OPINIONS**
>
> Critical readers form their own opinions about important topics in a text.

Research

Conduct a survey to see how each member of your class responded to the two questions above. Compile the results. What percentage of the class believes tests are a good way to measure learning? What percentage believes they are a bad way to measure learning? For those who responded that tests are not a good way to measure learning, find out what other forms of measurement they suggest. You may also need to do some research online to find out more about other ways to measure learning.

Writing

Write two paragraphs. The first paragraph will describe the results of your class's response to the first question. The second paragraph will discuss their suggestions for other ways to measure learning.

Improving Your Reading Speed

Good readers read quickly and still understand most of what they read.

A Read the instructions and strategies for Improving Your Reading Speed in Appendix 3 on page 271.

B Choose either Reading 1 or Reading 2 in this unit. Read it without stopping. Time how long it takes you to finish the text in minutes and seconds. Enter the time in the chart on page 272. Then calculate your reading speed in number of words per minute.

Finding Supporting Details

As you learned in Skills and Strategies 2 on page 21, each paragraph has a main idea that contains a topic and a claim. Writers need to provide statements that give specific information to make their readers believe that claim. These statements are called *supporting details*. Supporting details are usually examples, numbers, facts, and reasons. Learning to identify supporting details will help you understand what you read.

Examples & Explanations

①The focus of education today is becoming increasingly international. ②In the past, students focused on studying the history and geography of their own country. ③These days, however, students study the history and geography of other countries as well as their own. ④They also learn how to communicate with different cultures by studying a second and sometimes third language. ⑤Finally, today many students study overseas. ⑥Each year over three million students leave their country to study overseas. ⑦Educational leaders know that today's students need skills as well as knowledge about the world.

Sentence 1 contains the main idea of the paragraph: *The focus of education today is becoming increasingly international.*

Sentence 2 provides some background information about what happened in the past. This is useful, but does not give details that support the claim.

Sentences 3–6 support the main idea with specific details.

Sentence 7 is a conclusion sentence. It restates the main idea.

The Language of Supporting Details

Writers use the following transition words to signal a supporting detail.

WORDS THAT SIGNAL SUPPORTING DETAILS	WORDS THAT SIGNAL EXAMPLES	WORDS THAT SIGNAL A REASON OR EXPLANATION
to begin with	for example	because
also, in addition	for instance	for this reason
first, second, next	including	so, as a result
furthermore	such as	since
moreover		therefore
another		
last, finally		

Strategies

These strategies will help you identify supporting details.

- First identify the main idea using the strategies you learned in Skills and Strategies 2 on page 21. Highlight the main idea as you read.

- Look for examples, facts, numbers, and reasons that support the main idea. Note transition words that introduce these supporting details.

- Number supporting details as you read. Check that these details support the main idea by looking back and rereading the main idea that you highlighted.

- One way to practice this skill is by writing an outline of an important paragraph. This is a good strategy to check if you understand the main idea and if you can find the supporting details. Outlining also helps you remember the information. An outline lists only the most important information. It is written in a short form that does not need complete sentences. The following is an example of a simple outline.

> *Main idea: The focus of education is becoming international.*
> *a. students study about other countries*
> *b. students learn second / third language*
> *c. 3 million students study overseas*

Skill Practice 1

Read the following pairs of sentences. Write *M* next to the sentence that is a main idea. Write *S* next to the sentence that is a supporting detail.

1. ___ A For example, a study in the United States found that students in small classes graduated from high school at higher rates than students who were in large classes.

   ___ B Although many factors affect student success, class size is one of the most important.

2. ___ A In the past, U.S., Canadian, and British universities have attracted the largest number of international students, but today many students are choosing to study in other countries.

   ___ B As a result, Singapore will increase the number of its international students to 150,000 in 2015.

3. ___ A People learn information in different ways.

   ___ B For instance, some people find it easier to learn things by listening.

4. ___ A Therefore, many parents read to their children at bedtime.

   ___ B Educational research has found that parents play an essential role in a child's education.

Skill Practice 2

The following groups of sentences are parts of a paragraph. Write _M_ next to the sentence that is a main idea. Write _S_ next to the two sentences that are supporting details.

1. _____ A Students need to think and ask questions about things they are learning.

   _____ B Education is not only about learning and remembering facts.

   _____ C In addition, learning how to be a responsible member of society is very important.

2. _____ A A student in Poland, for example, can access online information from a library in Toronto.

   _____ B Today, technology is changing the way instructors teach.

   _____ C There are also online help centers where students from anywhere in the world can get help with their homework.

3. _____ A Moreover, some brilliant people, such as Albert Einstein, did not do well on tests at school.

   _____ B Some students perform badly on a test because they are so nervous.

   _____ C A test does not always show how much a student knows and understands.

4. _____ A Over half of U.S. college students are in their thirties because they have worked between secondary school and college.

   _____ B Moreover, some colleges in western countries offer "senior school" to students who are over fifty-five. 55

   _____ C Education does not begin at the age of five and end when a student graduates from college.

Skill Practice 3

Read the following paragraphs. The main ideas are given to you. Find the supporting details in the paragraph, and write them on the blank lines, like an outline.

1. One-room schoolhouses were schools where children of all ages learned together in one classroom. In the nineteenth and first half of the twentieth centuries, there were many of these schoolhouses in farming areas of the United States, Australia, and New Zealand. It was not easy being a teacher in this kind of school. First, the teacher had to learn how to teach with no training. The teacher was often a previous student of the school and sometimes as young as 16 years old. She had to arrive at the schoolhouse early in order to light a fire and sweep the floors. She often cooked breakfast for the children, who were hungry after walking or riding a long distance to get to school. Then she had to teach all subjects to children of all ages.

Main idea: It was not easy being a teacher in a one-room schoolhouse.

Supporting detail: _____

Supporting detail: _____

Supporting detail: _____

Supporting detail: _____

2   Bilingual education means teaching school subjects in two languages. Many countries have bilingual education programs. In the United States, however, not everyone thinks these programs are a good idea. In bilingual U.S. schools, children of immigrants learn math, social science, and history in their own language while they are still learning English. Some people argue that immigrants have always had to learn English in order to be successful in the United States. They also say that the best and quickest way to learn English is to speak it in all classes. Finally, they believe that it will be harder for children if they speak two languages at school.

Main idea: Not everyone in the United States thinks that teaching school subjects in two languages is a good idea.

Supporting detail: _①__some_people_argue_that_____

Supporting detail: _____they_also_say_that_____

Supporting detail: _____it_will_be_harder_for_children__

3   From the 1870s to the 1930s, thousands of Native American children were sent away from their parents to live in boarding schools. The goal of these schools was to teach Native American children how to be Americans. On the first day, teachers gave the children new English names and cut their long hair. The children were permitted to speak only English; if teachers heard children speaking in their native language, they hit them. The boarding schools were a long way from home, and many children did not go home for many years. Moreover, the schools forced the children to study the Bible and did not allow them to practice their own religion. Today, however, people understand that a person can be Native American and American at the same time.

Main idea: Boarding schools forced Native American children to give up their culture.

Supporting detail: _____

Supporting detail: _____

Supporting detail: _____

Supporting detail: _____

Connecting to the Topic

Read the definition of *alternative*, and then discuss the following questions with a partner.

> **alternative** (*adj*) offering something that is different, especially from what is usual

1 What do you think *alternative* means when it is used in phrases such as *alternative fuel* or *alternative music*? Give some examples.

2 What do you think *alternative education* means? What do you think might be some examples of *alternative education*?

3 Was the high school you attended alternative, or was it traditional?

Previewing and Predicting

> Reading the first sentence of each paragraph and looking at graphs can help you predict what a text will be about.

A **Read the first sentence of each paragraph in Reading 3, and look at the graph (Figure 2.2) on page 71. Then put a check (✓) next to the questions you think will be answered in the reading.**

_____ A Why are alternative high schools becoming popular?

_____ B Why do some people decide not to go to university?

_____ C What is homeschooling?

_____ D Is public education successful?

_____ E Why is distance learning popular?

_____ F How are university entrance exams changing?

_____ G How many students are studying in other countries?

_____ H How many students are studying online?

B **Compare your answers with a partner's.**

While You Read

As you read, stop at the end of each sentence that contains words in bold. Follow the instructions in the box in the margin.

◀)) Alternative Education

1   Most people agree that public education has been successful – students learn skills that help them improve their lives. However, many parents and business leaders are criticizing public education. Some parents argue that schools are too concerned with standardized tests. Business leaders, on the other hand, believe that most schools do not teach the skills needed in today's world. Bill Gates, founder of Microsoft, describes American schools as **obsolete**. He states that schools were designed in the 1950s, and that they have not changed to fit the needs of today's workplace. Because of this criticism, parents and business leaders are looking for different ways to teach children. These different approaches are known as *alternative education*. Alternative education can take place in a school, a home, or online.

2   Alternative high schools are becoming popular, especially in the United States. These schools often have a very different curriculum than traditional high schools. Some teach more of the arts, for example, while others concentrate on the sciences. Because of the global **demand** for an increasing number of highly skilled workers, many alternative high schools today concentrate on technology. In San Diego, for example, a group of business leaders was worried about the shortage of skilled people for the high-tech workplace. So, in 2000, they decided to start a school called High Tech High. Businesses such as Cisco Systems, IBM, and Microsoft provided funding.

3   At High Tech High, students learn actively from hands-on experience. For example, they design and build their own projects. Instead of taking tests, students are evaluated on their projects. In addition to their class work, all students work outside the classroom in local businesses and organizations. This school has been so successful that there are now 11 High Tech Schools, for students ages 5 to 18.

4   *Homeschooling* is another form of alternative education. In this system, parents become the teachers, and the home becomes the school. Parents choose homeschooling for many different **reasons**. Some disagree with

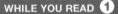

WHILE YOU READ ❶
The next sentence explains the meaning of *obsolete*. Highlight the words that help you understand the meaning.

WHILE YOU READ ❷
Which part of speech and definition is correct for *demand* in this sentence?
a) (*n*) A need or desire
b) (*v*) To ask strongly for something

WHILE YOU READ ❸
Highlight the supporting details as you continue to read.

Some parents choose to homeschool their children.

standardized tests; some do not like a traditional curriculum. Others choose to homeschool because they want to emphasize religious instruction, which is not always available in traditional schools. Parents may also see homeschooling as an opportunity to spend more time with their children. In general, they believe they can do a better job of teaching their children than schools.

5   For all of these reasons, a growing number of families are choosing homeschooling. How large is this number? Most countries do not keep statistics on homeschooling, so the numbers are approximate. It is estimated that Canada has about 80,000 homeschool families – a number that has been growing each year. In Great Britain, the government estimated that there were 50,000 homeschool families in 2007, and it is expected that the number will grow. The United States has the largest number of homeschool families with around two million children homeschooled each year.

6   The fastest growing form of alternative education is *distance learning* – taking classes online. There are many reasons why students become distance learners. Location is one important factor. Distance learners can live in one city and take classes from another city – or even another country – without ever leaving home. Because classes are online, all they need is a computer and Internet access. This means that students do not have to leave their home country in order to experience an international **education**.

7   Another important advantage of distance learning is convenience. Learners can study when they want to. They do not need to attend classes at a particular time. This allows people with full-time jobs to continue their education in their free time – in the evenings or on weekends. Many online courses also allow students to work at their own pace. In other words, the students in the course do not have to follow the same **schedule**. Some students may complete a course quickly; others may take much longer.

8   Online courses are becoming more and more common throughout the world. There are even high schools and universities that are completely online. These online institutions have no buildings. Students and teachers log in remotely and all assignments and tests are done online. In the United States, online courses have been gaining in popularity every year. In 2010, of the approximately 20 million students studying in postsecondary

WHILE YOU READ 4

Highlight the main idea of paragraph 6.

WHILE YOU READ 5

Look in the next sentence for clues to the meaning of *schedule*. Highlight the clues that help you understand the meaning.

Figure 2.2 Enrollment in U.S Colleges and Universities – 2002–2010

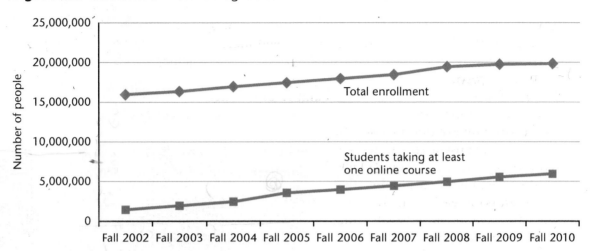

Source: Sloan Consortium

institutions, more than six million of them were studying at least one of their courses online. (See Figure 2.2) This figure is increasing by 10 percent every year.

9   The future for alternative education looks very strong. Because a growing number of people are dissatisfied with traditional education, it is likely that alternative programs, such as alternative high schools, homeschooling, and distance learning will continue to expand globally. It is also likely that as technology continues to change, people will develop new forms of schooling. Some people even believe that in the future, all schools will become alternative and offer more choices in how and what people learn.

Main Idea Check

Match the main ideas below to five of the paragraphs in Reading 3. Write the number of the paragraph on the blank line.

_____ A The number of people who are going to school online is growing every year.

_____ B One school uses an alternative curriculum to prepare students for careers in technology.

_____ C People choose homeschooling for several reasons.

_____ D People choose distance education because it is convenient.

_____ E People choose alternative education because they are not satisfied with traditional schools.

A Closer Look

Look back at Reading 3 to answer the following questions.

1 In paragraph 1, it says that Bill Gates describes American schools as obsolete. Which paragraphs describe an alternative education model that he would like the best?

a Paragraphs 2 and 3
b Paragraphs 4 and 5
c Paragraphs 6 and 7

2 Why did business leaders decide to start High Tech High, according to paragraph 2? Circle all that apply.

a They did not like the arts curriculum.
b They wanted to meet global demand for technology.
c They wanted to prepare skilled workers for their companies.
d They thought students needed more work experience.

3 Primary school students can attend High Tech Schools. True or False?

4 Most countries keep statistics on homeschooling. True or False?

5 According to paragraph 5, which country has the most homeschool families?

a Canada
b The United States
c Great Britain
d Europe

6 According to Figure 2.2, what percentage of U.S. college and university students are taking at least one course online?

a About 5 percent
b About 30 percent
c About 60 percent
d Almost 100 percent

7 It is possible to get a university degree completely online. (True) or False?

8 According to paragraph 9, what are the two reasons why alternative education will continue to grow?
   (a) Technology will lead to new forms of education.
   b There will be global demand for skilled workers.
   c Traditional schools will be obsolete.
   (d) More people will be unhappy with traditional schools.

Skill Review

In Skills and Strategies 4, you learned that writers support their main points with details such as examples and explanations. Identifying the supporting details is an important reading skill.

Paragraph 4 discusses reasons for homeschooling (Main Idea 1). Paragraphs 6 and 7 discuss reasons for distance learning (Main Idea 2).

Main Idea 1: *There are several reasons why parents decide to homeschool their children.*

Main Idea 2: *Distance learning offers several advantages.*

A Read the following supporting details for these two main ideas. Then sort the supporting details. Write *1* on the blank lines before the supporting details for Main Idea 1, and write *2* on the blank lines before the supporting details for Main Idea 2.

1 _____ Religious instruction may be an important part of education for some people.

2 _____ Students want to choose their own schedule.

3 _____ Parents want to spend more time with their children.

4 _____ Some people believe schools are too traditional.

5 _____ Not everyone learns at the same pace.

6 _____ Some learners don't want to travel to school.

B Find a sentence or phrase in Reading 3 that matches each detail in step A.

Definitions

Find the words in Reading 3 that complete the following definitions. When a verb completes the definition, use the base form, although the verb in the reading may not be in the base form.

1 To _____ means to say something bad about someone or something. (v) Par. 1

2 When someone is worried, they are _____ about someone or something. (adj) Par. 1

3 Something that is _____ is no longer used. It has been replaced by something newer. (adj) Par. 1

4 _____ are methods or ways of doing something. (n pl) Par. 1

5 A lack of something that is needed is called a/an _____. (n) Par. 2

6 _____ are a collection of numerical facts. (n) Par. 5

7 _____ means almost exact. (adj) Par. 5

8 A/An _____ is a specific place. (n) Par. 6

9 Someone who is _____ with something is unhappy about it. (adj) Par. 9

10 If something is probably true, it is _____. (adj) Par. 9

Words in Context

Complete the passages with words and phrases from Reading 3 in the box below.

alternative	design	estimate	high-tech
concentrate on	especially	hands-on	workplace

1 Some students don't like academic subjects. Instead they want to take courses that
include _____ projects. They want to _____ furniture or fix
       a   b
machines. They believe this kind of course will prepare them better for the
_____. It is important for schools to provide this kind of
   c
_____ education for students who do not do well in traditional schools.
   d

2 A government report says there will be a significant increase in the number of
_____ jobs in the next 10 years. Experts _____ that the
   e   f
number will double during that time. Job growth will be _____ strong in
                                                  g
computer systems. They suggest that students _____ math and science
                                                      h
courses in school.

Critical Thinking

Reading 3 states that some universities and high schools are completely online.

A In small groups, consider the advantages and disadvantages of online schools. Make a chart like the one below. One example has been done for you.

ADVANTAGES	DISADVANTAGES
	Students would not be able to play sports like in traditional schools.

B With your group, discuss possible ways to reduce the disadvantages of online education.

Research

Survey your classmates and do online research to find out about online learning. Take notes on what you find. Find answers to the following questions.

- Has anyone in your class taken an online course?
- What did they like? What didn't they like?
- What kinds of online courses are offered at the schools or universities that you researched?
- What kinds of online courses are your classmates interested in?

Writing

Write two paragraphs. The first paragraph will describe the advantages of distance learning. The second paragraph will describe its disadvantages.

Connecting to the Topic

Discuss the following questions with a partner.

1 How well do you think your schoolwork has prepared you for your job?

2 Of all the skills you learned in school, which ones do you think are the most important? Why?

3 What other skills are important for today's workplace?

4 Are there any skills you do not have but would like to learn?

Previewing and Predicting

When you preview a text, look to see if the text is divided into sections. Also, look to see if the sections have headings. Read the headings, and think about why the writer divided the text in this way.

A Read the section headings in Reading 4. Decide what content will be in each section. Then write the number of the section (*I–V*) next to the topic that best describes it.

SECTION	TOPIC
	A description of skills people need today
	An evaluation of how different countries are teaching twenty-first century skills
	An explanation of why twenty-first century skills are essential
	An explanation about how people use skills while they are working
	Background information about how the meaning of *literacy* has changed through history

B Compare your answer with a partner's.

While You Read

As you read, stop at the end of each sentence that contains words in bold. Follow the instructions in the box in the margin.

Skills for the Twenty-First Century

I. The Changing Meaning of Literacy

1   Education and jobs have been closely connected for many years. In the eighteenth century, being literate meant you could sign your name. In the nineteenth century, industrialization spread across the western world, and jobs began to change. People needed more skills to do these jobs, so literacy meant reading and writing. By the end of the twentieth century, technology had significantly changed, and many jobs required some computer skills. At this time, the meaning of literacy expanded to include these skills. At the beginning of the twenty-first century, education and business leaders began trying to find out what skills students need to be successful in today's workplace. One thing is certain: twenty-first-century skills are very different from skills people **needed in the past**.

II. Defining Twenty-First-Century Skills

2   Today, experts believe that in order to be successful in the workplace, most students need digital skills, such as information literacy. Students skilled in information literacy can do **three things**. First, they can find information, such as text, videos, and audio files, from different sources. Next, they know how to evaluate these sources to make sure the information is current and accurate. For example, a website must be written by an expert and use recent information. Finally, students are able to use a range of technology tools and software programs to present their information to others. In other words, they must be able to use technology to find, organize, analyze, evaluate, and communicate information.

3   Excellent communication is also essential for the twenty-first century. Good communication includes many skills. A person must be able to talk

> **WHILE YOU READ 1**
> What is the topic of paragraph 1? What claim is the author making? Highlight the topic and the claim.

> **WHILE YOU READ 2**
> Highlight the supporting details in this paragraph as you read.

The ability to work in groups is an important skill.

or write about their ideas in a way that other people can clearly understand. In addition, communication includes working well in a group. In most businesses, groups of people must collaborate to solve problems and think of new ideas. Each group member must listen carefully, ask questions, and explain ideas clearly. Lastly, good communication includes knowing how to work with people from different cultures. People in today's businesses come from all over the world. So, in this global economy, speaking a second language is a real advantage.

4   A third skill is critical thinking. Critical thinking is really a set of skills. It requires solving problems in creative ways and changing plans when something does not work. It also includes **curiosity**. In other words, critical thinkers ask questions about the world around them. They ask *Why?* and *Why not?* Many schools are trying to encourage these critical thinking skills. For example, in Singapore, educators have designed a national math curriculum that requires more critical thinking and less rote learning, or just memorizing information.

WHILE YOU READ ③

Look in the next sentence for the meaning of *curiosity*. Highlight the words that help you understand the meaning.

III. Using Twenty-First-Century Skills at Work

5   How do people incorporate these skills into their work? Consider the following example. A few years ago, three friends were talking about the problems of sending video by e-mail. Video files are very large, so when one friend tried to send a video, it took a very long time. Often the e-mail rejected the file and returned it to the sender. The friends then had an idea. Why not design a website that lets people send videos easily? People could share their videos with anyone, anywhere. This idea was the beginning of YouTube – one of today's most popular websites. Chad Hurley, Steve Chen, and Jawed Karim, the three friends, launched the website in February 2005. By summer of the following year, YouTube was the fastest growing site on the Internet. It was a huge success. In October 2006, just 20 months after its **launch**, they sold YouTube to another Internet success, Google, for $1.6 billion.

Chad Hurley and Steve Chen, founders of YouTube

6   Hurley, Chen, and Karim used twenty-first-century skills to start YouTube. All three had strong academic backgrounds and digital skills. They were graduates in computer science, engineering, and the arts. When they encountered a problem, they solved it by thinking creatively. They worked well together and communicated their ideas clearly and effectively to **investors** who then agreed to lend them money. Finally, the three friends understood that great ideas need to be global. They designed a website where someone in Australia can upload a video that is instantly available to a person in Italy.

WHILE YOU READ ④

Use context clues to figure out the meaning of *launch*. Is it (a) funding, (b) beginning, or (c) visit?

WHILE YOU READ ⑤

Use context clues to define *investors*. Highlight the words that help you understand the meaning.

IV. How Well Are Schools Teaching These Skills?

7   Are schools around the world teaching twenty-first-century skills? There are wide differences across the world in teaching digital skills. On the one hand, in some regions of Africa, South East Asia, and Latin America, many schools do not have access to technology. For example, only about five percent of people with Internet access live in Africa. On the other hand, just two countries, the United States and China, are home to about 35 percent of the world's Internet users. Internet use is growing, especially in Asia, where the number of users increased by 44 percent between 2001 and 2011. However, this difference in access to technology, called the "digital divide," remains a problem. Because of the digital divide, not all countries are able to teach digital skills.

8   Most countries are also focusing on communication skills – particularly teaching second languages. Students across the world learn English since it is an international language. European countries begin to teach English in primary school, and in China, children start studying English in kindergarten at the age of four. In addition to studying at home, each year thousands of students travel to English speaking countries to improve their English. Around 725,000 international students study in the United States, 400,000 study in Great Britain, and 475,000 study in Australia. This shows that many countries are successful in teaching a second language.

9   Countries where English is the first language are not doing so well in teaching a second language. Compared to China and Europe, a much smaller number of American children learn another language. Only about 15 percent of Americans speak a language other than English well, and many of these are immigrants. In Europe, more than half of the population speaks a second language well. So countries like the United States are falling behind the rest of the world in teaching second languages.

10   It is difficult to estimate how well schools are teaching critical thinking. Because standardized testing is common around the world, many education experts believe that rote learning is still emphasized in most schools. This is partly because it is much easier to test rote learning in a standardized test than it is to test critical thinking. As long as most countries continue to use traditional tests, it is likely that teachers will continue to encourage more rote learning than critical **thinking**.

V. The Importance of Twenty-First-Century Skills

11   The United Nations estimates that 80 percent of all economic activity in industrial nations comes from human skills and knowledge. Therefore, business and education leaders believe that it is essential for schools to teach twenty-first-century skills. They believe that these skills improve the lives of individuals as well as the economies of nations. So today, education and employment are still very closely connected as schools try to change with the rapidly changing world.

WHILE YOU READ 6

Highlight the definition of *digital divide*.

WHILE YOU READ 7

Highlight the main idea of paragraph 10.

Main Idea Check

Match the main ideas below to five of the paragraphs in Reading 4. Write the number of the paragraph on the blank line.

_____ A The men who started YouTube used today's skills.

_____ B Some countries cannot teach digital skills to all of their citizens.

_____ C Good communication is important for the twenty-first-century workplace.

_____ D People who live in English-speaking countries often do not learn a second language.

_____ E Information literacy can be divided into three skills.

A Closer Look

Look back at Reading 4 to answer the following questions.

1 Which statement is *not* correct according to the first paragraph?

   a The meaning of literacy has changed over time.

   b Literacy today means the ability to read and write.

   c In the twenty-first century, computer skills have become a part of literacy.

   d The first meaning of literacy was the ability to sign your name.

2 What is the purpose of the last sentence of paragraph 2?

   a It repeats the main idea of the paragraph.

   b It introduces a new idea.

   c It provides more information to a supporting detail.

   d It gives background information.

3 Why does the writer use the example of YouTube? Circle all that apply.

   a It makes the article more interesting.

   b It helps the reader understand how skills are used in businesses today.

   c YouTube is a successful company because Google bought it for a lot of money.

   d YouTube is a global company.

   e It is an example that illustrates the main idea of the reading.

4 According to paragraph 4, which of the activities below use critical thinking? Circle all that apply.

   a Using new information to solve an old problem

   b Reading a map

   c Asking for reasons

   d Reporting on a meeting

5 According to paragraph 10, why is it difficult to evaluate how well critical thinking skills are taught?

   a Standardized tests never include critical thinking exercises.

   b It is easier to test for rote learning.

   c Most countries use standardized tests that test memorized learning.

   d Students who study critical thinking do not take tests.

6 Why will teachers probably continue to teach rote learning, according to paragraph 10?

   a Rote learning is an important skill in today's world.

   b Students need to learn how to remember information.

   c All standardized tests evaluate a student's ability to analyze information.

   d The most common standardized tests evaluate memorized information rather than critical thinking.

7 According to paragraph 11, there is a direct connection between education and the world economy. **True or False?**

Skill Review

> In Skills and Strategies 4, you learned that one way to practice and remember supporting details is to make an outline. Outlining can help you understand the information in a text and prepare for a test.

A Make an outline for paragraphs 3 and 9 by listing the supporting details under the main ideas.

Paragraph 3

Main idea: Communication skills are essential for the twenty-first century.

   a _____

   b _____

   c _____

Paragraph 8

Main idea: Many countries are teaching English as an international language.

   a _____

   b _____

   c _____

B Compare your outlines with a partner's.

Definitions

Find the words in Reading 4 that complete the following definitions. When a verb completes the definition, use the base form, although the verb in the reading may not be in the base form.

1 Someone who knows a lot about a subject is called a / an _____ *Expert*.
   (*n*) Par. 2

2 To _____ means to work together on something. (*v*) Par. 3 *Collaborate*

3 To _____ means to need something or make something necessary.
   (*v*) Par. 4 *require*

4 _____ means a strong desire to learn about something new. (*n*) Par. 4 *curiosity*

5 If you _____ somebody or something, it is more likely to happen.
   (*v*) Par. 4 *encourage*

6 To _____ means to begin or introduce something new. (*v*) Par. 5 *launch*

7 _____ means you successfully produce the results you want. (*adv*) Par. 6 *effectivly*

8 People who provide money to a business are known as _____s. *investors*
   (*n pl*) Par. 6

9 To _____ something is to give it temporarily. (*v*) Par. 6 *lend*

10 Large geographical areas are called _____. (*n pl*) Par. 7

Synonyms

Complete the sentences with words from Reading 4 in the box below. These words replace the words or phrases in parentheses, which are similar in meaning.

accurate	creative	encounter	incorporated
analyzed	current	essential	range

1 The television program reported on (recent) _____ events in Europe.
   (*adj*) Par. 2

2 She checked her test to make sure all the answers were (correct) _____.
   (*adj*) Par. 2

3 The store sells a wide (variety) _____ of products. (*n*) Par. 2

4 The doctor (studied carefully) _____ the patient's blood. (*v*) Par. 2

5 The business students thought of some (original and unusual) _____ ideas
   for new products. (*adj*) Par. 4

6 We (included) _____ everyone's suggestions in the final report. (*v*) Par. 5

7 I hope that we don't (experience) _____ bad weather on our trip.
   (v) Par. 6

8 It is (very important) _____ to arrive early at the airport. The lines are very
   long. (adj) Par. 11

Academic Word List

**The following are Academic Word List words from Readings 3 and 4 of this unit. Use
these words to complete the sentences. (For more on the Academic Word List, see
page 257.)**

alternative (adj)	approximate (adj)	design (v)	estimated (v)	incorporated (v)
analyze (v)	creative (adj)	encounter (v)	expert (n)	range (n)

1 I am not very traditional so I prefer _____ music.

2 My sister is very _____. She is always has original ideas for how to
   do things.

3 After the students finished their research, they _____ the new
   information into their projects.

4 A company from New York was hired to _____ the new airport.

5 The workman _____ that it would cost $500 to repair the car.

6 The teacher asked her students to _____ the information and present
   their findings to the class.

7 Western companies sometimes _____ problems when they do business
   in other countries.

8 The website sold books on a/an _____ of topics, from the economy to
   the arts.

9 If you are very sick, it is important to ask a medical _____ for advice.

10 The _____ number of students in each class is 50.

Critical Thinking

Reading 4 claims that twenty-first century students need skills in three important areas: digital literacy, communication, and critical thinking.

PERSONALIZING

Thinking about how new information applies to your own life can help you understand a text better.

A **Discuss the following questions with a partner:**

1 Are these skills important for you? Why or why not?

2 Did your high school focus on each of the three skills?

3 How well did your school teach each skill? For example, did your school encourage critical thinking, or did it focus on rote learning?

B **Share your answers with your class.**

Research

Survey some of your classmates. Find answers to the following questions.

- How well did their education prepare them in digital skills, communication skills, and critical thinking skills?
- Where did they learn these skills?

Writing

Write three paragraphs. Each paragraph will discuss one of the three skills above. Explain why they are important, and describe the experiences of your classmates.

Improving Your Reading Speed

Good readers read quickly and still understand most of what they read.

A Read the instructions and strategies for Improving Your Reading Speed in Appendix 3 on page 271.

B Choose either Reading 3 or Reading 4 in this unit. Read it without stopping. Time how long it takes you to finish the text in minutes and seconds. Enter the time in the chart on page 272. Then calculate your reading speed in number of words per minute.

PRONOUN CONNECTORS

Writers use pronouns to connect words and ideas within and across sentences. A *pronoun* is a word that replaces a *noun*. The noun it replaces is called an *antecedent*. The antecedent always comes before the pronoun. In the following example, the pronouns are in **bold**, and their antecedents are underlined.

Today schools often focus on children's emotional and physical needs as well as on **their** academic needs.

The pronouns *this* and *these* can refer to whole ideas that the writer introduces earlier in the sentence or in the previous sentence.

Students in many countries work very hard to get into the best universities. **This** is not easy because the universities only admit a small number of students.

Exercise 1

Find the antecedents to the pronouns in bold in the following sentences. Write the antecedents on the blank lines.

1 Parents choose homeschooling for many reasons. **They** may want to emphasize religious instruction, or **they** may disagree with standardized testing.

They _____

they _____

2 The fastest growing type of alternative education is distance learning. **This** is not surprising because **it** is so convenient.

This _____

it _____

3 The students agreed to collaborate on their final project. **They** thought **this** was the best way to finish **it** quickly.

They _____

this _Project_ _____

it _Project_ _____

4 Primary education is compulsory in most countries, and **it** is usually free. **This** means that most children have the opportunity to gain at least basic literacy skills.

it _____

This _____

Exercise 2

Make a clear paragraph by putting sentences A, B, C into the best order after the numbered sentence. Look for pronouns and repeated key words to help you. Write the letters in the correct order on the blank lines.

1 Some U.S. educational leaders believe that the SAT admission test is unfair.

   B   A   C

A This test often includes topics such as sports and business.	**B** These leaders argue that although girls get better grades than boys in high school, they are more likely to score lower on the SAT.	**C** These topics are more familiar to boys, so it makes sense that they score higher.

2 Boarding schools started approximately 1,000 years ago in England.   C   A   B

A Later, in the twelfth century, the Pope ordered all churches to open schools.	**B** This expanded the number of schools.	**C** They began in churches because the religious leaders were the only literate people in the community.

3 Assessment is a challenge for teachers of distance learning classes.   B   A   C

A This means they have to design questions that make it difficult to cheat.	**B** Teachers have to assess students who are not in a classroom.	**C** To make sure of this, teachers often write long and complicated tests.

4 There are many different types of programs and degrees in higher education.

   C   A B   B

A Students can also take a technical program.	**B** Admission to this type of program is often easier as fewer academic courses are required.	**C** There are bachelor's and master's degrees in the sciences and the arts for students with a strong academic background.

5 In the United States, many schoolchildren have a very long summer vacation.

   B   C   A

A They needed their children to help work in the fields.	**B** It can last almost three months.	**C** The three-month vacation began when most people in the country were farmers.

3

THE WORLD OF BUSINESS

SKILLS AND STRATEGIES

- The Vocabulary of Numbers
- Information in Graphs and Charts

The Vocabulary of Numbers

> Academic writing often includes information about numbers. Writers use a range of vocabulary to talk about numbers. Understanding this vocabulary is an important part of becoming a strong academic reader.

Examples & Explanations

The words in bold in the following paragraph are examples of words and phrases that refer to numbers.

①The price you pay for gas at the gas station is directly connected to the cost of oil. ②Oil is measured in barrels, and in recent history, the cost of a barrel of oil has **sharply increased**. ③In January 1970, the **average cost** of a barrel of oil was below $20. ④By 1975, this **had doubled to** over $40 – **an increase of** more than **100 percent**. ⑤The cost continued **to rise rapidly**, and in 1980, it reached $90. ⑥In the next five years, it **fell again** by $60, but this **decline** ended in the early 1990s when the cost began to **significantly grow** again. ⑦By 2005, a barrel of oil cost $50; and it **continued to rise** to just under $100 a barrel in 2010. ⑧This was an increase of more than **500 percent** in about 40 years.

In sentence 2, *increased* is a verb. In sentence 4, *increase* is a noun. Words like *increase*, *rise*, and *decline* are used in both noun and verb form.

Writers use synonyms to add variety to sentences. For example, in sentences 2–7, the following words all mean the same thing: *to rise, to grow, to increase*.

In sentences 2 and 6, the writer uses adverbs such as *sharply* and *significantly* to show the amount or speed of a change.

Numbers can express many things: value of money, time periods, amounts. In sentence 8, an amount is expressed as a percentage.

Note that in sentences 3–8, the writer uses time words to talk about the change in cost over the years: *in January 1970, in the next five years, by 2005, in about 40 years*.

The Language of Numbers

The following words are used to introduce and describe numbers.

GROWING NUMBERS	FALLING NUMBERS	WORDS TO DESCRIBE CHANGE
to double / triple	to decline / a decline	dramatic / dramatically
to go up	to decrease / a decrease	rapid / rapidly
to grow / a growth	to drop / a drop	sharp / sharply
to increase / an increase	to fall / a fall	significant / significantly
to rise / a rise	to go down	slight / slightly
		slow / slowly
		steady / steadily

Strategies

These strategies will help you understand the language of numbers.

- Use any numbers in a reading to help you understand the vocabulary that refers to those numbers. For example, in the sentence: *The cost of oil doubled from $20 to $40*, the number 40 is twice as much as 20; therefore, you can guess that *doubled* means increased by twice the number.

- Remember that there are many synonyms with this type of vocabulary. Learn the vocabulary in groups of synonyms. For example, learn the vocabulary in the Language of Numbers chart on page 88 under each heading: Growing Numbers, Falling Numbers, and Words to Describe Change.

- Make sure you figure out the part of speech – particularly for words that are the same in noun and verb form. For example: *Oil increased* (v). . . . *This was an increase* (n). . . . This will help you as you read.

Skill Practice 1

Use the vocabulary from the Language of Numbers chart on page 88 to complete the statements below Table 1. Use the correct verb tenses. There may be more than one possible answer.

1 From 1900 to 1920, the price of butter _____ from 23 cents to 63 cents per pound. This was a/an _____ of around 300 percent.

2 In 1930, however, it _____ to 44 cents.

3 In the 20 years between 1930 and 1950, the cost of butter rose _____ .

4 It _____ again from 1950 to 1999.

5 In the last 30 years of the twentieth century, the cost of butter _____ to $2.48.

6 The cost of butter has continued to _____ in the twenty-first century.

Table 1 Cost of Butter in the U.S. from 1900 to 2012

YEAR	COST PER POUND OF BUTTER
1900	$0.23
1920	0.63
1930	0.44
1950	0.71
1970	0.87
1999	2.48
2011	3.65
2012	3.49

Source: *The Value of a Dollar: Prices and Incomes in the United States*

Skill Practice 2

Use the vocabulary from the Language of Numbers chart on page 88 to answer the following questions about Table 2. Write complete sentences and use the correct verb tenses. Check your answers with a partner.

1 How did the cost of eggs change from 1900 to 1920?

_____

_____

2 Describe the change in cost from 1920 to 1930.

_____

_____

3 What happened to the price from 1930 to 2000?

_____

_____

4 Describe the change in cost from 2000 to 2012.

_____

5 What do you think will happen to the price of a dozen eggs in the future?

_____

Table 2 Cost of Eggs in the U.S. from 1900 to 2012

YEAR	COST PER DOZEN EGGS
1900	$ 0.18
1920	0.71
1930	0.39
1950	0.57
2000	0.91
2011	1.25
2012	1.88

Source: The Value of a Dollar: Prices and Incomes in the United States

Skill Practice 3

The minimum wage is the lowest amount a company can pay a worker for an hour's work. Write five sentences about Table 3. Use a variety of vocabulary from the Language of Numbers chart on page 88.

Table 3 Minimum Wage in the U.S. from 1938 to 2009

YEAR	MINIMUM WAGE PER HOUR
1938	$ 0.25
1960	1.00
1980	3.10
1991	4.25
2000	5.15
2009	7.25

Source: U.S. Department of Labor, Bureau of Statistics

Connecting to the Topic

Discuss the following questions with a partner.

1 Think of a product that has *increased* in price recently.
   - Why do you think the price of this product has increased?
   - Are people now buying more or less of this product?
   - Have you bought this product recently? Why or why not?

2 Think of a product that has *decreased* in price recently.
   - Why do you think the price of this product has decreased?
   - Are people now buying more or less of this product?
   - Have you bought this product recently? Why or why not?

Previewing and Predicting

> Writers include graphs in order to present numerical information that supports a main idea of a reading. Therefore, reviewing graphs will help you predict what a text will be about.

A Read the title of Reading 1, and look at the graph (Figure 3.1) on page 92 and the photo on page 93. Then put a check (✓) next to the topics you think will be included in the reading.

_____ A Coffee prices

_____ B Why people like coffee

_____ C How many cups of coffee people buy

_____ D The connection between how many cups of coffee and price per cup

_____ E Places where coffee grows

_____ F Why coffee is not very good for you

B Compare your answers with a partner's.

While You Read

As you read, stop at the end of each sentence that contains words in bold. Follow the instructions in the box in the margin.

Supply and Demand in the Global Economy

1 There is a saying that a butterfly flapping its wings in Japan can cause a hurricane in North America. This saying illustrates what can happen in a global economy. An event in a business in one country can significantly affect businesses in other countries. This happened in July 2007 when an earthquake closed several Japanese power plants. These plants produced energy. Because the Japanese could not use their own energy, they needed to buy more oil from other countries. As a result, oil prices around the world rose. This shows that a natural disaster in one country can change the prices of a global product, such as oil, and can cause energy prices to increase around the world.

2 When someone or something wants or needs a product, it is called *demand*. In the example above, the Japanese demand for oil increased. When people want more of a product, **there is a growth in demand**.

3 Coffee is an example of a global product that is in growing demand. Every morning, over 166 million Americans wake up and drink their first cup for the day. As they drive to work, they stop at a coffee shop and buy their second cup. By the end of the day, the average American has drunk three cups of coffee. Therefore, the average demand for coffee at current prices in the United States is three cups per day per person. It is important

> **WHILE YOU READ** 1
>
> Look back at paragraphs 1 and 2. Highlight the words meaning *growth*.

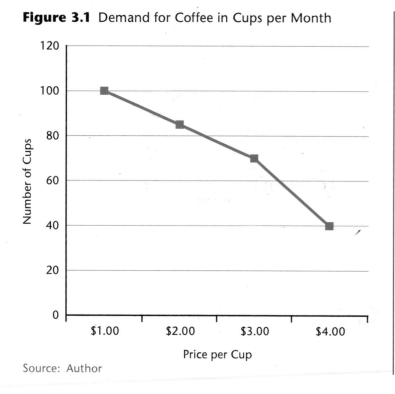

Figure 3.1 Demand for Coffee in Cups per Month

Source: Author

Table 3.1 Cost of Coffee in the U.S. from 1900 to 2012

YEAR	COST PER POUND OF COFFEE
1900	0.16
1920	0.35
1930	0.26
1950	0.90
1970	1.03
1980	2.45
1990	2.35
2000	3.54
2006	3.11
2012	5.69

Source: Author

to note that a person will buy three cups per day at current prices. If the price of a cup of coffee increases, the person may decide to drink only two cups per day. The **law of demand** states that as prices rise, demand falls. An average person will buy 70 cups of coffee each month if the coffee costs $3 a cup. However, if the cost increases to $4, the same person will now only buy 40 cups per month. (See Figure 3.1.)

4. Businesses want demand to increase so they can sell more products. However, they must also have enough of their product to sell. This is called *supply*. Supply and demand are closely connected. In the 1980s and 1990s, for example, the global demand for coffee grew rapidly, and so did the price. (See Table 3.1.) Coffee companies needed more coffee beans, so many farmers in countries such as Brazil and Vietnam grew more coffee – they increased the supply. The farmers received a good price for their coffee beans. However, by 2002, farmers had produced a surplus of this product. In other words, they were producing too much coffee – the coffee supply was 8 percent higher than the demand. As a result, coffee prices fell. Coffee farmers could not sell their beans at the previously high price, so they stopped growing coffee and grew a different crop.

5 A change in supply can have a global effect. Much of the world's corn is grown in the United States. In the past, corn was used mainly for human and animal consumption. However, since 2005, corn has also been used to produce ethanol – an alternative fuel for automobiles. From 2005 to 2007, the United States' supply of corn for food decreased by approximately 33 percent. This was because corn suppliers, the farmers, sold an increasing amount of this crop to ethanol producers. As a result of this drop in supply, corn skyrocketed to its highest price in 10 years. This price increase had a significant effect in Mexico, a country that imports corn from the United States. In a country where 50 percent of its population survives on less than $4 a day, Mexican families depend on tortillas, a basic and inexpensive food. Corn is the main ingredient of the tortilla. Therefore, when the price of corn doubled in March 2007, the cost of tortillas also doubled. A change in the supply of corn in the United States led to thousands of Mexicans gathering in the streets to protest this increase in the cost of the tortilla.

6 The laws of supply and demand are at the center of every business – from a very large global company to a small store that sells freshly cooked kebabs on a street corner in Turkey. Successful businesses today need to understand that in these days of global trade, a change in supply or demand in one part of the world can have major effects on the rest of the world.

WHILE YOU READ ❷

Read ahead and find the definition of the *law of demand*. Highlight it.

WHILE YOU READ ❸

Highlight the definition of *supply*.

WHILE YOU READ ❹

Highlight the claim in paragraph 5.

Main Idea Check

Match the main ideas below to their paragraphs. Write the number of the paragraph on the blank line.

_____ A Demand refers to the want or need for a product.

_____ B Businesses need to understand the laws of supply and demand.

_____ C An event in one country can affect businesses in other countries.

_____ D A change in supply in one country can affect prices in other countries.

_____ E The changing price of a cup of coffee illustrates the law of demand.

_____ F Supply and demand are related to each other.

A Closer Look

Look back at Reading 1 to answer the following questions.

1 Why did the writer of the reading include a saying about a butterfly and a hurricane in paragraph 1?

  a It explains the law of demand.

  b It shows that butterflies can cause hurricanes.

  c It helps the reader understand the main idea of the paragraph.

  d It helps the reader understand Japanese business.

2 According to paragraph 3, what will the average consumer do if the cost of a cup of coffee sharply increases?

  a Buy more coffee

  b Stop drinking coffee completely

  c Buy fewer cups of coffee

  d Buy the same number of cups, but complain

3 The example of coffee growers shows that when supply is higher than demand, prices rise. **True or False?**

4 Reread paragraph 4. Then complete the diagram of supply and demand. Put sentences A–E in the correct order of events. Write the correct letter in each box.

  A The price of coffee fell.

  B The demand for coffee increased.

  C Farmers grew less coffee.

  D Farmers grew more coffee.

  E There was a surplus of coffee.

5 According to paragraph 5, why did the price of corn rise from 2005 to 2007?

   ⓐ People were eating more tortillas, so demand grew.

   b The supply of corn increased.

   c The demand for corn decreased.

   ⓓ The supply of corn for people to eat decreased.

Skill Review

In Skills and Strategies 5, you learned that writers use a range of vocabulary to talk about growing numbers, falling numbers, and words to describe change. Understanding the language of numbers will help you in reading and writing tasks.

Look back at Figure 3.1 in Reading 1, and answer the following questions. If you need help, review the Language of Numbers chart on page 88.

1 Which statement is correct according to the table?

   a The cost of coffee increased steadily from 1900 to 2006.

   ⓑ From 1970 to 1980, the cost more than doubled.

   c The cost of a pound of coffee rose by 10 cents from 1980 to 1990.

2 Which statement is *not* correct according to the table?

   a From 1930 to 1990, the cost of coffee increased to $2.35 per pound.

   b In 2006, coffee cost 66 cents per pound more than it did in 1980.

   ⓒ From 1970 to 1980, the cost increased by almost 100 percent per pound.

3 In which period did coffee more than triple in price?

   a 1900–1920

   ⓑ 1930–1950

   c 1970–1980

4 Which statement best describes the main idea of the table?

   a The cost of coffee more than doubled from 1970 to 1980.

   b In 2006, coffee cost almost three dollars more per pound than it did in 1900.

   c In 1990, the cost of coffee fell by 10 cents per pound.

   ⓓ The cost of coffee increased steadily during the twentieth century.

Definitions

Find the words in Reading 1 that complete the following definitions. When a verb completes the definition, use the base form, although the verb in the reading may not be in the base form.

1 To _____illustrate_____ means to explain something by giving examples. (v) Par. 1

2 Large industrial buildings or factories are called _____plants_____. (n pl) Par. 1

3 A grain, fruit, or vegetable that is grown for food is called a/an _____crop_____. (n) Par. 4

4 A/An _____effect_____ is a result, or an impact. (n) Par. 5

5 _____approx_____ means about, or a little more or a little less than. (adj) Par. 5

6 To increase sharply means to _____ky_____. (v) Par. 5

7 To _____survive_____ is to live. (v) Par. 5

8 A/An _____ingredient_____ is one part of something – usually food. (n) Par. 5

9 If you _____protest_____, you show that you strongly disagree with something. (v) Par. 5

10 A/An _____major_____ problem is a very serious problem. (adj) Par. 6

Words in Context

Complete the sentences with words from Reading 1 in the box below.

affects	energy	fuel	previously
consumption	event	note	surplus

1 The election of Barack Obama was an important _____event_____ in U.S. history.

2 There is a/an _____surplus_____ of apples, so the price has dropped because farmers cannot sell them all.

3 Using the sun and the wind is a natural way to produce _____fuel energy_____.

4 When the cost of oil increases, it _____affects_____ the prices of many other products.

5 It is important to _____note_____ that some countries do not have a minimum wage.

6 Mexico is now producing electronic parts that were _____ made in Sweden.

7 _____ of beef in China is increasing because the Chinese are eating more of this product than in the past.

8 In Brazil, 40 percent of all automobiles use _____fuel_____ made from ethanol; the remaining 60 percent use gas.

Critical Thinking

Writers often use examples to explain key terms. In
Reading 1, the writers use the example of cups of coffee to
explain the term *demand*.

A **Complete the following statements with a partner
using information from the reading.**

1 Demand is _____

2 Supply means _____

3 The law of demand states that _____

B **With a partner, think of your own examples to explain the terms. For instance,
you could discuss how the cost of gas or cell phones increases and decreases.**

Research

**Work with a group. Think of a food or drink product that the people in your group
buy several times a month. For example, you could choose bottled water or pizza.
On average, how many times a month do the people in your group buy this product
at today's price. Suppose the price increased by 10 percent, 50 percent, or more.
Agree as a group how many times a month you would then buy the product. Enter
the number of times in the chart.**

PRODUCT:	
	NUMBER BOUGHT PER MONTH
At today's price	
After an increase in price of 10%	
After an increase in price of 25%	
After an increase in price of 50%	
After an increase in price of 100%	
After an increase in price of 200%	

Writing

**Use your research to make a graph in order to explain the law of demand. Refer to
Figure 3.1 on page 92 if you need help. Then write a paragraph to explain the law
of demand. Begin your paragraph with a definition of the term *demand*. Use your
research to explain how demand for the product changes as the price changes.**

Connecting to the Topic

Discuss the following questions with a partner.

1 What kinds of items do you have with you in class? These might be an electronic dictionary, an MP3 player, a smart phone, or a jacket. Where do you think these items were made?

2 What type of car do you own – or what type of car would you like to own? Where do you think this car is made?

Previewing and Predicting

> Look to see if a reading is divided into sections. Then look for headings. These can help you predict what a text will be about

A **Read the section headings in Reading 2, and think of a question that you expect each section to answer. Then choose the question below that is most like your question. Write the number of the section (I–III) next to that question.**

SECTION	QUESTIONS
	What is a *skilled worker*?
	What is *outsourcing*?
	What kind of workers do employers want?
	What does *mobile* mean?
	What kinds of jobs require skilled workers?
	How does outsourcing save money?
	What is a *global workforce*?

B **Compare your chart with a partner's.**

While You Read

As you read, stop at the end of each sentence that contains words in bold. Follow the instructions in the box in the margin.

The Workforce of the Twenty-First Century

I. Supply and Demand for Skilled Workers

1   Today, modern businesses must have workers with strong technology skills in order to be successful. They need workers who can design and create products using modern technologies. In other words, there is a strong global demand for skilled workers. However, the demand for skilled workers is greater than the supply. India, for example, believes it will need 500 million skilled workers in the next 20 years. Therefore, just like coffee, when the demand is high and the supply is low, the cost goes up. This means that high-tech workers can ask for, and get, high salaries.

II. Outsourcing: A Practice that Saves Money

2   Today's companies must be flexible. They may decide to move parts of the manufacturing process to different countries This is called **outsourcing**. Usually, jobs are moved to developing countries. Outsourcing began with low-skilled jobs in businesses, such as clothing and shoe manufacturing. Outsourcing saves money because workers in developing countries are willing to work for less money than European or North American workers. In fact, companies usually cut their costs by 30–70 percent when they outsource part of their business to a developing country.

3   There are several advantages to outsourcing. Outsourcing increases employment opportunities in some developing countries. This encourages developing nations to improve their education in order to meet the demand for workers. It also allows global companies to increase profits and growth. A third advantage is that there are more opportunities for skilled employment in developed countries. For example, although manufacturing of computers is often outsourced to developing countries, the global demand for specialists who design these computers continues to increase.

4   However, there are also disadvantages to outsourcing. Some workers in developed countries criticize this practice. They believe that they are losing their jobs because of outsourcing. In the United States, workers blame outsourcing for the loss of jobs in manufacturing, for example. Although it is difficult to know precisely how many jobs are outsourced, it is estimated that the United States outsourced about 3 million manufacturing jobs between 1996 and 2006. In addition, business leaders expect around 2.4 million jobs in business and technology will be outsourced by 2014.

III. A Mobile, Global Workforce

5   Another change in the twenty-first-century workforce is that it is mobile. In other words, today's workers are willing to move away from home in order to get a good job. There are several reasons for **this**. In the

WHILE YOU READ 1
Highlight the definition of *outsourcing*.

WHILE YOU READ 2
What does *this* refer to? Highlight it.

past, language, and political differences prevented people from traveling to other countries to work. Now English is the global language, and people all over the world learn it. This allows people from different countries to communicate more easily. There is also more freedom to move across national borders. Europeans, for example, can travel and work more easily in many different European countries because of new laws within the European Union. As an example, more than a million Polish workers have left their homes to find employment in other European countries.

6   A mobile workforce brings benefits to the countries where people move in order to find work. It increases the supply of workers, so companies can hire employees quickly. Because of this, governments are trying to attract skilled workers to **their** countries. Countries such as Canada, New Zealand, and China are changing their laws; they want to make it easier for skilled people to move to these countries. They are also trying to encourage foreigners to attend their universities because students often stay in that country after they graduate.

WHILE YOU READ 3

Who does *their* refer to? Highlight it.

7   A mobile workforce can also help the economy of the country that a worker leaves. This is because workers often send part of their salaries back to their families in their countries. Money sent back to a country is called *remittances*. Remittances help the economies of those countries. For example, in 2011, Indians working in other countries sent $58 billion U.S. dollars back to India. In fact, $351 billion U.S. dollars was sent back to developing countries in 2011, and this figure is expected to rise to $593 billion by 2014. The total amount of remittances worldwide has been growing and experts expect it to reach 590 billion U.S. dollars **by 2014**. (See Figure 3.2.)

WHILE YOU READ 4

Which sentence contains the main idea of paragraph 7?
a) First sentence
b) Last sentence

8   The world's economy and workforce have changed significantly in the last 100 years. There is an increasing demand for skilled workers. Jobs are also moving as outsourcing continues to grow. The global workforce is more mobile, and workers move across borders in order to find work. These changes bring both challenges and opportunities in the twenty-first century.

Figure 3.2 Money Workers Sent Home to Developing Countries in 2011

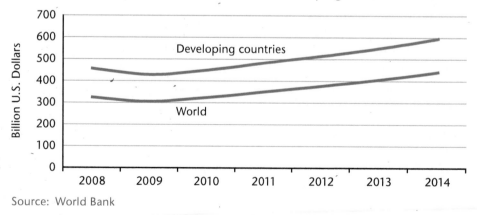

Source: World Bank

Main Idea Check

Here are the main ideas of paragraphs 2–7 in Reading 2. Match each paragraph to its main idea. Write the number of the paragraph on the blank line.

_____ A Outsourcing is growing because it saves money for businesses.

_____ B Mobile workers send some of their money home.

_____ C There are several reasons why today's workforce is more mobile than in the past.

_____ D There are advantages to outsourcing.

_____ E Countries try to attract foreign workers because they help the economy.

_____ F There are also disadvantages to outsourcing.

A Closer Look

Look back at Reading 2 to answer the following questions.

1 Which statement is *not* correct according to paragraph 1?
   a High-tech workers can get high salaries.
   b The demand for skilled workers is higher than the supply of skilled workers.
   c The world will need 500 million workers in the next 20 years.
   d There is a strong demand for skilled workers.

2 Paragraph 2 claims that workers in developing countries are willing to work for less money. Which statement would *not* support this claim?
   a It costs less to live in these countries.
   b The supply of jobs is higher than the demand for workers in this part of the world.
   c It is difficult to get a job in some areas of developing countries.
   d Demand for work is not high in these areas of the world.

3 The number of all computer jobs in the United States is declining because of outsourcing. **True or False?**

4 Which statement is *not* given in paragraph 5 as a reason for today's more mobile workforce?
   a There are fewer differences in language and politics, so it is easier to work in other countries.
   b Changes in laws have made it less difficult to cross national borders.
   c Higher standards of education have increased the supply of international workers.
   d More people are willing to move to get good jobs.

5 Which two reasons does the writer give in paragraphs 6 and 7 to explain the benefits of a mobile workforce?
   a The supply of workers in a country increases.
   b It is easier for people to move to other countries.
   c National economies improve when workers send money home.
   d Foreigners can study in good universities.

6 According to paragraph 7 and Figure 3.2, which sentence is *not* correct?

  a Remittances worldwide are increasing at approximately the same rate as remittances to developing countries.

  b From 2010 to 2014, it is expected that money sent home to developing countries will increase by over $100 billion U.S. dollars.

  c Across the world, the amount of money sent home in 2009 was more than $400 billion U.S. dollars.

  d The amount of money sent home to developing countries more than doubled from 2007 to 2011.

Skill Review

In Making Connections on page 85, you learned that writers use pronouns to make connections between sentences within a paragraph. Understanding these connections is an important reading skill.

The following sentences are from Reading 2. Find the nouns or noun phrases that the pronouns in bold refer to. Write them on the blank lines.

1 Therefore, just like coffee, when the demand is high and the supply is low, the cost goes up. **This** means that high-tech workers can ask for, and get, high salaries.

  This _____

2 Another change in the twenty-first-century workforce is that **it** is mobile.

  it _____

3 Now many people speak English as the global language, and people all over the world learn **it**. **This** allows people from different countries to communicate more easily.

  it _____

  This _____

4 A mobile workforce can also help the economy of the country that a worker leaves. **This** is because workers often send part of **their** salary back to their families in their countries.

  This _____

  Their _____

5 The total amount of remittances worldwide has been growing, and experts expect **it** to reach $590 billion U.S. dollars by 2014.

  it _____

Vocabulary Development

Definitions

Find the words in Reading 2 that complete the following definitions. When a verb completes the definition, use the base form, although the verb in the reading may not be in the base form.

1 To _____ something is to make something new. (v) Par. 1

2 If something is _____, it is becoming modern or advanced. (adj) Par. 2

3 If you are _____ to do something, you are ready and eager to do it. (adj) Par. 2

4 People who know a lot about a particular topic are known as _____. (n pl) Par. 3

5 A/An _____ is an activity that is done regularly. (n) Par. 4

6 To say that someone is responsible for something bad is to _____ them. (v) Par. 4

7 _____ is exactly. (adv) Par. 4

8 A group of people who work for a company or country is called a/an _____. (n) Par. 5

9 When you _____ someone, you arrange for that person to work for you. (v) Par. 6

10 _____ are things that are difficult and need a lot of work to solve or do correctly. (n) Par. 8

Word Families

A The words in **bold** in the chart are from Reading 2. The words next to them are from the same word family. Study and learn these words.

B Choose the correct form of the words from the chart to complete the following sentences. Use the correct verb tenses and subject-verb agreement. Use the correct singular and plural noun forms.

NOUN	VERB	ADJECTIVE
attraction	**attract**	attractive
employment	employ	—
flexibility	—	**flexible**
manufacturing	manufacture	—
prevention	**prevent**	—

1 The new law _____ people from working more than 50 hours a week.

2 The Nike company _____ many of its products in Thailand and Vietnam.

3 My friend prefers a/an _____ work schedule so he can spend more time with his family.

4 The new factory will _____ employ _____ hundreds of workers.

5 She used the new computer program to produce a very _____
advertisement.

6 Many companies try to _____ skilled workers with good pay and
long vacations.

7 _____ and farming are both important to a country's economy, but
farming is often more important in developing countries.

8 Fire _____ is a concern in California, so many people cut down trees near
their homes.

9 The new policy gives workers more _____ in their hours. They can come
in early and leave early.

10 Many people in developing countries must leave their homes to find _____.

Academic Word List

**The following are Academic Word List words from Readings 1 and 2 of this unit. Use
these words to complete the sentences. (For more on the Academic Word List, see
page 257.)**

affects (*v*)	challenge (*n*)	energy (*n*)	illustrate (*v*)	precisely (*adv*)
approximately (*adj*)	consumption (*n*)	flexible (*adj*)	major (*adj*)	previously (*adv*)

1 An increase in the price of oil _____ the prices of many other products.

2 Educating all children to be successful in today's workforce is a/an _____
facing all countries.

3 The teacher gave several good examples to _____ supply and demand.

4 In 2006, Mexican workers in the United States sent home _____
$26 billion (U.S.).

5 When the cost of coffee increased, _____ went down.

6 When it is very cold, people use more _____ to heat their homes.

7 Many jobs that were _____ done in the United Kingdom are now
outsourced to developing countries.

8 Economists cannot say _____ what the demand for skilled workers will
be. They can only estimate the numbers.

9 Lack of Internet access is a/an _____ problem facing some
developing countries.

10 The company hired her because she was very _____; she could work any
time in the day or evenings and even some weekends.

Critical Thinking

Reading 2 states that there are several advantages of a
mobile workforce. However, there may also be disadvantages.

A Imagine you are from a developing country and are going
to give a speech discussing the advantages and disadvantages
of workers leaving your country to work overseas.

- Reread Reading 2, Section III: A Mobile, Global Workforce.
  Highlight the advantages of a mobile workforce.
- Think of other advantages and disadvantages.
- Use your highlighted information and notes to complete the following table.

ADVANTAGES	DISADVANTAGES

B Give your presentation to your class.

Research

Choose a developing country. Go online and find answers to the following questions.

- How many workers leave this country in order to find work?
- Which country or countries do they move to, and what kind of work do they do there?

Writing

Write two paragraphs. The first paragraph will describe your research. The second
will talk about whether you are willing to go overseas for a job and why or why not.

Improving Your Reading Speed

Good readers read quickly and still understand most of what they read.

A Read the instructions and strategies for Improving Your Reading
Speed in Appendix 3 on page 271.

B Choose either Reading 1 or Reading 2 in this unit. Read it without
stopping. Time how long it takes you to finish the text in minutes and
seconds. Enter the time in the chart on page 272. Then calculate your
reading speed in number of words per minute.

Information in Graphs and Charts

Many academic texts include important information in graphic form. Often information is easier to understand when it is presented in this way. There are many different forms of graphic information. The most common ones are *bar graphs*, *line graphs*, *tables*, and *pie charts*. Good readers pay attention to the information in graphic material. They try to see the connection between the information in the graphic material and the text, and this makes it easier for them to understand the text.

Examples & Explanations

①Internet use is growing all over the world. ②The developed countries in Europe, North America, and Australia have the largest percentage of their population using the Internet (see Figure 1), but this is changing. ③Since 2000, the number of Internet users in many parts of the developing world has jumped more than 1,000 percent (see Figure 2).

If you look at Figures 1 and 2 before reading the paragraph, you can guess that the text will be about Internet use around the world. Sentence 1 shows your guess is correct.

Sentence 2 says that countries in the developed world have the largest percentage of their population who use the Internet. Figure 1 shows this is true. It shows that almost 80 percent of people in North America use the Internet, but only about 10 percent of people in Africa use it.

Sentence 3 is about change. It says that since 2000 there has been more than a 1,000 percent increase in Internet use in developing countries. Figure 2 shows that this is true with two regions of the world: Africa and the Middle East. These two regions both have an increase in use above 1,000 percent.

Figure 1 Percentage of Population Using the Internet in 2010

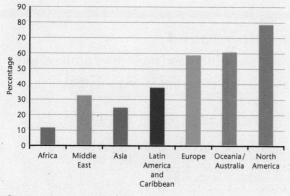

Source: Internet World Stats

Figure 2 Percentage of Internet Growth from 2000 to 2010

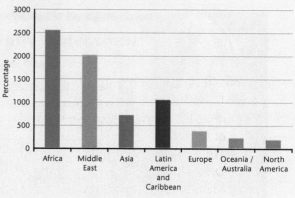

Source: Internet World Stats

Strategies

These strategies will help you connect information in graphs and charts to the text more effectively.

- Look at graphic material before you begin reading. This will give you a good idea of what the text will be about.
- When you study the graphic material, you should look at the title and other words. These will help you understand what the graphic material is about.
- Look at the axes. Axes are the vertical and horizontal lines on line and bar graphs. For example, in Figure 1 on page 106, the vertical axis shows the percentage of the population. The horizontal axis shows different regions of the world.
- Quickly read through the text to see if there is a reference to the graphic material. It may say something in parentheses like *(See Table 1.2)* or *(Figure 2.1)*. This will help you see where the graphic information fits into the information in the text.
- When you take notes on a text, don't forget to take notes on the graphic material, as well. Write down one or two sentences about what the graphic information shows.

Skill Practice 1

Study Figure 3. Then answer the question that follows.

Figure 3 Energy Sources Used to Produce Electricity in the U.S. in 2010

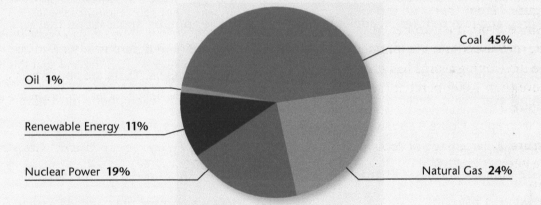

Oil **1%**

Renewable Energy **11%**

Nuclear Power **19%**

Coal **45%**

Natural Gas **24%**

Source: Energy Information Administration, 2011

Which of the following statements do you think will *probably not* be in a reading that includes this pie chart?

a In 2010, nearly half of the electricity in the United States used coal as its source of energy.
b The United States must do something to reduce its dependence on foreign oil.
c Only 1 percent of energy in the United States comes from oil.
d Many people do not realize that nuclear power is used to produce nearly one-fifth of the electricity in the United States.

Skill Practice 2

Study Figure 4. Read the title and make sure you understand the vertical and horizontal axes. Then complete the paragraph that follows by using the graph to write in the correct numbers on the blank lines.

Figure 4 Apps for Three Smart phones (in thousands)

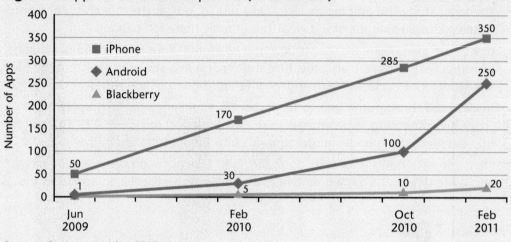

Source: Business Insider, 2011

In the early days of the twenty-first century, a new kind of phone – the smart phone – appeared. With a smart phone, you can send text messages, search the Internet, play games, and take pictures. In addition, smart phones have apps, or, applications, that you can download from the Internet. There are apps for many different purposes: for finding out about the weather, for finding friends, for reading newspapers. There are apps for almost everything. Because each phone works a little differently, each phone must have its own apps. Figure 4 shows the figures for three smart phones. It shows that in June 2009, there were _____ apps for the iPhone, but only _____ for

the Android. By October of 2010, however, the number of apps for the Android was growing. It reached _____ thousand. There was a more dramatic increase in the next four months, when the number of Android apps rose to _____ .

During those four months, the number of apps for the iPhone also increased from

_____ to _____ . The number of apps for the Blackberry was still

quite low in February, 2011 – only _____ thousand. When you look at total sales of apps for all phones, you see that in less than two years, the number of apps grew from less than _____ to more than _____ . In other words, the smart phone app business is doing very well.

Skill Practice 3

Work with a partner. Study Figure 5. Read the title and make sure you understand the vertical and horizontal axes. Then read the paragraph and discuss the questions that follow with a partner.

Figure 5 Predicted U.S. Total Green Building Market Value 2010–2015

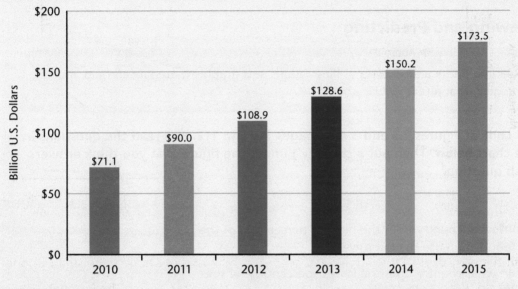

Source: *Fast Company*

A *green* building is one that does not use much energy and water and does not produce much waste and pollution. It also generally provides a healthy work environment. As a result, green buildings are good for business and for workers. Figure 5 shows the increase in green building since 2010. It also shows the growth that experts expect in the future. Green building in the United States has grown steadily since 2010, from over $70 billion to almost $109 billion in 2012. From 2012 to 2015, green building is expected to grow more quickly. This is partly because the government is encouraging businesses to build green offices and factories. By 2015, experts expect the value of green buildings to be almost $175 billion. That is a 144 percent increase since 2010. This is good news for U.S. workers and for the environment.

1 What is a "green" building?

2 What are the advantages of a green building?

3 What was the value of green buildings in the United States in 2010?

4 What was the increase in the value of green buildings between 2010 and 2011?

5 The writer says that the increase in the value of green buildings between 2000 and 2015 is likely to be about 144 percent. How did the writer get this number?

6 Why does the writer say that Figure 5 shows good news for the U.S. workers?

Connecting to the Topic

Discuss the following questions with a partner.

1 How often do you use the Internet?

2 What do you use the Internet for?

3 How would your life be different without the Internet?

Previewing and Predicting

> Reading a title and looking at illustrations and graphic material can help you predict what a text will be about.

A **Look at Figures 3.3 and 3.4 on pages 111 and 112, and read the questions in the chart below. Then put a check (✓) under the figure that you think answers each question.**

QUESTION	FIGURE 3.3	FIGURE 3.4
1 In what country does the highest percentage of the population use the Internet?		
2 In what country does the lowest percentage of the population use the Internet?		
3 What country has the highest GNI per person?		
4 What country has the lowest GNI per person?		
5 What country has a higher percentage of Internet use? Singapore or South Korea?		
6 Which country has a higher GNI per person? Germany or Japan?		

B **Compare your answers with a partner's.**

While You Read

As you read, stop at the end of each sentence that contains words in bold. Follow the instructions in the box in the margin.

◀))) Communication Technology in Business

1   Many government and business leaders think that information and communication technology is the key to the future prosperity of all nations. They argue that new technology is not just good for business – it is good for individuals, too. They believe that new developments in technology help businesses work more quickly and effectively. This ability improves their productivity and increases their profits. These companies can then contribute to the success of nations and their citizens.

2   Technology has changed how people in business communicate with one another. E-mail messages and cell phone calls began as the main communication tools of the late twentieth century. In the twenty-first century, **tools such as video chatting, file sharing, and social networking have become important tools for business.** These tools let people work together more efficiently. They allow them to collect and share different kinds of information in text, pictures, audio, and video, for example. All of these forms of communication use the most important development in communication technology: the Internet. Figures 3.3 and 3.4 suggest how communication technology and prosperity may be related.

WHILE YOU READ 1

As you read ahead, highlight the details that support this idea.

WHILE YOU READ 2

What do the numbers on the vertical axis of Fig. 3.3 mean?
a) Percentage of people in each country who use the Internet
b) Percentage of world's Internet users who live in that country.

Figure 3.3 Internet Use: Percent of the Population in 2011

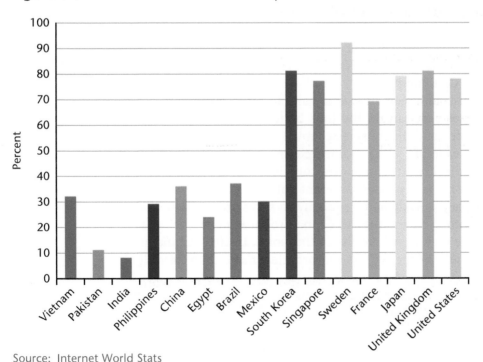

Source: Internet World Stats

Figure 3.4 Gross National Income (GNI) per Person in U.S. Dollars, 2010

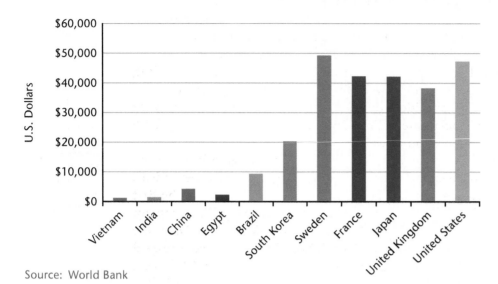

Source: World Bank

3   Global communication can help businesses in several ways. First, employees in different parts of the world can all work as a team to solve a problem, create a new product, or attract new customers. The global team can use new technology to communicate with all its members at the same time. In addition, when some team members in one part of the world are sleeping, team members in another part of the world can continue working on the same project. The global workday never ends. Global companies work around the clock. This saves time and increases productivity.

4   Global communication also increases productivity because it helps companies divide up their jobs and **distribute tasks** to different companies around the world. One company does not have to complete every part of the job by itself; instead, it can give some parts to other businesses. These are often businesses that can do the jobs better and for a lower price. However, to be successful, the businesses must be in constant communication. One good example is the motorcycle manufacturing industry in China. Hundreds of different companies contribute to the production of motorcycles. Each company has a different role in the process, so they need to communicate quickly and frequently to solve problems and work efficiently. The motorcycle industry in China produces motorcycles faster and at a lower price than anywhere else in the world. In 2010, China made more than 50 percent of the world's motorcycles, more than 24 million of them.

5   Communication in global businesses must be fast and efficient, but it also must be effective. People who do business all over the world need good work relationships. These kinds of relationships usually develop when people see each other every day. This is not always possible for teams with members all over the world. Fortunately, new communication tools

WHILE YOU READ ❸
Read ahead to find an example of *distribute tasks*. Highlight the example.

make it possible for team members to get to know one another and share ideas online. People who cannot meet face-to-face can still collaborate by using video chat programs such as Skype or FaceTime. These programs allow people to see each other when they talk. They can see **facial expressions** – a smile or a frown – and look at documents together. They can also use social networking sites, such as Facebook, VKontakte, Orkut, or LinkedIn. Social networking websites allow groups of people to share information, interests, and ideas on the Internet. The main focus of these sites was originally social interaction, but now businesses are using them for professional collaboration as well.

WHILE YOU READ 4
Read ahead for a clue to the meaning of *facial expressions*. What type of clue is it?
a) Definition
b) Example
c) Contrast

6   These new tools are also very important in encouraging **innovation**, that is, new approaches and ideas. In order to get the best new ideas, sometimes businesses go outside of the company for help. One of the first companies to try this was a Canadian gold mining company. The company, Goldcorp, was losing money. In 2000, it decided to ask experts all over the world to give it ideas for improving its mining. They promised a reward for the most valuable ideas. Suggestions came from all over the world. More than 80 percent of them were useful, and they resulted in more than $8 million in profits. Innovation happens very quickly today. As a result, many companies cannot depend only on their own scientists and engineers for solutions. They will need to ask experts all over the world. It doesn't matter where the experts live or work; they just need to be connected.

WHILE YOU READ 5
Read ahead in the sentence for a definition of *innovation*. Highlight it.

7   Sometimes companies do not ask only experts; they go directly to the public. For example, in 2009, Netflix, a company that allows people to watch films and television programs on their computers, asked for help from the public. They wanted to improve their ability to predict what kinds of films their customers would like. They offered a prize to the person or group who could do this. The winner, who did not work for Netflix, received a million dollars. For many companies, this kind of consumer participation is at the center of their business. The online companies eBay and YouTube do not have their own products. Instead, the public provides the products. eBay simply brings buyers and sellers together online. YouTube brings video producers and viewers together online. All of these developments are possible because of the increasing availability of powerful global communication tools. These tools will continue to encourage innovation and the growth of new businesses, which can promote development and prosperity.

New technology allows for face-to-face interaction.

Main Idea Check

Here are the main ideas of paragraphs 2–7 in Reading 3. Match each paragraph to its main idea. Write the number of the paragraph on the blank line.

_____ A Global communication allows people in business to work around the world and around the clock.

_____ B Global communication helps companies because it allows them to distribute work to companies in different parts of the world.

_____ C Some companies use consumer participation to consult people all over the world.

_____ D Communication tools allow companies to consult experts all over the world.

_____ E The Internet is the most important development in communication technology.

_____ F Internet tools can help people in different parts of the world develop good work relationships.

A Closer Look

Look back at Reading 3 to answer the following questions.

1 According to paragraph 2, which communication tools have become important in the twenty-first century? Circle all that apply.
a E-mail
b Video chatting
c Social networking
d Mobile phone calls
e File sharing

2 According to paragraph 3, how does global communication help businesses? Circle all that apply.
a It allows people in different locations to collaborate.
b It increases sales.
c It encourages consumers to come together online.
d It allows work to continue around the clock.

3 What are two tools that help with online collaboration, according to paragraph 5?
a Teamwork
b Social networking
c Task distribution
d Video chatting

4 Why does the writer use the example of Goldcorp in paragraph 6? Circle all that apply.
   a To show that it is important to keep secrets in business
   b To show how global communication can use the knowledge of experts all over
     the world
   c To give an example of how the Internet makes it possible for people outside of the
     company to send in ideas
   d To show how the Internet increases national prosperity
   e To show how communication encourages innovation

5 According to paragraph 7, what is the Netflix prize an example of?
   a An Internet communication tool
   b Consumer participation
   c Global communication
   d Social networking

6 Which of the following activities is *not* given in the reading as a way for businesses to
  use the Internet?
   a To share information
   b To increase GNI
   c To collaborate
   d. To sell new products

Skill Review

In Skills and Strategies 6, you learned that academic texts often include
important information in graphic form. Understanding graphic information can
help you understand the text better.

A Look back at Figures 3.3 and 3.4, and answer the following questions.

1 Which statement best describes the relationship between GNI per person and the
  percentage of Internet use in a country's population?
   a Countries in Europe and North America have the highest percentage of Internet use.
   b Countries with a high per person GNI also have a high percentage of Internet use.
   c Internet use depends on the size of the population.

2 Which of these two statements do you think is true?
   a As GNI rises, there is an increase in the percentage of the population that uses
     the Internet.
   b As Internet use increases, people make more money, and GNI increases.

B Compare your answers with a partner's.

Vocabulary Development

Definitions

Find the words in Reading 3 that complete the following definitions. When a verb completes the definition, use the base form, although the verb in the reading may not be in the base form.

1 To _____share_____ is to have or use something with other people. (v) Par. 2

2 A/An _____team_____ is a group that works or plays together. (n) Par. 3

3 _____members_____ are people who are part of a group. (n pl) Par. 3

4 If something is _____constant_____, it continues for a long time or happens very often. (adj) Par. 4

5 _____interaction_____ means talking or doing things with other people. (n) Par. 5

6 _____mining_____ is digging below the ground for such materials as gold or coal. (n) Par. 6

7 A/An _____reward_____ is something given in exchange for good work. (n) Par. 6

8 _____suggestions_____ are possible plans or ideas. (n pl) Par. 6

9 _____costumers_____ are people who buy things. (n pl) Par. 7

10 To _____promote_____ is to advertise something so that people will buy it or use it. (v) Par. 7

Words in Context

A Use context clues to match the first part of each sentence to its correct second part and to understand the meaning of the words in **bold**.

1 The people in the village did not have enough to eat, so
2 I believe that hard work is
3 The development of the Internet has led to
4 The discovery of large quantities of natural gas has led to
5 Each country will
6 The project was very large and complicated, so the manager decided to
7 In order to improve their products and service, the company has asked for
8 The British and Italian managers e-mailed each other for months before

a new ideas and **innovation**, especially in the media and education.
b have an important **role** in the peace talks.
c the **participation** of consumers.
d the government **distributed** five pounds of rice to each family.
e the **key** to success.
f they met **face-to-face**.
g give each employee separate **tasks** to complete.
h increasing **prosperity** in Brazil.

B Compare your answers with a partner's. Discuss what clues helped you match the parts of the sentences and helped you understand what the words in bold mean.

Critical Thinking

Reading 3 claims that communication in global business must be fast, efficient, and effective. Today, people use a variety of tools to communicate in this way. They use portable devices such as laptops, tablets, and smart phones. They also use Internet sites such as Facebook and Skype. The demand for these communication tools can be connected to the topic of *supply and demand* in Reading 1 of this unit.

SYNTHESIZING

Critical thinking includes connecting new information to information you learned in previous readings.

A With a partner, discuss the following questions. If necessary, review Reading 1.

1 How would you describe the demand for these portable devices? Is it increasing? Decreasing?

2 Is the demand for these products global, or is it limited to developed countries?

3 What is happening to the supply of these products? Are there more available today than in the past, for example?

4 The law of demand explains the relationship between demand and cost. Using this law, explain what is happening to the cost of many of these products.

B Share your answers with the rest of your class.

Research

Work in a group. Ask the members of your group what types of communication tools they use. You could talk about social networking sites, video chatting, or Internet tools for sharing files, music, videos, or information.

Writing

Write two paragraphs. Each paragraph will describe a communication tool that you or your classmates use.

Connecting to the Topic

Read the definition of *sustainable*, and then discuss the following questions with a partner.

> **sustainable** (*adj*) causing little or no harm to the environment and therefore able to continue for a long time

1 What do you think *sustainability* means as it relates to business?

2 Do you think we will have enough energy for the future? Enough water? Enough wood? Explain your answers.

3 Do you think businesses can help the environment? Explain your answer.

Previewing and Predicting

> Reading the title and section headings and looking at graphic material can help you predict what a text will be about.

A Read the title and first two sentences of each section in Reading 4. Look at the graphs in each section. Decide what content will be in each section. Then write the number of the section (*I–III*) next to the topic that best describes it.

SECTION	TOPIC
	Why consumers want sustainable products
	Changes to make businesses more sustainable
	Fossil fuels and air pollution
	Sustainable products
	Human damage to the environment
	The solar power business

B Compare your answers with a partner's.

While You Read

As you read, stop at the end of each sentence that contains words in bold. Follow the instructions in the box in the margin.

◄)) Business and Sustainability

I. Introduction

1   Are human beings harming their world? There are increasing concerns that **we are damaging our environment**. People are using up natural resources such as water, land, fossil fuels (for example, oil and gas), wood, and minerals. Humans are also polluting the water and air. However, the biggest concern about the environment today is climate change. Many scientists believe that the world is getting warmer and that human activity is the cause of this change. This global warming may lead to problems, such as floods, droughts, and changes in the weather and in plant and animal life. The consequences could be very serious. Many businesses are beginning to respond to consumers' environmental concerns. They are thinking about how they can make their products and do business in ways that will not damage the environment so much and will promote sustainability.

WHILE YOU READ ❶
Read ahead to find three supporting details for this claim. Highlight them.

II. Sustainable Products and Services

2   *Sustainability* is our ability to meet the needs of people today without decreasing our ability to meet the needs of people in the future. When a process is sustainable, it can occur again and again without negative consequences. For example, **using gasoline in a car is not a sustainable process. It has three negative consequences.** First, it pollutes the air. Second, it uses oil. The supply of oil will eventually run out because it is a nonrenewable resource. Finally, cars also emit carbon dioxide (CO_2) into the air. The increased level of CO_2 is one of the main causes of global warming. Our use of fossil fuels, such as gasoline, will cause the level of CO_2 to rise even more in the future. (See Figure 3.5.)

WHILE YOU READ ❷
Read ahead to find the three supporting details for this idea. Highlight them.

Figure 3.5 Global Emissions from Fossil Fuels from 1850 to 2010

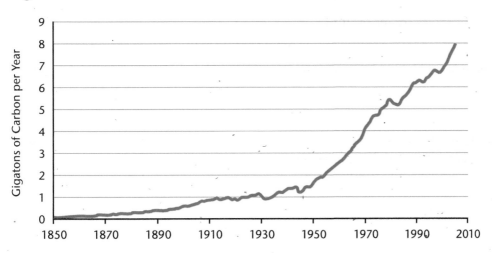

Source: The Global Carbon Project

Figure 3.6 World Annual Solar Panel Costs and Sales from 2008 to 2011

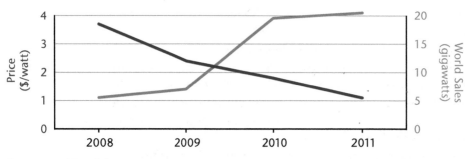

3   In contrast, using energy from the sun or wind to heat our homes is an example of a sustainable process because it does not pollute or increase CO_2 levels. In addition, solar and wind energy are renewable; they will not run out. The public wants alternatives for energy like these. Global companies are responding to this new demand. They sell alternative energy solutions, such as wind and solar power, to governments and communities all over the world. **Interest** in solar energy in particular has grown because new technology has made it less expensive. (See Figure 3.6.) There has also been an increase in the development of wind power. It grew by more than 30 percent in Europe in 2010, and the increase was even higher in developing countries.

4   Many consumers want businesses to be environmentally responsible, that is, to reduce their use of energy and other nonrenewable resources and to decrease their negative impact on the environment. Businesses are responding to these concerns in several ways. There is an increasing demand for *green* products and services, which will not harm the environment. Businesses are starting to meet this demand with new products. One of the best-known green products is the hybrid car. These cars use both gasoline and electricity for power. Electricity is a cleaner source of power than gasoline. Hybrid cars are quieter and use less energy and emit less CO_2 than traditional cars. In spite of these advantages, in 2011, less than 3 percent of the cars sold in the United States were hybrids. It is higher in other countries, especially Japan.

5   Consumers are also demanding that companies make familiar products more sustainable. For example, furniture has traditionally used wood from trees that take a long time to grow. Many of these trees come from tropical forests in Brazil, Malaysia, and Myanmar. Using these woods can destroy the forests and the animals that live in them. These forests are also significant because they help decrease the levels of CO_2 all over the world. Some large international companies, like Sweden-based Ikea, use other, more sustainable woods in their furniture. They use a lot of **bamboo**, which is a type of wood that grows very quickly and is a more renewable resource than other tropical woods.

WHILE YOU READ **3**
Highlight words in this paragraph that show change.

WHILE YOU READ **4**
Read ahead for a definition of *bamboo*. Highlight it.

III. Business Practices that Protect the Environment

6   Businesses are starting to make more sustainable products. However, they are also making other changes in order to decrease their impact on the environment. Volvo, the Swedish car manufacturer, builds hybrid cars in factories that use only renewable energy. These factories do not pollute or contribute to global warming. Businesses that cannot make these big changes can make small ones. For example, they can plant gardens on the roofs of their office buildings and factories. These gardens help keep the buildings warmer in winter and cooler in summer so they need less energy. The plants in these gardens also lower CO_2 levels.

7   Recycling resources such as paper, plastic, and glass is another way that businesses can help protect the environment. **Recycling**, or reusing old materials in new ways, has become an important business because the price of new materials is rising. Paper is one of these products. Demand for paper has increased and the supply of wood has decreased. As a result, paper has become more expensive. This makes paper recycling profitable, especially in countries with growing economies. China, for example, has a rising demand for paper. Paper recycling in China saves more than 50 million tons of wood every year – and that is a lot of trees.

8   Why are businesses making all of these changes? They are paying more attention to their responsibility in protecting the environment for **two main reasons**. First, this can save money. The shoe and clothing company Nike has been working to reduce its impact on the environment. The company wants to make its products primarily from cheaper, recycled materials. For example, it manufactured the official shirts for the South Africa Games in 2010. Each shirt was made from eight recycled plastic bottles. The second reason to be environmentally responsible is that it can improve a company's image. Nike can advertise its products as green. Sometimes consumers will pay more for a product if they think it is good for the environment.

9   The idea of sustainability is very popular with today's consumers. However, sustainability works best if it is also profitable. Businesses are more willing to do something good for the environment if it is also good for them. Walmart, the world's largest company, has been famous primarily for low prices, not for sustainability. In 2006, the company decided to show the world it was serious about helping the environment. It began to sell a "green" lightbulb that lasts longer but uses much less energy than traditional lightbulbs. By 2007, it had sold more than 100 million "green" lightbulbs. Then Walmart started using them in its own stores and instantly saved $6 million in electricity costs. This shows that green business can be good business.

WHILE YOU READ 5

Read ahead in this paragraph to find a definition of *recycling*. Highlight it.

WHILE YOU READ 6

Read ahead to find two supporting details. Highlight them.

Main Idea Check

Match the main ideas below to five of the paragraphs in Reading 4. Write the number of the paragraph on the blank line.

_____ A Businesses are responding to the demand for sustainable products.

_____ B Business can be sustainable and profitable.

_____ C Sustainable processes do not harm the environment.

_____ D Recycling is an important way to help protect the environment.

_____ E Solar and wind power are sustainable sources of energy.

A Closer Look

Look back at Reading 4 to answer the following questions.

1 According to paragraph 1, what is the biggest environmental challenge today?
   a Water pollution
   b Air pollution
   c Global warming
   d Drought

2 Reread paragraph 2. What are three negative consequences of using fossil fuels?
   a An increase in global warming
   b Air pollution
   c Water pollution
   d Decrease in nonrenewable energy resources
   e Decrease in renewable energy resources

3 Reread paragraphs 1 and 2. Then complete the diagram about the process of global warming. Put phrases A–D in the correct order of events. Write the correct letter in each box.

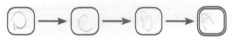

   A Droughts and floods
   B Global warming
   C CO$_2$ emission
   D Burning of fossil fuels

4 Using a car with a hybrid engine is an example of a completely sustainable process.
   True or False?

5 According to paragraphs 3 and 7, in what ways are solar power and paper recycling similar?
   a Their use has increased as their price has increased.
   b The price of both has dropped, but they still don't have much impact.
   c Both are more popular in China than other parts of the world.
   d Their popularity and profitability have both increased.

6 What business practices do Nike and Walmart share?
   a They have helped to replant tropical forests.
   b They understand that commitment to the environment is good for their image.
   c They recycle their products.
   d They promote organic farming.

Skill Review

In Skills and Strategies 6, you learned that academic texts often include important information in graphic form. Understanding graphic information can help you understand the text better.

A Look back at Figures 3.5 and 3.6 and answer the following questions.

1 According to Figure 3.5, when did the acceleration in CO_2 emissions from fossil fuels begin?

2 Why do you think it happened at that time?

3 Based on the information in Figure 3.5, what do you think is the future of CO_2 emissions?

4 In Figure 3.6, what is the vertical axis on the right? What is the vertical axis on the left?

5 According to Figure 3.6, when did the acceleration in the sales of solar panels begin?

6 What do you think might explain this increase in sales?

B Compare your answers with a partner's.

Definitions

Find the words in Reading 4 that complete the following definitions. When a verb completes the definition, use the base form, although the verb in the reading may not be in the base form.

1 To _____use up_____ something is to finish the available supply of it.
 (v – 2 words) Par. 1

2 _____resources_____ are supplies of useful or valuable things. (n pl) Par. 1

3 _____Climate_____ is the general weather conditions in a place. (n) Par. 1

4 _____droughts_____ are long periods of time with no rain. (n pl) Par. 1

5 If something happens _____eventually_____, it happens in the end or finally. (adv) Par. 2

6 To _____run out_____ means to finish something so that there is no more of it.
 (v – 2 words) Par. 2

7 If something is _____renewable_____, it can be replaced after it is used. (adj) Par. 3

8 A/An _____hybrid_____ is a mix of two or more things. (n) Par. 4

9 _____Primarily_____ means mainly or mostly. (adv) Par. 8

10 A/An _____image_____ is the idea that people have of someone or something.
 (n) Par. 8

Words in Context

Complete the following passages with words from Reading 4 in the box below.

damage	floods	pollute	solar
emit	level	reduce	tropical

1 There are often serious rainstorms in _____ countries. When there is a
 a
 lot of rain, the _____ of water in rivers and lakes often rises and can cause
 b
 _____. These disasters often injure people and _____ homes
 c   d
 and businesses.

2 Some experts believe that _____ energy is one good way to help our
 e
 planet. Using energy from the sun can _____ our dependence on fossil
 f
 fuels. Another important advantage of this type of energy is that it does not
 _____ dirt and chemicals so it does not _____ the air
 g   h
 or water.

Academic Word List

The following are Academic Word List words from Readings 3 and 4 of this unit. Use these words to complete the sentences. (For more on the Academic Word List, see page 257.)

constant (*adj*)	distributed (*v*)	innovation (*n*)	participation (*n*)	role (*n*)
consumers (*n*)	image (*n*)	interaction (*v*)	promote (*v*)	teams (*n*)

1 There is a / an _____ demand for more oil. The world always needs more energy.

2 There are many Internet tools that encourage _____ between people in different locations.

3 Every year there seems to be a new _____ in mobile phone technology.

4 The manager _____ a newsletter to all of the workers.

5 The World Health Organization tries to _____ good health for all the citizens of the world.

6 The class was divided into _____. They competed against one another to see who got the best score in the game.

7 Many businesses ask for the _____ of the public in new projects. They want to know what ordinary people think about their products.

8 Most businesses are very concerned about their _____. They want the public to have a positive view of them.

9 Parents play an important _____ in their children's development.

10 It is important for businesses to pay attention to what _____ want.

Critical Thinking

Experts and leaders argue about whether humans are really damaging the environment. They argue about the importance of sustainability. They also have different views about how much we should depend on nonrenewable energy sources.

A With a partner, review Reading 4, and decide whether the author would agree or disagree with the following statements. Underline the sentences in the text that help support your answers.

1 Humans are damaging the environment.

2 We should use more renewable energy.

3 People should buy green products.

4 People and businesses should recycle.

B Discuss your answers with the rest of your class.

> **UNDERSTANDING POINT OF VIEW**
>
> Critical readers notice when a writer has a point of view. They are aware that a writer's point of view may affect how the writer reports facts.

Research

Do some research to find three things that ordinary people can do to promote sustainability. Then find answers to the following questions.

- Do you do any of the things to promote sustainability that you found out about in your research?
- Do you choose products because they promote sustainability? Are you willing to pay more for them?

Writing

Write two paragraphs. The first paragraph will describe the results of your research. The second paragraph will describe the things you are willing and not willing to do to promote sustainability. Explain your reasons.

Improving Your Reading Speed

Good readers read quickly and still understand most of what they read.

A Read the instructions and strategies for Improving Your Reading Speed in Appendix 3 on page 271.

B Choose either Reading 3 or Reading 4 in this unit. Read it without stopping. Time how long it takes you to finish the text in minutes and seconds. Enter the time in the chart on page 272. Then calculate your reading speed in number of words per minute.

CAUSE-AND-EFFECT CONNECTORS

Writers often connect ideas by using words and phrases that signal cause and effect. These words show how one event or action can cause or be caused by another event or action. Some of these words and phrases are *as a result, to result in, to lead to, to cause, because, since, therefore,* and *so.*

In the following example, the words in **bold** show the effect that one event or action has on another event or action.

> An event in a business in one country can significantly affect businesses in other countries. For example, an earthquake closed several Japanese power plants. **As a result**, the Japanese needed more oil from other countries. **Therefore**, oil prices around the world rose. This shows how a natural disaster in one country **caused** a change in prices of a global product.

Exercise 1

Find words or phrases that signal cause and effect in the following paragraphs. Highlight them. Then write C above the causes and E above the effects. The first one has been done for you.

1   Many scientists believe that the use of fossil fuels has led to environmental damage. When fossil fuels such as oil and gasoline burn, they emit CO₂. Higher CO₂ emissions cause the world's temperatures to rise. Higher temperatures have resulted in floods and fires.

2   Rising oil prices can cause changes in the price of other energy sources. Corn is an alternative source of energy. As oil prices rise, some businesses may start to produce ethanol, a fuel made from corn. As a result of growing demand, corn prices may increase dramatically.

3   A decline in the economy can be good for education. When the economy is good, there are lots of jobs that pay well. As a result, students leave school to find jobs. When the economy declines, there are fewer jobs, so students stay in school.

4   In today's economy, jobs can often move around the world. Global businesses want to keep their labor costs low. So they may move their factories to another country if the labor there is cheaper. This practice is called *outsourcing* and can result in unemployment in the countries with higher labor costs.

Exercise 2

Make a clear paragraph by putting sentences A, B, and C into the best order after the numbered sentence. Look for cause-and-effect words, repeated key words (see page 41), and pronouns (see page 85) to help you. Write the letters in the correct order on the blank lines.

1 *Price fixing* is an illegal practice in most countries. ____ ____ ____

| A It occurs when all the producers of a product, such as oil, coffee, or milk, agree to ask the same price for it. | B The result is higher prices for consumers. | C Because these producers have all agreed to one price, they can make that price as high as they want. |

2 One example of a recycling business is aluminum. ____ ____ ____

| A Therefore, recycling old aluminum cans is more profitable than making new ones. | B Recycling aluminum is sustainable, but it is also profitable. | C When the price of aluminum goes up, cans become more expensive. |

3 Some products, such as cars and computers, contain parts that are made all over the world. ____ ____ ____

| A As a result of this, they can produce computers and cars at attractive prices for the consumer and make bigger profits. | B So they manufacture parts in different countries where the costs are lower. | C Computer and car companies want to keep their costs down. |

4 Business success can lead to philanthropy. ____ ____ ____

| A These leaders want to do something useful with their success. | B In the communication technology business, many leaders have become very rich at an early age. | C As a result, many of them, like Bill Gates at Microsoft, have become philanthropists. |

5 The Internet company Google is trying to stay ahead of other Internet businesses. ____ ____ ____

| A However, many other companies are now trying hard to take business away from Google. | B The company has been a huge success, with more people using Google than any other search tool. | C As a result, Google has had to create new products and services to stay successful. |

4

POPULATION CHANGE AND ITS IMPACT

SKILLS AND STRATEGIES

- Collocations
- Scanning for Specific Information

Collocations

When you are reading, you may notice that sometimes the same words frequently appear together. For example, you may notice *developing country* or *home country*. The noun *country* can appear with an adjective, such as *developing*, or another noun, such as *home*. When two or more words often appear together, we call this a *collocation*. *Developing country* is a collocation, and *home country* is another collocation. It is important for you to notice and learn collocations because it helps you see groups of words and read more quickly.

Examples & Explanations

The students learned **job skills** as well as academic subjects.

In the evening, we always listen to the **news report** on television.

Writers use noun + noun collocations, for example, *job* + *skills*, because they can fit a lot of information into just two words. The first noun in a noun + noun collocation acts like an adjective and modifies the second noun in some way.

Serious crime is often a problem in urban areas.

Some nouns frequently occur with a set of adjectives. The adjective *serious* and the noun *crime* often appear next to or near each other. Together these two words form a collocation. Many words could be used to describe a "big" or "great" crime, but *serious* is the most often used adjective and would be the most natural choice.

His home is a **long way** from his job so he has to leave early in the morning.

The adjective *long* and the noun *way* often appear next to or near each other. Together these two words form a collocation. Other words, such as *great* and *far*, might be used to describe *way*, but *long way* is the most common collocation.

The Language of Collocation

Many different combinations of words form collocations. The following are some common collocations often used in academic writing.

NOUN + NOUN	ADJECTIVE + NOUN
education policy	careful analysis
communication technology	global economy
government statistics	powerful influence
immigration rate	serious problem
oil prices	steady growth
world news	strong support

Strategies

These strategies will help you notice and learn collocations.

- When you encounter a new vocabulary word, look at the adjectives and other nouns near it.
- Pay attention to two nouns, or adjectives and nouns, that appear together frequently. These might be collocations. Look up one of the words in a learner dictionary. Many learner dictionaries include lists of collocations in their entries.
- Use these collocations when you write and speak.

Skill Practice 1

Read the following paragraph. Find the noun + noun collocations and highlight them. There are seven collocations in the paragraph. The first one has been done for you.

Last month business leaders had a meeting at city hall to discuss health and safety in the workplace. There are many immigrants in the city's factories, and leaders are concerned about the workers' language ability. If workers cannot read safety instructions, there could be an accident. The leaders decided on this policy to make sure that their employees stay safe and healthy: (1) Factory managers will read instructions to the employees. (2) If the workers cannot understand the instructions, the managers will find someone who speaks their language to explain the instructions to them. (3) All factory workers must wear safety glasses.

Skill Practice 2

Read the following paragraph. Find the adjective + noun collocations and highlight them. There are six adjective + noun collocations.

The population of the world has grown significantly in the second half of the twentieth century. Although the world population did not grow as fast as in the first half of the century, the Earth's population doubled from three billion to six billion people between 1960 and 1999. People were healthier and lived longer than at any time in human history. However, during the same period, changes in the global environment began to accelerate: there was a sharp increase in pollution levels and a continuous decline in natural resources. There is now widespread concern about climate change, and there is strong support for the conclusion that the sea level is rising. What will happen if this population increase continues?

Skill Practice 3

Here are some other common adjective + noun collocations. Read them. Then read the paragraph below. Fill in each blank line with one of these collocations.

careful attention	ethnic groups	low rates	steady decline
economic condition	healthy food	significant difference	strong evidence

The annual rate of infant mortality is the number of infants (babies) who die before their first birthday divided by the total number of births during the year. That number is then multiplied by 1,000. Experts pay _____ to this number. They use this rate to evaluate the _____ of a country. When people get
good medical care and _____, infant mortality decreases. There is
_____ that the rate increases during wars and other conflicts. For example, in 2011, Afghanistan, Somalia, and Sudan had very high rates of infant mortality. In contrast, Monaco and Singapore had very _____. In the United States, there has been a/an _____ in the mortality rate, from 26 per 1,000 births in 1960 to 6.06 per 1,000 births in 2011. There is a/an
_____ in this rate across different _____. The rate for African Americans is more than double the national average.

Connecting to the Topic

Discuss the following questions with a partner.

1 Is it good for a country to have a rising population? A falling population? A population that stays the same? Explain your answers.

2 What countries do you think have rising populations? What countries do you think have falling populations?

3 What can a government do to change the size of its population or to change how fast it is rising or falling?

Previewing and Predicting

> Looking at illustrations and graphic material can help you predict what a text will be about.

A **Look at the graph (Figure 4.1) on page 134, the map (Figure 4.2) on page 135, and the picture on page 136. Then read the information in the chart below. Decide if each item is about the *developed world* or the *developing world*. Put a check (✓) in the correct column.**

	DEVELOPED WORLD	DEVELOPING WORLD
Population of 1.6 billion in 2000		
More than 2.2 births per woman in 2008		
Fewer than 2.2 births per woman in 2008		
Predicted to be more than 7 billion in 2050		
Predicted to increase by more than 2 billion between 2000 and 2010		
Population of more than 5 billion in 2010		

B **Compare your answers with a partner's.**

While You Read

As you read, stop at the end of each sentence that contains words in bold. Follow the instructions in the box in the margin.

Population Trends

1   Demography is the study of population. It can tell us the percentage of a country's population in a specific age range, for example, whether there are more people over or under 65. Demography is also the study of population trends. These trends include increases or decreases in a country's population. This information is important because changes in population can have an enormous impact on a country's future. One important demographic trend is that the world population has been growing rapidly since the nineteenth century. However, this change is not the same in all parts of the world. The population of the developing world is growing much faster than the population of the **developed world**. (See Figure 4.1.)

2   **Two factors may explain this growth in the global population.** One of the most important factors is life expectancy. Life expectancy is the average age that people die, and it is closely related to a country's development. As the nations of the world develop and become more industrialized, life expectancy figures have risen everywhere. One reason is that development brings better hygiene and healthcare, so life expectancy is usually higher in more developed countries. In Japan, for instance, life expectancy is 83 years. Life expectancy has improved significantly in the less developed countries, too. In 1950, the average life expectancy in developing countries was 44 years. By 2009, the figure had risen to about 66 years.

3   Another important factor is a nation's **fertility rate**. The fertility rate is the average number of children per woman. Average fertility rates decreased worldwide from 5.0 children per woman in 1950 to 2.47 in 2009, but the size of this decrease is not the same everywhere. (See Figure 4.2.)

> **WHILE YOU READ** ➊
> Look back in paragraph 1 to find three noun + noun collocations. Highlight them.

> **WHILE YOU READ** ➋
> Read ahead in paragraphs 2 and 3, and highlight two details that support this statement.

> **WHILE YOU READ** ➌
> Find the definition for *fertility rate*. Highlight it.

Figure 4.1 Population Trends in Billions in the Developed and Developing World – 1950 to 2050

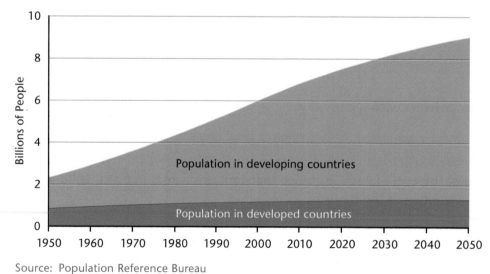

Source: Population Reference Bureau

Figure 4.2 World Fertility Rates – 2008

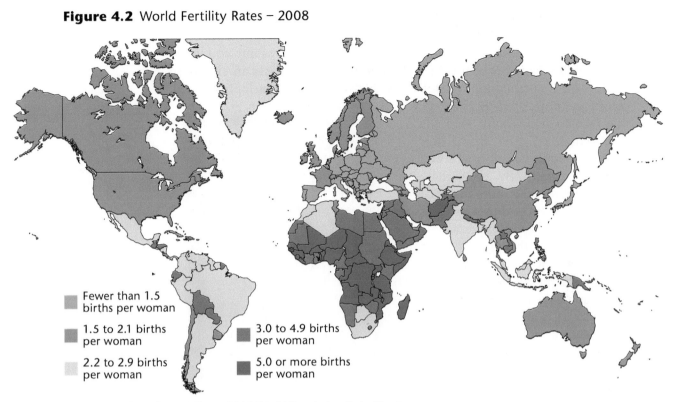

Fewer than 1.5
births per woman

1.5 to 2.1 births
per woman

2.2 to 2.9 births
per woman

3.0 to 4.9 births
per woman

5.0 or more births
per woman

Source: Haub and M.M. Kent, *2008 World Population Data Sheet.*

Like life expectancy, a country's fertility rate is related to its development. For example, in a less developed country where a major industry is agriculture, people need to have large families to work on the land. However, as machines start to do more of this type of work, families don't need as many children to help. The fertility rate is also frequently related to a woman's education level. In developing countries, if a woman has a good education, she is likely to have fewer children. Ethiopia is a dramatic example of this. Ethiopian women with no education have an average of 6.1 children; women with at least a secondary education have an average of 2.0 **children**.

4   A large population uses lots of resources. Starting in the 1950s, many countries became concerned about their skyrocketing populations. How could these nations support so many people? **As a result,** some of these countries made great efforts to control their population growth by encouraging people to have smaller families. Some countries with very large populations, such as China and India, have been leaders in population control. In the 1970s, China began its "one child" policy. This policy restricts most families to only one child. The government provides financial and educational rewards for families with one child and penalties for families who do not follow the policy. India's effort to control its population has emphasized education for girls and women. These programs show that it

WHILE YOU READ 4

Find the main idea of paragraph 3. Highlight it.

WHILE YOU READ 5

What cause is *as a result* connected to? Highlight it.

is possible for government policies to control fertility rates and slow population growth.

5   Although population growth may be slowing down in some countries, such as China and India, there are still many concerns about an explosion in the world's population. This is especially true in the developing world, where the population is growing the fastest. (See Figure 4.1.) In 1960, almost 70 percent of the world's people lived in developing countries. By 2000, that figure had reached more than 80 percent, and it continues to rise. Some demography experts are concerned that this growth is in countries that cannot afford to support such large populations.

A poster at a clinic encourages smaller families.

6   In some developed countries, in contrast, a major concern is the decline in population. In Japan, South Korea, Singapore, and in most of Europe, fertility rates are now too low to replace the current population. In some countries, the fertility rate is as low as 1.2 births per woman. This is much lower than the rate of 2.1 births per woman that is needed to replace the existing population. This falling fertility rate is a problem because a smaller number of younger workers have to support a larger older population. Many of the older people are retired, that is, no longer working. According to the United Nations, by 2050, almost a quarter of the world's population will be older than 65.

7   Some governments are trying to solve the problem of falling fertility rates by encouraging people to have more children. In particular, they are making it easier for women to work and have a family at the same time. In many European countries, the government pays for maternity leave and childcare for working mothers. Some governments also offer financial rewards to families who have more than two children. The Russian government began to offer $9,000 for second and third children in 2007. The program has been successful in raising the number of births in that country. In Singapore and Japan, two unusual government programs try to help young, busy single professionals meet each other. The governments hope that some of them will get married and start families.

8   All of these programs show that governments take changes in their populations very seriously. Demographic trends have important consequences for nations and their citizens. Increases and decreases in fertility rates and life expectancy do not just affect one country – they can affect the whole world.

Main Idea Check

Here are the main ideas of paragraphs 2–7 in Reading 1. Match each paragraph to its main idea. Write the number of the paragraph on the blank line.

_____ A The population continues to grow in the developing world.

_____ B Life expectancy is an important factor in population growth.

_____ C Some governments have programs to encourage larger families.

_____ D Some countries have programs to control their population growth.

_____ E Fertility rates contribute to population trends.

_____ F In some developed countries, the population is decreasing.

A Closer Look

Look back at Reading 1 to answer the following questions.

1 Which of the following is *not* stated paragraph 1?
   a The world population is rising.
   b The number of people older than 65 is larger than the number of people younger than 65.
   c The population of the developing world is growing faster than the population of the developed world.
   d The world population started to grow more rapidly in the nineteenth century.

2 According to paragraph 3, why are large families often an advantage in developing countries?
   a A large number of children increases the population.
   b Many members of the family contribute to a family's farm or business.
   c The government supports large families.
   d The children can help friends and neighbors in the village.

3 How does India's policy of education for girls and women help lower fertility rates, according to Paragraph 4?
   a The women get money from the government to go to school.
   b Education is important for development.
   c Educated women are permitted to have only one child.
   d Women with an education have fewer children.

4 A rate of 1.2 children per woman is needed to replace an existing population.
   True or False?

5 According to paragraph 6, why are experts concerned about the falling population in the developed world?

   a It may cause problems with the countries in the developing world.

   b A healthy economy requires a large working population to support those who cannot work. When the population falls, not enough people are working.

   c Because they have more workers, the population in the developing world will soon have to support people in the developed world.

   d If current trends continue, some countries may slowly disappear.

6 According to the reading, what are governments doing to encourage larger families? Circle all that apply.

   a They provide services for working women.

   b They give penalties to couples with only one child.

   c They help single young people to meet each other.

   d They give prizes for large families.

   e They give money to couples with more than two children.

Skill Review

In Skills and Strategies 7, you learned that English has many noun + noun collocations. Noticing these collocations will help you read more quickly. Using collocations when you speak and write is also important.

A The chart below contains words from noun + noun collocations in Reading 1. Combine words from the first column in the chart with words from the second column to make noun + noun collocations. Make a list of the collocations. Then use the collocations to complete the sentences below.

population	rate
government	level
fertility	range
age	growth
education	programs

1 In some countries, there are _____ that encourage couples to have more than two children.

2 In the United States, girls often reach a higher _____ than boys. This is because girls stay in school longer.

3 The _____ for fertility in women is from about twelve to the late forties but this can vary in individual women.

4 Rapid _____ is an important issue in developing countries. Experts are concerned there will not be enough food for all of the people.

5 In developed countries, the _____ is so low that soon there will be many more old people than young people.

B Compare your answers with a partner's.

Definitions

Find the words in Reading 1 that complete the following definitions. When a verb completes the definition, use the base form, although the verb in the reading may not be in the base form.

1 _____ is the academic study of groups of people and the characteristics of those groups. (*n*) Par. 1

2 The _____ is the number of people in a city, country, or other area. (*n*) Par. 1

3 _____ are the general directions of changes or developments over time. (*n pl*) Par. 1

4 _____ are numbers. (*n pl*) Par. 2

5 To _____ is to provide things necessary for life. (*v*) Par. 4

6 _____ matters are matters related to money. (*adj*) Par. 4

7 _____ are punishments for breaking a law or a rule. (*n pl*) Par. 4

8 A/An _____ is a sudden and large increase, or a burst with a loud sound. (*n*) Par. 5

9 To _____ someone or something is to take the place of someone or something. (*v*) Par. 6

10 Someone who is _____ is no longer working. (*adj*) Par. 6

Words in Context

Complete the sentences with words or phrases from Reading 1 in the box below.

according to	existing	restricts	specific
agriculture	hygiene	single	take seriously

1 The report stated that fewer Americans are getting married. A growing number of them, 82 million, are _____.

2 It is time for us to _____ climate change more _____.

3 One _____ factor – life expectancy – can explain this demographic trend.

4 Technology has improved _____. For example, there are new kinds of rice that can grow in dry areas.

5 _____ a study by the United Nations, the ratio of working people to retired people is changing quickly.

6 The new policy _____ the number of people who can go to universities. Only the top 5 percent will be admitted.

7 Good _____, such as washing your hands frequently, can prevent illness.

8 We need to use our _____ natural resources wisely so they do not run out.

Critical Thinking

In Reading 1 you learned the population is growing in some parts of the world and decreasing in other parts of the world. The chart below contains predictions by the United Nations about population trends for the next 300 years.

Figure 4.3 Actual and Expected Population Figures by Continent 2000–2300

YEAR	AFRICA	ASIA	LATIN AMERICA AND THE CARIBBEAN	OCEANIA	NORTH AMERICA	EUROPE
			POPULATION (MILLIONS)			
2000	795.7	3,679.7	520.2	31.0	315.9	728.0
2100	2,254.3	5,019.2	732.5	46.1	473.6	538.4
2200	2,008.2	4,681.7	680.8	45.5	508.8	573.7
2300	2,112.7	4,943.2	722.7	48.4	534.1	611.3

Source: United Nations

A Review the chart and discuss the following questions with a partner.

1 How would you describe future global population trends?

2 What do you think will be some of the consequences of these population trends?

3 What role do you think governments should play in controlling population growth in different parts of the world in the future?

B Share your answers with your class.

Research

Do some online research about the demographics of your home country. Find answers to the following questions. Then discuss the answers with a partner or your class.

- What is the population today?
- What was the population in 1900?
- Is the government encouraging larger or smaller families? How?

Writing

Write two paragraphs. The first paragraph will describe the results of your research. The second paragraph will discuss what you think will happen in the future and why.

Connecting to the Topic

Discuss the following questions with a partner.

1 Today many people leave the country where they were born. What are some possible reasons for this?

2 Would you leave the country where you live now to live somewhere else for a short time? Why or why not?

3 Would you leave the country where you live now to live somewhere else forever? Why or why not?

Previewing and Predicting

Reading the first sentence of each paragraph is a quick way to predict what a text will be about.

A Read the first sentence of paragraphs 2–7 in Reading 2, and think of a question that you expect the paragraph to answer. Then choose the question below that is most like your question. Write the number of the paragraph (*2–7*) next to that question. The first paragraph has been done for you.

PARAGRAPH	QUESTION
	Where do immigrants typically go when they leave their countries?
	Is migration good for the countries that migrants leave?
	Are there negative effects of global migration?
	Do immigrants always move to countries richer than their home countries?
2	What kind of people are migrants?
	What effects does global migration have on host countries?

B Compare your chart with a partner's.

While You Read

As you read, stop at the end of each sentence that contains words in bold. Follow the instructions in the box in the margin.

🔊 Global Migration

1   In today's global world, money and products move across international borders every day. People **move across borders**, too. As they move from one country to another, they are pushed and pulled by economic, social, and political forces. The number of people who cross international borders has been rising. (See Figure 4.4.) In 2010, about 214 million people, or about 3 percent of the global population, were living outside their country of origin. Most of these people came from Mexico, India, Russia, and China.

WHILE YOU READ ❶

Read ahead to the next sentence for the definition of *move across borders*. Highlight it.

2   **Migrants** are people who move their homes from one place to another. When they come to a new country and remain there, they are called *immigrants*. Migrants come from many different backgrounds. They are wealthy and poor, educated and illiterate. Some come alone to a new country; others come with their families. Some come for a few years; others stay forever. The one thing they all share is the hope for a better life. Migration has become a global issue because it has a large impact on the homeland that the immigrant is leaving as well as on the immigrant's new host country. It also, of course, has an impact on the lives of the immigrants themselves and their families.

WHILE YOU READ ❷

Highlight the definition of *migrants*.

3   The typical migrant moves from a poor country to a richer country to find work. In 2010, about 73 million people went from a poor country to a richer one. In some countries, such as Qatar and Singapore, migrants can work only for a limited period of time. They are not permitted to stay in

Figure 4.4 Countries with the Largest Number of Immigrants in 2010

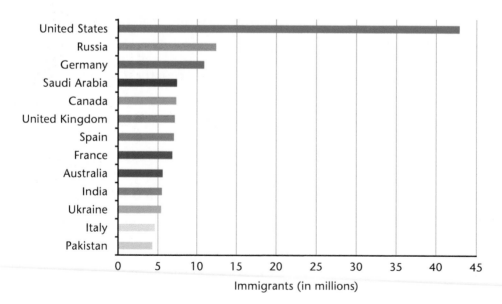

Source: *World Bank: Migration and Remittances Factbook 2011*

the country forever, and they may not become citizens. In some of these countries, the percentage of migrants is very high. For example, 87 percent of the population of Qatar in 2010 was migrants. In many other countries, especially in Europe and North America, however, immigrants intend to make the new country their home.

4   **Although** most migrants move to richer countries, almost as many people move from very poor countries to other countries that are not rich. The United Nations estimates that there are almost 74 million of these migrants. For example, many Dominicans come to the United States as immigrants. However, the Dominican Republic is also a host country for many people from Haiti. There were about a million migrant workers in Libya before the 2011 revolution; most were from other countries in Africa. These migrants can make much more money in these countries than they could make in their homelands.

WHILE YOU READ ③

What is the main idea of paragraph 4? Highlight it.

5   These migration trends can have a positive impact on prosperous host **countries**. Many developed countries have a labor shortage, that is, there are not enough workers. In these countries, migrants can fill some of these jobs, especially jobs that do not require a specific skill. They can also allow skilled workers in the host country to be more productive. **This** helps the economy of the host country. For example, in the United States, many immigrants provide childcare so that both parents can work.

WHILE YOU READ ④

Look back in this sentence to find an adjective + noun collocation. Highlight it.

WHILE YOU READ ⑤

What earlier information does *This* refer to? Highlight it.

6   Migration can also help the immigrants' homeland because immigrant workers often send part of their income back to their families in their home country. They sent home 440 billion dollars in 2010. For some countries, this money is a major part of their GDP, which is the total value of what a country produces in a year. It would be difficult for migrants' home countries to survive without it.

7   The economic and social effects of widespread migration are not always positive, however. For the host country, services for immigrants, such as healthcare and education, are expensive. Some residents of the host country also fear that immigrants will take their jobs away. In addition, if the cultures of the host country and the immigrants are very different, this can lead to misunderstandings between the two groups. However, it is the immigrants'

These are migrant workers in Dubai.

homelands that feel the greatest impact of migration. These countries lose their most productive workers as a result of migration. Migration can also divide families, so some towns and villages in immigrants' homelands lose many of their residents. Finally, migrants invest their skills and energy in another country, instead of in their homeland. As a result, few new jobs or other opportunities are created in those countries. Global migration has economic, political, and social consequences for all nations.

Main Idea Check

Here are the main ideas of paragraphs 3–7 in Reading 2. Match each paragraph to its main idea. Write the number of the paragraph on the blank line.

_____ A A large number of immigrants go from very poor countries to countries that are not rich.

_____ B Global migration can be positive for host countries.

_____ C Immigrants usually move from poor countries to rich countries.

_____ D Some of the impact of world migration is negative.

_____ E Immigration can be helpful to immigrants' homelands.

A Closer Look

Look back at Reading 2 to answer the following questions.

1 Look back at Figure 4.4. Put the following continents in the order of the number of immigrants they receive. Use *1* for the continent that receives the most immigrants and *3* for the continent that receives the fewest.

_____ Europe

_____ Asia

_____ North America

2 According to paragraph 2, what do most immigrants share?
a They are poor.
b They want a better life.
c They don't like their homelands.
d They come with their families.

3 According to paragraphs 3 and 4, how do the numbers of (a) immigrants who move to countries that are only a little more prosperous than their homelands compare to (b) immigrants who move to rich countries?
a (a) is a larger than (b)
b (b) is larger than (a)
c (a) and (b) are about the same

4 According to paragraph 5, less skilled immigrants do jobs that allow professionals in the host country to be more productive. What kind of jobs would be examples of for less skilled immigrants? Circle all that apply.
a Cleaning
b Engineering
c Childcare
d Working in gardens and farms
e Teaching

5 The Dominican Republic is a host country for migrants. **True or False?**

6 Think about the effects of the items in the list below. Are the effects felt by the immigrants' homeland (*HL*) or host country (*HC*)? Are these effects positive (*P*) or negative (*N*)? Choose one from each of the first two columns. The first one has been done for you.

HL / HC	P / N	
HL	*P*	Money is sent back to migrants' homelands.
		There are fewer people left to work in the homelands.
		Professionals in the host country become productive.
		Migrants provide needed labor.
		Migrants need expensive services in the host country.
		Migrants contribute to the host country's prosperity.

Skill Review

In Making Connections on page 127, you learned that writers use words and phrases to signal cause and effect. Finding these cause-and-effect relationships deepens your understanding of the text.

A Review the introduction to Making Connections on page 127, and read the final paragraph of Reading 2 again. Find four sentences in the paragraph in which the writer expresses a cause-and-effect relationship, and highlight the words or phrases that signal this relationship. Then fill in the chart below with the cause, the effect, and the transition words used in each of the four sentences.

CAUSE	EFFECT	TRANSITION WORDS OR PHRASES

B Share your chart with your class.

Definitions

Find the words in Reading 2 that complete the following definitions. When a verb completes the definition, use the base form, although the verb in the reading may not be in the base form.

1 _____ are the lines that divide one country from another. (*n pl*) Par. 1

2 A / An _____ is a subject or problem that people are thinking about. (*n*) Par. 2

3 Your _____ is the country where you were born. (*n*) Par. 2

4 If something is _____, it shows the normal and expected characteristics of a group. (*adj*) Par. 3

5 If you are _____, you are very successful, and you make a lot of money. (*adj*) Par. 5

6 _____ means all workers. (*n*) Par. 5

7 To _____ is to make it possible. (*v*) Par. 5

8 _____ is the money you get for doing work. (*n*) Par. 6

9 Something that is _____ happens or exists in many places. (*adj*) Par. 7

10 _____ are people who live in a place. (*n pl*) Par. 7

Word Families

A The words in **bold** in the chart are from Reading 2. The words next to them are from the same word family. Study and learn these words.

NOUN	VERB	ADJECTIVE
intention	**intend**	—
migration	*migrate*	—
origin	*originate*	*original*
permission	**permit**	—
wealth	—	**wealthy**

B Choose the correct form of the words from the chart to complete the following sentences. Use the correct verb tenses and subject-verb agreement. Use the correct singular and plural noun forms.

1 Immigrants usually move from poor countries to _____ countries.

2 Some immigrants change their _____ plans to return home; instead, they stay in their new country.

3 Global _____ is mainly a result of economic forces.

4 His _____ was to remain in Canada after he finished his university education.

5 A country's development is related to its _____ . Most developing countries are poorer than developed countries.

6 Most countries do not _____ tourists to stay for more than six months.

7 Most of the immigrants in the United States are of Mexican _____ .

8 Many immigrants _____ to return home after they have made enough money.

9 People, animals, and products all _____ across international borders.

10 Students usually have _____ to remain in the host country longer than tourists.

Academic Word List

The following are Academic Word List words from Readings 1 and 2 of this unit. Use these words to complete the sentences. (For more on the Academic Word List, see page 257.)

financial (*adj*)	issue (*n*)	migration (*n*)	restrict (*v*)	trends (*n*)
income (*n*)	labor (*n*)	residents (*n*)	specific (*adj*)	widespread (*adj*)

1 The _____ of the city pay a tax that helps pay for their schools.

2 The manager asked for _____ ideas for the new projects.

3 My _____ went up last year because I got a better job.

4 The increase in crime led to _____ fear in the town.

5 An analysis of last year's economic _____ suggests that the government's policies have been a success.

6 I keep my _____ documents, such as tax and bank information, in a safe place.

7 Global _____ increased to new levels as more than 200 million people moved from one country to another.

8 The cost of _____ went up last year because workers made more money.

9 Most countries _____ the number of immigrants they allow to enter each year.

10 Immigration is a very important _____ in the world today.

Critical Thinking

Reading 2 explores how migration connects developed and developing countries and how these different types of countries rely on one another in different ways.

EXPLORING OPINIONS

Critical readers form their own opinions about important topics in a text.

A Work in a group. Discuss the following questions.

1 Think about a developing country in which a high percentage of its labor force works outside the country. Is this a positive or negative situation for the developing country? Why or why not?

2 Think about a developed country in which skilled and professional workers rely on less skilled labor of immigrants from other developing countries. Is this a positive or negative situation for the developed country? For the immigrants?

B Share your answers with your class.

Research

Research the topic of migration for the country where you live now or a country where you have lived in the past. Find answers to the following questions.

- Do many people leave the country to live somewhere else? How many? Where do they go?
- Do many people come to the country from somewhere else? How many? Where do they come from?

Writing

Write two paragraphs. The first paragraph will discuss the people who leave the country that you researched and why. The second paragraph will discuss the people who come to that country. Where have they come from and why?

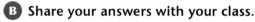

Improving Your Reading Speed

Good readers read quickly and still understand most of what they read.

A Read the instructions and strategies for Improving Your Reading Speed in Appendix 3 on page 271.

B Choose either Reading 1 or Reading 2 in this unit. Read it without stopping. Time how long it takes you to finish the text in minutes and seconds. Enter the time in the chart on page 273. Then calculate your reading speed in number of words per minute.

Scanning for Specific Information

As a student, you often have to read for the main idea of a reading in an academic text. This involves careful, thoughtful reading. However, there are also many times when you need to find a specific piece of information from a reading – a number, a name, a definition, or an example. In this case, it is not necessary to read the complete text carefully. A better strategy is scanning. *Scanning* is moving your eyes very quickly through a reading until you find the information you are looking for. For example, in an economics class, your teacher may ask you to find the definition of the terms *supply* and *demand*. You do not have to read the whole text carefully because you are searching for only two specific pieces of information. You can quickly scan for the terms, and, when you find them, you can read more carefully to find the information you are looking for.

Examples & Explanations

Historically, diseases have played an important role in population rates. For example, the Black Death killed about one-third of Europe's population between 1347 and 1351. In recent years, the most dangerous disease has been HIV / AIDS. This disease has had a significant impact on the southern part of Africa – particularly on the small country of Botswana. Botswana's population is declining because of deaths due to HIV / AIDS. Around 25 percent of Botswana's adults have HIV, and life expectancy has fallen from 65 years in 1990 to 53 years in 2011. Other countries in this area of Africa also have high rates of HIV / AIDS. Unless scientists find a cure for HIV / AIDS, this disease will continue to have an important effect on the population of southern Africa.

Imagine you are reading this paragraph in order to find out why the population of Botswana is declining. You can quickly scan through the paragraph for the answer and focus on the key word *Botswana*.

Quickly move your eyes through the paragraph. Focus on the center of each line, and move your eyes quickly down, looking left and right along each line. Don't say the words to yourself or move your lips. Stop when you come to the word *Botswana*. Now read more slowly until you find out why the population of Botswana is declining: *Botswana's population is declining because of deaths due to HIV / AIDS.*

Strategies

These strategies will help you scan for specific information.

- Decide what specific information you are looking for.
- Focus on a key word in the text, and quickly scan for that word. Quickly move your eyes through the text.
- Don't say the words to yourself. Try not to move your lips.
- Scan quickly until you find the key word. When you find it, slow down and see if the information you are looking for is there. If it is not, speed up again and look for the next time the key word appears.

Skill Practice 1

Read the following questions. Focus on the word or date in bold. Quickly scan the paragraph for that key word or date. Then write the answers on the blank lines.

1 What was the world's largest city in **1800**?

_____

2 What was the world's largest city in **1900**?

_____

3 Which city in **India** has a population of over 20 million?

_____

4 What will be the population of this city in **2020**?

_____

In the past, the population of cities grew faster in developed countries. Today, in contrast, the population of cities in developing countries is skyrocketing. In 1800, Beijing was the only city in the world with a population of over 1 million people. However, as Europe became more industrialized in the nineteenth century, cities there grew rapidly. By 1900, London was the world's largest city. The next nine largest cities were all in Europe and the United States. However, most of the largest cities in the world today are in developing countries. Mexico City, Delhi in India, and São Paulo, Brazil all have populations of 20 million or more. By 2020, it is estimated that these cities will each have over 25 million people. In contrast, the population of cities in developed countries is growing at a much slower rate.

Skill Practice 2

Read the following questions. Underline the key word in each question. Then focus on that key word, and scan the paragraph to find the answers. Write the answers on the blank lines.

1 Who was Thomas Malthus?

_____

2 When did he write about overpopulation?

_____

3 Define the term *Malthusians*.

_____

4 According to Malthus, what events would slow population growth?

_____

The name Thomas Malthus is not very well known today, but his ideas have had a lot of influence in the world of demography. In 1798, he wrote an article, which raised an important question: Will the world face a problem of overpopulation? Malthus was an English economist who was interested in demography. At that time, life in Europe was improving: people had enough to eat, and fewer children were dying at a young age. As a result, the population was growing. Malthus feared that this was going to cause serious problems in the future. He believed that the world's population was growing faster than food production. Therefore, Malthus argued that there would not be enough food for everyone unless war, disease, or smaller families reduced population growth. Many people still agree with his theories today. They are known as *Malthusians*. Malthusians argue that the population is rising most rapidly in developing countries but that most of the people in these countries are poor. These countries are not producing enough food for this growing population. So Malthusians still believe the answer to the question is, "Yes, the world does face a problem of overpopulation."

Connecting to the Topic

Discuss the following questions with a partner.

1 Do you prefer living in a city or outside of a city?

2 Most people in the world now live in cities. What are some possible reasons for this?

3 Think of a city you know well. If possible, look at a map of the city or draw a map of the city.
   a What do you know about the history of this city? When and why did it grow?
   b Where are the best shops, restaurants, and entertainment?
   c Where do wealthy people live? Where do poorer people live?

Previewing and Predicting

Reading the title of a reading and the first sentence of each paragraph can help you predict what a text will be about.

A Read the title of the reading and the first sentence of each paragraph in Reading 3. Then put a check (✓) next to the questions you think will be answered in the reading.

_____ A Why are most of the world's largest cities in developing countries?

_____ B What percentage (%) of the world's population lives in cities?

_____ C Is crime a problem in today's large cities?

_____ D Did some cities develop because they are close to the sea?

_____ E Why do some people prefer to live far away from cities?

_____ F What are some of the differences between European and North American cities?

B Compare your answers with a partner's.

While You Read

As you read, stop at the end of each sentence that contains words in bold. Follow the instructions in the box in the margin.

The Growth of Cities

1   In 1800, only 3 percent of the world's population **lived in urban areas**; most of the world's population lived in rural, or farming, areas. According to the United Nations, today more than 50 percent of the world's population lives in urban areas. Recent urban growth has been in developing countries, and their cities are continuing to grow very quickly. The United Nations predicts that the urban population of developing nations will grow from 3.3 billion in 2007 to 6.4 billion in 2050. In the future, the United Nations predicts that almost all population growth will be in cities.

2   Cities have developed for many **different reasons**. The first cities grew up around marketplaces, where people traded food and goods. Because of trade, major cities were established along large rivers or around harbors. Religion also played an important role in the development of urban areas. As religions became more organized, people built settlements around important religious buildings. Later, cities became the centers for government. They also provided security in a dangerous world. They were built on top of hills and often were surrounded by walls. Finally, and perhaps most importantly, cities attracted growing numbers of people with ideas about art and science. The cities then became the centers of culture.

3   By the nineteenth century, the largest cities were in Europe. Europeans planned cities around a central business district. The best shops and restaurants were often located in this sector. Wealthy people lived in an area that circled the central business district. Factories and low-quality housing were built away from this center, so poorer people lived in the suburbs. This pattern continues today. In many European cities, the richest residents live close to the center, whereas the poorest residents live far from the center.

WHILE YOU READ ❶

What percentage of the world's population lives in urban areas now? Focus on the key word *percent* while you scan ahead. Highlight the answer.

WHILE YOU READ ❷

Highlight the reasons that explain why cities developed.

Figure 4.5 Global Urban and Rural Population – 1950–2050

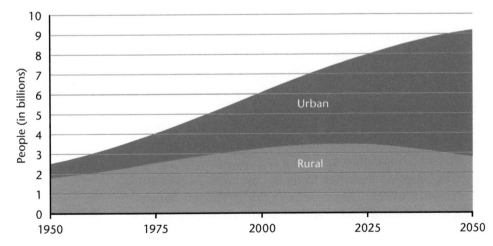

Source: United Nations: World Urbanization Prospects, The 2007 Revision

Figure 4.6 Models of Typical European and North American Cities

Typical European City

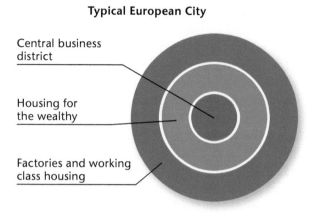

Central business district

Housing for the wealthy

Factories and working class housing

Typical North American City

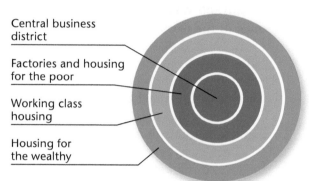

Central business district

Factories and housing for the poor

Working class housing

Housing for the wealthy

4   In contrast, many North American cities have evolved **differently**. A well-known sociologist, Ernest Burgess, studied Chicago in the 1920s. He described the development of the city as a series of rings. The inner ring was the central business district. However, wealthy people did not live in the next ring, as they did in European cities. Instead, this ring had factories and poor housing. The third ring had better housing, but it was still for the working class, that is, people who did physical labor. The fourth ring was the suburbs, where the wealthy lived – in large houses with big yards. Not every North American city follows Burgess's model; however, it does explain why many cities in the United States have poor communities close to the central business districts and wealthy suburbs far away from the central areas.

5   Today, most of the world's largest cities are in the developing countries. In these cities, as in Europe, most wealthy residents live close to the city center. These centers have the best stores, the finest restaurants, and the most expensive apartments. Thousands of people migrate to these cities to look for work. However, many of the cities cannot provide housing for them. **As a result** of this internal migration, these new residents move into areas known as squatter settlements, or slums. In these settlements, very few services are available because neither the residents nor the city can afford them. For example, people often have to carry water by hand, and they do not have electricity. Millions of people around the globe live in these squatter settlements.

6   Cities have developed in different ways around the world but they also share some features. A city in the United States looks very different from an older European city, which is different from a rapidly growing city in a developing country. Yes, cities do have one thing in common: people move to cities looking for opportunities. This creates exciting, vibrant communities. Unfortunately, as migration from rural to urban areas continues to rise, cities face many challenges. The most critical challenge is providing services to this **growing urban population**.

WHILE YOU READ 3

What two topics are contrasted in paragraphs 3 and 4?
a) The rich and the poor
b) European and North American cities

WHILE YOU READ 4

Read ahead in the paragraph to find a noun + noun collocation. Highlight it.

WHILE YOU READ 5

What is the main idea of paragraph 6? Highlight it.

Main Idea Check

Match the main ideas below to their paragraphs. Write the number of the paragraph on the blank line.

_____ A There are several reasons why cities have developed throughout history.

_____ B Many cities in the developing world cannot provide housing to all of their residents.

_____ C Cities have developed differently, they share one thing.

_____ D North American cities were planned differently from European cities.

_____ E In European cities, the wealthy live close to the center, and the poor live far from the center.

_____ F The world's urban population is large and rapidly growing.

A Closer Look

Look back at Reading 3 to answer the following questions.

1 According to paragraph 1, which statements are correct? Circle all that apply.
   a In the past, more people used to live in rural areas than urban areas.
   b Cities are growing more quickly in developed rather than developing countries.
   c Experts believe that the population is growing at the same rate worldwide.
   d Urban areas in developing countries are growing very quickly.

2 It is estimated that the number of people living in cities in developing countries will almost double in the first half of the twenty-first century. **True or False?**

3 Which statements are true according to Figure 4.5? Circle all that apply.
   a The number of people living in rural areas declined steadily from 1950.
   b Experts believe that the rural population will begin to decline in 2025.
   c The world's population will continue to grow sharply until 2050, when it will begin to fall.
   d As the world's population grows, most people will live in urban areas.

4 Which reason is *not* given to explain why cities developed in specific locations?
   a Religion   c Trade
   b Security   d Weather

5 Which statements are correct according to paragraphs 3 and 4? Circle all that apply.
   a European and North American cities are similar in design.
   b Cities in European countries and developing countries are similar in that the rich live close to the city center.
   c All North American cities are designed as a series of rings around a central suburban area.
   d All cities usually have a wealthy central area.
   e In North American cites, the wealthy are likely to live in the suburbs.

6 In many North American cities, the wealthy work in the central business district but live far away from it. **True or False?**

7 Why do many people live in squatter settlements?
  a These settlements provide good housing at low prices.
  b The people cannot afford better housing.
  c City governments have built these settlements for the poor.
  d There are a lot of jobs available in these settlements.

Skill Review

In Skills and Strategies 8, you learned that sometimes you need to scan for specific information. To find specific information, you focus on key words and search for words connected to these key words. You do not need to read the complete text.

Read each of the following questions. Focus on the word or date in bold. Then quickly scan for that item in Reading 3. Write the correct answer on the blank line below.

1 What percentage of the population lived in cities in **1800**?

_____

2 According to the reading, how many people lived in urban areas in developing countries in **2007**?

_____

3 Where were the largest cities in the **nineteenth century**?

_____

4 Who was **Ernest Burgess**?

_____

5 Who lived in the **fourth ring** of North American cities according to Burgess's series of rings?

_____

6 What is another word for **squatter settlements**?

_____

Definitions

Find the words in Reading 3 that complete the following definitions. When a verb completes the definition, use the base form, although the verb in the reading may not be in the base form.

1 If something is of or in a city, it is _____. (*adj*) Par. 1

2 A/An _____ is a protected area of water where ships can land. (*n*) Par. 2

3 _____ are places where people come to live and where people have not lived in the past. (*n*) Par. 2

4 A/An _____ is a way something is done or organized. (*n*) Par. 3

5 A person who studies society is called a/an _____. (*n*) Par. 4

6 A/An _____ is a group of similar things that follow one other. (*n pl*) Par. 4

7 Areas outside of the city are called _____. (*n pl*) Par. 4

8 A/An _____ is an example that shows how something works. (*n*) Par. 4

9 _____ are things that people need such as electricity and water. (*n pl*) Par. 5

10 If something is _____, it is of the greatest importance. (*adj*) Par. 6

Synonyms

Complete the sentences with words from Reading 3 in the box below. These words replace the words or phrases in parentheses, which are similar in meaning.

communities	internal	sector	trade
evolved	rural	surrounded	vibrant

1 The accident damaged her (inside) _____ organs, including her heart and lungs.

2 Many poor (neighborhoods) _____ do not have water or electricity.

3 People who live in small villages often come to larger towns to (buy and sell) _____ things.

4 People from (country) _____ areas often move to the city to find jobs because there is not enough work on farms.

5 The hotel was very quiet and peaceful because it was (circled) _____ by fields and forests.

6 His small store (grew slowly) _____ into an international business.

7 San Francisco is a (lively) _____ city with lots of shops and restaurants.

8 Many artists have moved into a neighborhood that was previously an industrial (area) _____ of the city.

Critical Thinking

Reading 3 provides several reasons why cities develop.

A Think about your city or a city that you know well. Why did it develop in its location? Use paragraph 2 in Reading 3 to help you think of reasons. Are there any other reasons that are not mentioned in the reading? Write the reasons below.

Name of city: _____

- _____
- _____
- _____

B Share your answers with a partner.

Research

Review Figure 4.5 on page 153, which illustrates how many European and North American cities developed. Find a map of the city you discussed in the Critical Thinking task. Use this map to help you draw a plan of the city. Label your plan to show the suburbs, the financial district(s), shopping district(s), industrial area(s), the wealthy residential areas, the middle class suburbs, and the working class residential areas.

Writing

Write two paragraphs. The first paragraph will explain why your city developed in its location. Use the discussion in the Critical Thinking task to help you write this paragraph. The second paragraph will describe how your city is designed, or organized. Use the map from the research task to help you write the second paragraph.

Connecting to the Topic

Discuss the following questions with a partner.

1 Think about famous cities in the world you have been to or read about. Which of these cities do you think would be good to live in, and why?

2 What problems do you think these cities face today?

3 What will happen to these cities in the future? Will they get bigger? Will they solve their problems or face new ones?

Previewing and Predicting

Reading section headings and looking at illustrations and graphic material can help you predict what a text will be about.

A Read the section headings in Reading 4, and look at Table 4.1 on page 160 and the photos on pages 161 and 163. Then decide what content will be in each section. Write the number of the sections (*I–IV*) next to the topics that best describe it. Each section has two topics.

SECTION	TOPIC
	Traffic problems in major cities
	Breathing problems for residents of cities with bad air pollution
	People who cannot afford housing and have to live on the street
	Communities that use alternative energy
	Reasons why crime is high in some cities
	The largest cities in the past and the future
	A definition of megacities
	Planning for better urban living in the future

B Compare your answers with a partner's.

While You Read

As you read, stop at the end of each sentence that contains words in **bold**. Follow the instructions in the box in the margin.

◀)) Challenges Facing the World's Cities

I. Introduction

1   Throughout history **cities have offered hope and opportunity**. Today, 70 million people a year migrate from rural areas to cities. Most of these people migrate to find better jobs and to improve their lives. This migration has resulted in the development of megacities, that is, cities with a population of more than 10 million people. By 2020, there will be about 35 of these megacities, and most will be in developing countries. (See Table 4.1.) This urbanization brings many economic benefits. Most of any country's economic activity takes place in urban areas, so urbanization usually leads to increased prosperity. However, these huge cities also face serious social and environmental challenges.

WHILE YOU READ ❶

Scan ahead for the definition of *megacities*. Highlight it.

II. Social Challenges: Poverty, Housing, and Crime

2   Not everyone who comes to a city from a rural area can get a **good job**. Some people cannot find any job at all. As a result, poverty is a major problem in large cities, especially in developing countries. The World Bank estimates that over 3 billion people live in poverty, on less than U.S. $2.50 a day. Poverty leads to serious consequences. The results of poverty are often poor nutrition, poor health, low-quality housing, and little if any

WHILE YOU READ ❷

As you read, highlight the words that signal cause and effect.

Table 4.1 The World's Largest Cities in 1950 and 2020 (predicted)

RANK	LARGEST CITIES IN 1950	POPULATION IN MILLIONS	LARGEST CITIES IN 2020	POPULATION IN MILLIONS
1	New York, U.S.	12.5	Tokyo, Japan	37.3
2	London, U.K.	8.9	Mumbai, India	26.0
3	Tokyo, Japan	7.0	Delhi, India	26.0
4	Paris, France	5.9	Dhaka, Bangladesh	22.0
5	Shanghai, China	5.4	Mexico City, Mexico	22.0
6	Moscow, Russia	5.1	São Paulo, Brazil	21.6
7	Buenos Aires, Argentina	5.0	Lagos, Nigeria	21.6
8	Chicago, U.S.	4.9	Jakarta, Indonesia	20.8
9	Ruhr, Germany	4.9	New York, U.S.	20.4
10	Kolkata, India	4.8	Karachi, Pakistan	18.9

Source: citymayors.com/statistics/urban_2020_1.html

education. In addition, the cycle of poverty is difficult to break: if children are born into a poor family, they are more likely to get sick and less likely to get an education. As adults, they will find it difficult to get a good job, so they will be poor like their parents. Therefore, poverty usually persists from one generation to another.

3   The United Nations believes that one in seven people around the world lives in very poor housing or is homeless. It estimates that there are 100 million children living on the streets. In urban areas, one in three people lives in these conditions. Cairo, Egypt, is an example of a rapidly growing city that is facing housing shortages. The population of this city doubled between 1980 and 2006 to almost 20 million. Private investors built many new apartments, but these are very expensive. In 2011, there were around one million empty apartments because residents could not afford to buy or rent them. In contrast, 12 million residents of Cairo live in squatter settlements. One settlement, the City of the Dead, has become famous around the world for its unique housing. This settlement is a huge cemetery. The residents live in the tombs where people are buried. Families sit on the floor of these cold, dark tombs and eat their meals on the tombstones. It is estimated that over one million people in Cairo live in the City of the Dead.

4   Crime is another major problem of urban areas. A 2007 United Nations study found that more than 60 percent of people in the urban areas of developing countries had been victims of crime. Other studies have also found that the highest crime rates are in large cities. For example, in Brazil, Mexico, and Peru, the largest cities have the majority of crimes. However, not all big cities have a lot of crime. Tokyo, one of the largest cities in the world, does not have a high crime rate.

5   Historically, crime is most likely to rise during periods of rapid urbanization. In the nineteenth and early twentieth centuries, crime rates rose in European and North American cities when the rural poor were moving to these urban areas. This pattern continues today. Crime often increases when large numbers of people, especially young men, migrate to the city. Often these people cannot find jobs, and they live in difficult conditions. However, poverty is just one factor in rising urban crime rates. Some experts believe that the picture is more complicated. They argue that the crucial factor is not poverty; it is economic inequality. During periods of rapid urbanization, the rich and the poor often live near each other. This can lead to an increase in crime. For example, Johannesburg, a rapidly

growing city in South Africa, has a very high rate of economic inequality and one of the highest murder rates in the **world**.

III. An Environmental Challenge: Pollution

6   Another problem in growing cities is pollution. Visitors to Bangkok, Thailand, are often shocked by the large numbers of motorcycles, cars, and buses on the city's streets. The traffic is so bad there that an average Bangkok resident spends about 44 days each year sitting in traffic. The situation in Jakarta, Indonesia is similar. Five and a half million people come into Jakarta each day – 2.5 million by car and over 3 million by motorcycle. Emissions from all of these cars and motorcycles are a major cause of air pollution in these cities. It is not unusual for the people who breathe this air to have serious health problems, especially **respiratory illnesses**.

7   Because of the connection between pollution and illness, many cities are trying to clean up their air and water. One city in Brazil showed that it is possible to reduce pollution dramatically. In the 1990s, Cubatão was known as the Valley of Death. The oil and steel plants and chemical factories were polluting the city's air and poisoning the water. Fish died in the rivers, trees died in the forests, and people died of respiratory illnesses and cancer. The problem was so serious that the government and industries decided to do something to solve it. They invested millions of dollars to reduce the air pollution and clean up the water. Today, fish are returning to the rivers, trees are growing in the forests, and the residents of Cubatão are healthy **again**.

IV. Future Trends: The Environment

8   There are many environmental challenges. Many cities have problems with air pollution and heavy traffic. Rapid urbanization has led to an explosion of new buildings and the loss of parks and open spaces. However, in some places, **these trends** are changing. Architects, engineers, and politicians are starting to plan for a better future. They understand that growth does not need to create environmental problems. They are designing new cities that are environmentally smart. Design guidelines for "smart growth" include:

- smaller communities with parks and gardens
- use of alternative energies
- services and employment near where people live so they can walk to work
- green areas where people can plant trees, flowers, and vegetables
- efficient public transportation

9   A community in South London, England, has followed these guidelines of smart growth. This community, BedZED, has housing, health services, and employment all inside one community. Wind and solar power provide energy, and the buildings do not use fossil fuels. This alternative energy is

WHILE YOU READ 3

Look back in paragraph 5 and find two noun + noun collocations with *rate*. Highlight them.

WHILE YOU READ 4

What is the main idea of paragraph 6? Highlight it.

WHILE YOU READ 5

Look back in paragraph 7, and find four noun + noun and adjective + noun collocations. Highlight them.

WHILE YOU READ 6

What do *these trends* refer to? Highlight the antecedents.

cheaper, so residents pay only 10 percent of what other London residents pay for electricity. In BedZED, buildings collect and reuse rain water. They also have roof-top gardens, which help keep buildings cooler in the summers and warmer in the winters. Residents walk or bicycle to work. If they need a car, they use one of the community's biofuel cars.

10   BedZED has been so successful that other cities are designing communities using smart growth guidelines. China has been criticized for its heavy use of fossil fuels, such as oil and coal. Today, however, it is a leader in smart growth design. One of China's new cities is called Tianjin Eco-city. Engineers are building this city to house 350,000 residents. Wind and solar power will provide energy, and rainwater will be recycled. In order to reduce traffic emissions, 90 percent of its traffic will be public transportation, so people will not need cars. The design of the city will encourage people to walk. Residents can walk around the city using ground-level walkways as well as skybridges that connect the high-rise buildings. This remarkable city of the future is planned to start taking in residents in 2020.

11   Every minute 130 people leave their villages and move to a city, where they often face difficult living conditions. However, this migration is likely to continue because cities offer the best economic opportunities. For megacities, it is a huge challenge to meet the needs of these new residents. Poverty, squatter settlements, homelessness, crime, and pollution are real problems. Yet when people come together in the cities, great things can happen. People all around the world are making changes in their cities. Everyone wants to be sure that in this century, these cities will continue to be places where people want to live.

Plans for Tianjin Eco-city

Main Idea Check

Match the main ideas below to five of the paragraphs in Reading 4. Write the number of the paragraph on the blank line.

_____ **A** Rapid urbanization and economic inequality lead to increasing crime.

_____ **B** Air pollution is a significant problem in many cities.

_____ **C** One community in England has followed the principles of smart design.

_____ **D** Poverty is a significant problem in large cities.

_____ **E** One city successfully cleaned up its air and water pollution.

A Closer Look

Look back at Reading 4 to answer the following questions.

1 According to paragraph 1 and Table 4.1, which statement is *not* correct?
   a By 2020, experts predict that most urban growth will be in developing countries.
   b In 1950, over half of the megacities were in Europe and North America.
   c By 2020, there will be 10 cities with a population of 10 million people or more.
   d The Indian cities of Mumbai and Delhi will have the same population by 2020.

2 The population of Tokyo will double between 1950 and 2020. **True or False?**

3 Reread paragraph 2. Which of the following actions would most likely end the cycle of poverty?
   a Parents get more help from the government.
   b All family members, including the children, work.
   c Children have the opportunity to get an education.
   d More families stay in rural areas instead of moving to the cities.

4 Why is the City of the Dead in Cairo unique?
   a Its population doubled between 1980 and 2000.
   b It is a squatter settlement.
   c People live in a cemetery.
   d One million people live in this squatter settlement.

5 According to the reading, crime rates are rising in many megacities. **True or False?**

6 Which of the following is *not* listed in paragraph 5 as a factor in high crime rates?
   a Rapid urbanization
   b Economic inequality
   c Squatter settlements
   d Poverty

7 According to paragraphs 8 and 9, which environmentally smart developments are likely to save energy? Circle all that apply.

 a Efficient public transportation
 b Gardens and parks
 c Biofuel cars
 d Services and employment near where people live
 e Rooftop gardens

8 In Tianjin Eco-city, 90 percent of emissions will be reduced because people will use public transportation. **True or False?**

Skill Review

In Skills and Strategies 8, you learned that sometimes you need to scan for specific information. To find specific information, you need to identify key words and quickly scan for words connected to these key words. You do not need to read the complete text.

A **Read the following questions. Highlight the key words in each question. Then focus on those words, and scan Reading 4 to find the answers. Write the answers on the blank lines.**

1 How many megacities will there be worldwide by 2020?

_____

2 How many people worldwide are living in poverty according to the World Bank?

_____

3 What study found that 60 percent of people who live in urban areas had been victims of crime?

_____

4 How many people come into Jakarta each day by motorcycle?

_____

5 Why is the new Chinese city Tianjin Eco-city a good example of smart growth?

_____

B **Compare your answers with a partner's.**

Definitions

Find the words in Reading 4 that complete the following definitions. When a verb completes the definition, use the base form, although the verb in the reading may not be in the base form.

1 _____ are results or effects of something that has happened. They are often negative. (*n pl*) Par. 2

2 _____ is the food you eat to stay healthy. (*n*) Par. 2

3 A/An _____ is a set of events that repeat themselves. (*n*) Par. 2

4 To _____ is to continue to exist, often in spite of difficulty. (*v*) Par. 2

5 People who are about the same age in a family or society are a/an _____. (*n*) Par. 2

6 If something is _____, it is very unusual, or special. (*adj*) Par. 3

7 An area of land where dead people are buried is called a/an _____. (*n*) Par. 3

8 _____ are buildings where one person or a family is buried. (*n pl*) Par. 3

9 To _____ someone is to put a dead person under the ground. (*v*) Par. 3

10 _____ problems are related to the lungs and breathing (*adj*) Par. 6

Words in Context

Complete the passages with words from Reading 4 in the box below.

face	inequality	provide	similar
huge	poverty	rate	victims

1   A recent study of _____ in urban and rural areas looked at the poorest
        a
people in the world – those who live on less than one dollar a day. The study showed

_____ between rural and urban areas. Almost 75 percent of the poorest
        b
people live in rural areas. These results of the study are very _____ to the
                                                                                                                          c
results of a study that was done 10 years before. That study found that 77 percent of

the world's poor lived in rural areas. Together, the studies make it clear that the world

needs to _____ more help to the rural poor.
        d

2   The urban poor _____ many challenges in their lives. One of the
     e
biggest problems is that the crime _____ is higher in urban areas. As a
                                             f
result, poor people are often _____ of crimes. This is a / an
                                         g
_____ challenge, especially in the megacities of the developing world
         h
where there are not enough resources for the police.

Academic Word List

The following are Academic Word List words from Readings 3 and 4 of this unit. Use these words to complete the sentences. (For more on the Academic Word List, see page 257.)

community (*n*)	cycle (*n*)	internal (*adj*)	sector (*n*)	similar (*adj*)
consequences (*n*)	evolved (*v*)	persist (*v*)	series (*n*)	unique (*adj*)

1 The industrial _____ of the city is located far from the city center.

2 New York and Hong Kong developed for _____ reasons: both cities are located by deep harbors.

3 There will be serious _____ if city governments do not try to help people find jobs. Crime rates may increase, for example.

4 People who live in the same _____ often have similar interests and ideas.

5 Parents who live in poverty find it difficult to educate their children, who then grow up to be poor like their parents: it is a difficult _____ to break.

6 This city _____ from a small village to the huge city it is today.

7 In some countries, such as Egypt, _____ migration is a bigger challenge than international migration.

8 Every city is _____ because every city is different in some ways from all other cities.

9 Poverty and crime _____ in many large cities in spite of government efforts to reduce them.

10 The city produced a / an _____ of videos which showed how the city would evolve in the next 50 years.

Critical Thinking

Reading 4 discusses important social and environmental challenges facing large cities today.

A Work with a group, and identify some of the challenges raised in Reading 4. Then talk about ways to solve them. Use your ideas to complete the chart. The first challenge is provided as an example.

CHALLENGE:	SOLUTION:
very heavy traffic	

B Compare your answers with another group's.

Research

Choose a megacity with a population of over 10 million people. Use the Internet to find answers to the following questions.

- What is the population of this city today? Is it growing quickly or slowly?
- What are some challenges facing this city?
- Find some examples of what the city is doing to solve some of these problems.

Writing

Write two paragraphs. The first paragraph will describe the results of your research. The second paragraph will discuss what the city is doing to solve its problems.

Improving Your Reading Speed

Good readers read quickly and still understand most of what they read.

A Read the instructions and strategies for Improving Your Reading Speed in Appendix 3 on page 271.

B Choose either Reading 3 or Reading 4 in this unit. Read it without stopping. Time how long it takes you to finish the text in minutes and seconds. Enter the time in the chart on page 273. Then calculate your reading speed in number of words per minute.

CONTRAST CONNECTORS

Writers often connect ideas by showing how one idea is different from another idea. Writers may use words and phrases such as *however, on the one hand, in contrast, although, whereas,* and *but* to make these contrasts.

In the following example, the word ***however*** introduces a contrast between the two underlined ideas.

> In the nineteenth and early twentieth centuries, <u>crime rates were high in European and North American cities.</u> ***However***, <u>as these cities became fully urbanized, the crime rates fell.</u>

Exercise 1

Find words or phrases that signal contrast in the following paragraphs. Highlight them. The first one has been done for you.

1   The definition of a city is an urban settlement that has its own government. This government provides basic services to its residents. They include schools, water, electricity, and roads. Although all cities provide these services to some people, many cities cannot provide them to everyone.

2   All countries have experienced some changes in their population growth. This growth has occurred at different times in different parts of the world. Europe and North America had an explosion in population growth in the early nineteenth century. In contrast, many African and Latin American countries began to grow rapidly in the twentieth century.

3   Better hygiene and healthcare have increased life expectancy in many countries. A simple change, the introduction of soap in the nineteenth century, made a big difference in life expectancy. Medicines that prevent disease have made an even bigger difference. However, there are still some countries today where the life expectancy is low because of the low standard of hygiene and healthcare.

4   How do we know the population of different countries? Some countries like Canada and England count their inhabitants every 10 years. In contrast, France counts every seven years, and Japan and Australia count their inhabitants every five years. This information provides an estimate of the worldwide population.

Exercise 2

Make a clear paragraph by putting sentences A, B, and C into the best order after the numbered sentence. Look for transition words, pronouns, and repeated key words to help you. Write the letters in the correct order on the blank lines.

1 In the past, the majority of immigrants to the United States were single male adults. ___ ___ ___

| **A** Many of these women brought their children, so the number of immigrants under the age of 15 increased. | **B** Today, many immigrants are both men and women who come to the United States with their children. | **C** However, in the 1950s this changed because, for the first time, there were more female immigrants than male immigrants. |

2 Immigrants face many difficulties when they move to a new country. ___ ___ ___

| **A** The first challenge is finding a job. | **B** Learning a new language and understanding a different culture can be very hard. | **C** However, before they can find a good job, immigrants usually need to learn a new language. |

3 In the United States, there are both advantages and disadvantages to living in the suburbs. ___ ___ ___

| **A** However, people in the suburbs usually have to pay a high price for their house and will have to drive a long distance to get to work. | **B** Finally, although suburbs have lower crime rates than cities, people feel separated from the vibrant city life. | **C** A typical suburban house is much larger than a house in the city. |

4 Cities are finding ways to solve traffic problems. ___ ___ ___

| **A** In U.S. cities, on the other hand, the traffic is getting worse. So soon these cities may have to follow Singapore's example. | **B** In Singapore, for example, the number of drivers has decreased because they have to buy a license to drive during these times. | **C** One trend is to make people pay if they drive during the busiest times. |

5 The countries of East Asia have different population patterns. ___ ___ ___

| **A** In contrast, only one-third of all Chinese live in urban areas. The majority live in smaller farming communities. | **B** In total, three-quarters of Japanese and South Koreans live in urban areas. | **C** In Japan and South Korea, large populations live in a few major cities, such as Tokyo and Osaka in Japan and Seoul in South Korea. |

5

DESIGN IN EVERYDAY LIFE

SKILLS AND STRATEGIES

- Vocabulary Study
- Taking Notes from a Reading

Vocabulary Study

When you read in English, you will meet many new words. Some of these words will be important for you to learn and remember; some may not be so important. What should you do when you meet new words that you want to learn and remember? You should write down the new words with a definition and an example sentence. You should study them frequently. You can do this if you keep the words and their definitions in a vocabulary notebook or on vocabulary cards. Cards work best because you can change the order of the words when you study them. Cards are also more portable.

Examples & Explanations

Architecture is the art and science of building. One important choice in architecture is building materials. In the eighteenth century, most large buildings were made of stone. Stone made the buildings heavy and dark. In the nineteenth century, the invention of new materials, such as steel and concrete, changed buildings on the outside and inside. Stone walls were very heavy and thick. In contrast, walls made of concrete and steel were much thinner but stronger. This combination of steel and concrete also made it possible to construct much taller buildings with very large windows and recesses. The outside walls were so strong that new buildings also needed fewer walls on the inside for support. These changes on the outside and inside meant buildings could be light and open.

The words in color may be unfamiliar to you. As you read, you may need to guess or look up their meaning to understand the paragraph. After you have finished reading, you will need to decide which words from the reading you want to study and remember. It may not be possible to remember every new word, so you need to choose just the most important words and study them.

Choose words that are useful. A word might be useful in general or useful to you as an individual. In this paragraph, generally useful words include *materials* and *construct*. However, based on your interests or your work, perhaps the words *architecture*, *steel*, and *concrete* are also words you would like to remember. In contrast, the word *recess* is less common than the other words, so it is probably less important to study.

Once you have chosen the new words to study, you can make vocabulary cards. Each card should include the word, its definition, and how it is used in a sentence.

Strategies

These strategies will help you study new vocabulary words.

- First, make sure you understand the meaning of the new word. Check the definition in a learner dictionary, and follow the steps in Skills and Strategies 3 on page 44.

- For the new words you choose to study, make vocabulary cards like the example on the right. On one side of the card, write the word and an example sentence – either the sentence in which you found it or an example sentence from the dictionary. This will help you remember how the word is used in context. On the other side, write a definition of the word in English.

- Mix up the cards, and study them in a different order each time.

- Study your cards often but for short periods of time. This is more effective than studying them less often for a long period of time.

- Start by looking at the side with the word and the example sentence, and think of the meaning. After you know the words fairly well, change the direction. Look at the side with the meaning, and think of the word.

- To help you remember the word, try to use it. For example, say the word aloud, write it down, or use it in a new sentence.

- Use an electronic dictionary to listen to the pronunciation of the word. Practice saying it out loud.

Side 1

> *materials*
>
> *The only <u>materials</u> you need are paper and a pencil.*

Side 2

> *the things that you need to make or do something*

Skill Practice 1

Read the following paragraph. The words in color may be unfamiliar to you. Use context clues to figure out their meaning, or look up their meaning in a dictionary. Choose three words that you think are important for you to study. Make a card for each word. On one side, write the word and an example sentence. On the other side, write a definition.

Naoto Fukasawa is an innovative designer. He designs living spaces, furniture, and other everyday objects. He started his career designing Seiko watches in Japan. In 1989, he found a job in the United States. At that time, he didn't speak very much English, so he tried to create designs that were simple to understand. He didn't need many new words to explain his designs. His idea was to design things that fit well into people's lives. For example, he designed a bedside lamp with a small bowl in it where people can put their glasses or keys before they go to sleep. He designed a cell phone that feels like a smooth rock that slides easily into a pocket. He also designs furniture and appliances. Some of his designs are in the Museum of Contemporary Art in New York City.

Skill Practice 2

Read the following paragraph. Some of the words may be unfamiliar to you. Choose three words that you think are important for you to study. Make a card for each word. On one side, write the word and an example sentence. On the other side, write a definition.

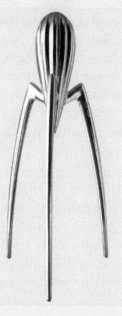

Philippe Starck is one of the world's premier designers. He designs everything from toothbrushes to hotels. When he was a child, he liked building things better than going to school. He left school before graduation and went to work. He became famous after he designed an apartment for the French President, François Mitterand. Starck designs luxurious hotels and homes; however, he is best known in the United States for bringing his design of everyday objects to stores where ordinary people shop. Today, he designs motorcycles, trains, and even spacecraft. However, the design that remains his most famous is much smaller. It looks like a huge spider but is actually a lemon squeezer.

Skill Practice 3

Reread the Example paragraph on page 172 and the two paragraphs in Skill Practices 1 and 2. Choose four more words to study. Make cards for them, and study them for a few minutes. Then, work with a partner and test each other on your 10 new vocabulary words.

Connecting to the Topic

Read the definition of *design*, and then discuss the following questions with a partner.

design (*n*) the way in which something is planned and made

1 Look at the title of the reading on the next page. What do you think "everyday objects" are? Give three examples.

- _____
- _____
- _____

2 When you buy everyday objects, such as a camera, chair, or microwave, what is most important to you? The appearance? The cost? The design? Explain your answer.

3 Have you ever bought something and then discovered that it was difficult to use? Describe why it was difficult.

Previewing and Predicting

> Looking at illustrations and reading the first sentence of each paragraph is a quick way to predict what a text will be about.

A Look at the illustrations and read the first sentence in each paragraph in Reading 1. Then put a check (✓) next to the topics you think will be included in the reading.

_____ A Principles of design

_____ B Examples of bad design

_____ C Design in the economy

_____ D Emotional responses to design

_____ E History of design

_____ F Famous designers

B Compare your answers with a partner's.

While You Read

As you read, stop at the end of each sentence that contains words in bold. Follow the instructions in the box in the margin.

The Design of Everyday Objects

1   We use many different products every day: cars, watches, pencils, and hundreds of other things. Why do these products look the way they do? Why do they work the way they do? The answer is design. Design combines art and engineering to create objects that are a part of our lives.

2   The design of everyday objects has changed in the past 300 years. Early designers were craftsmen who made tools, clothing, furniture, and other objects by hand. For farmers and working people, craftsmen made simple, useful objects. For wealthy people, they made beautiful things. They carved furniture, made gold jewelry, and created fine clothes. The design and creation of these decorated objects required a lot of time and skill. The objects showed the world that the owners were very rich. However, industrialization in the nineteenth century changed the role of design in society. Machines could carve, paint, and decorate hundreds of these everyday objects at a low cost. Whereas in the past, only craftsmen could make beautiful objects; now machines could mass-produce them at a low **cost**. This change meant that these objects were no longer symbols of wealth; they were available to everyone.

3   In the twenty-first century, although most products are mass-produced, they still require design. Some, like pencils, are simple; others, like cameras, are far more complex. All of these products follow three basic principles of design. The most basic design principle is *functionality*. A functional product does what it is supposed to do: a bottle holds liquid, a lightbulb provides light, and a DVD stores sounds and images. Design should not conflict with functionality. For example, the main function of a chair is to provide a place to sit. The design of the chair in the photo to the left prevents people from sitting in it. Although the design of the chair in the photo is beautiful, its design conflicts with its **function**.

4   The second design principle is *usability*. Is it clear how to use the object? If it is not easy for a consumer to understand how to use an object, then it does not have a good design. Many consumers complain that some products have become too complex. Some people report that they do not use all of the functions of their mobile phones or their televisions, for example. They simply don't

WHILE YOU READ 1

What two ideas are in contrast in this sentence? Highlight them.

WHILE YOU READ 2

Look back in paragraph 3 to find a noun + noun collocation. Highlight it.

Well designed products are easy to operate.

understand how to make them work. This does not happen only with high-tech products. It can be confusing to control the temperature in a shower. It can be difficult to decide whether to push or pull a door. Experts say that this is the result of poor design.

5   **One design expert**, Donald Norman, says that many products fail the basic test of usability. However, a few simple changes could improve their usability. According to Norman, products should provide visual signals. For example, a long horizontal bar across a door tells the user to push the door. A short vertical handle on one side of a door tells the user to pull the door. A product should also tell users if they have used it correctly. For example, when an oven is turned on, a light should show that the oven is on. Finally, a well-designed product should prevent users from doing something wrong. If batteries must go in one direction, the product design should make it impossible to put them in the other direction.

6   Problems with usability often occur because designers do not think about the users. Perhaps designers of complex mobile phones think more about selling their product than about using it. If they include lots of new functions in the phone, the company can advertise all of the things that the phone can do. This may persuade consumers to buy it. However, when consumers take the phone home and try to use it, they may not like it because it is too complicated.

7   Functionality and usability are central design principles, but there is one more very important consideration – the *emotional response* to the product. This is the third principle of design. How does the product make the user feel? Does it bring pleasure? A product can do this in many ways: in how it looks, feels, sounds, or even smells. You can have a positive emotional response to a simple object, such as a chair or a computer mouse. A well-designed computer mouse feels good in your hand and is a pleasure to use.

WHILE YOU READ ❸

What is the main idea of paragraph 5? Highlight it. What examples are given to support it? Highlight them.

WHILE YOU READ ❹

Look back in paragraph 6 to find a cause-and-effect relationship. Highlight the cause and the effect.

8   Objects can bring other emotional responses, too. Today, consumers don't just want objects that work well and look good; they want objects that show the world who they are. In other words, they want their objects to express their personal identity. For example, some people may prefer a luxury car with leather seats. Others may like a small, fast car. In order to satisfy this desire to express personal identity, designers offer the same product in many different colors and patterns.

9   Some experts believe that the next big challenge in design will be sustainability. Good product design can reduce waste and reuse resources. Designers will need to balance functionality and usability with the need to reduce our negative impact on the **environment**. However, designers may not have to worry too much about whether sustainable designs produce an emotional response. Many consumers already have a positive emotional response to products that use less energy and can be recycled.

WHILE YOU READ 5

Look back in the sentence for an adjective + noun collocation with *impact*. Highlight it.

10   Good design today pays attention to the three basic design principles: functionality, usability, and emotional response. Some products will emphasize some principles more than others. For example, look at the watches in the photos below. The first watch has many different functions; it does not just tell the time. It is functional but may be difficult to use. The second watch emphasizes usability. It has only a few functions, but it is easy to use. The last watch is a good example of the emotional impact of objects. It tells time, but the important thing about this watch is what it says about the person who wears it.

Main Idea Check

Match the main ideas below to five of the paragraphs in Reading 1. Write the number of the paragraph on the blank line.

_____ A Usability is an important design principle.

_____ B An object can be an expression of personal identity.

_____ C Many products are not very usable and could be improved.

_____ D Functionality is the most basic design principle.

_____ E Some designers pay more attention to sales than usability.

A Closer Look

Look back at Reading 1 to answer the following questions.

1 According to paragraph 2, which statement is *not* true?
   a Machines changed the role of design.
   b Decorated objects were expensive in the eighteenth century.
   c Mass production made decorated objects available to more people.
   d Industrialization required a lot of time and skill.

2 All products are functional. **True or False?**

3 What are some characteristics of a well-designed and usable product according to paragraph 5? Circle all that apply.
   a It is beautiful.
   b It has visual signals that show how it works.
   c It includes many advanced functions.
   d It makes people feel good.
   e It shows the users that they are using it correctly.

4 According to paragraph 6, why do designers of high-tech products include a lot of functions in them?
   a They hope all of the functions will attract buyers.
   b They enjoy exploring new technology.
   c They think the functions will make the products less expensive.
   d They think the functions will increase the product's usability.

5 Choosing an expensive watch can be an expression of personal identity. **True or False?**

6 According to paragraph 9, why do some consumers choose sustainable products?
   a They have a positive feeling about using these products.
   b They are less expensive than other products.
   c They don't want products with a lot of extra functions.
   d These products are very functional.

7 Which watch on page 178 is less functional than the other two?
   a Watch 1
   b Watch 2
   c Watch 3

Skill Review

In Skills and Strategies 9, you learned that making and studying vocabulary cards for new words is a good way to learn and remember new words. Increasing your vocabulary will help you read more quickly and with a better understanding.

A There are several words related to design in Reading 1. They are essential for understanding the reading. Look up the following words in a learner dictionary. The first one has been done for you.

● mass-produce (*v*) (Par. 2) *to make a lot of a product, using machinery in a factory*

● principle (*n*) (Par. 3) _____

● functional (*adj*) (Par. 3) _____

B Make vocabulary cards for the new words above. Put the sentence in which the words occur in Reading 1 on one side of the card. Put the definition on the other side.

C Review Reading 1.

1 Choose two other new words.
2 Make a card for each word.
3 Write a new sentence with each new word.

D Use your cards to test your classmates on new vocabulary.

Definitions

Find the words in Reading 1 that complete the following definitions. When a verb completes the definition, use the base form, although the verb in the reading may not be in the base form.

1 To _____ is to cut into wood or stone. (*v*) Par. 2

2 Something that is _____ has a lot of parts. (*adj*) Par. 3

3 Something that is _____ is simple but very important. (*adj*) Par. 3

4 _____ are rules that explain how things work. (*n pl*) Par. 3

5 To _____ something is to keep or save it for future use. (*v*) Par. 3

6 To _____ is to oppose or disagree with. (*2-part verb*) Par. 3

7 Something that is _____ is related to seeing. (*adj*) Par. 5

8 To _____ someone is to make him or her do or believe something by giving good reasons. (*v*) Par. 6

9 _____ is enjoyment or happiness. (*n*) Par. 7

10 A/An _____ item is very comfortable and expensive. (*adj*) Par. 8

Words in Context

Complete the sentences with words from Reading 1 in the box below.

confusing	identity	owner	prefer
decorated	leather	pay attention to	symbols

1 Most expensive shoes are made from _____.

2 The walls were _____ with beautiful blue and yellow flowers.

3 The star and new moon are _____ of Islam.

4 Do you _____ coffee or tea with your lunch?

5 The instructions for the CD player were very _____. It was not clear where to put the batteries.

6 The car was parked in the same place for more than a year. No one knew who the _____ was.

7 If you _____ lectures and readings, you will do well on tests.

8 Teenagers often express their personal _____ by wearing unusual clothes and having interesting hairstyles.

Critical Thinking

In Reading 1, the writer states that consumers often buy objects that show the world who they are. They want to own and use objects that express their personal identity.

A Think about the objects that you own. Then, explain your answers to the following questions to a partner.

1 Which object do you find difficult to use?
2 Which object is very well designed?
3 Which object is not very functional but produces a positive emotional response?
4 Which object expresses your identity well?

B Share your answers and examples with the rest of your class.

Research

Research the history of an everyday object that you use, such as a toaster or a pencil. Find answers to the following questions.

- How has the design changed since its origin?
- Has it improved?
- Have there been changes in functionality, usability, or the emotional response the object produces?
- Could the design be better? How would you improve it?

Writing

Think of an object that is poorly designed. Write two paragraphs. The first paragraph will describe the object and explain why it is not well designed. The second paragraph will explain how to improve it. Refer to the three basic principles of design in your paragraph.

Connecting to the Topic

Discuss the following questions with a partner.

1 Where do you use computers the most? At a desk? On your bed? On a bus or a train?

2 What is the position of your body when you use a computer? Are you sitting? Are you lying down? Is your back straight?

3 What happens if you work on a computer for a long time? Do you feel uncomfortable? Which parts of your body hurt?

Previewing and Predicting

Reading a title and looking at illustrations and graphic material can help you predict what a text will be about.

A Read the title of Reading 2, and then look at Figure 5.1 on page 184 and the photo on page 185. Think of the position of people's bodies when they use computers. Then put a check (✓) next to the items you see in the figure or in the photo.

	FIGURE 5.1	PHOTO
Feet flat on the floor		
Back straight		
Keyboard flat		
Support for arms		
Support for back		
Wrists straight		
Monitor at eye level		

B Compare your answers with a partner's, and discuss the following question.

What do you think *ergonomics* means?
a The study of computer languages
b The study of how people relate to their physical environment
c The study of human physical movement

While You Read

As you read, stop at the end of each sentence that contains words in bold. Follow the instructions in the box in the margin.

◀)) Ergonomics

1   Ergonomics is an important part of good design. It is the science of designing objects and equipment for safe and comfortable human use. Sometimes it is called "human engineering." Ergonomic products include tools, furniture, and other objects that are more than just functional; they are also designed for safe and comfortable use.

2   The features of electronic devices, such as computers and mobile phones, are good examples of ergonomics. On older phones and computers, every time, you want to write, select, change, or perform some other function, you have to press a key. If you use your phone or computer a lot, all of these small movements can put a strain on your joints, that is, the places where one bone meets another bone. After several hours, your hands, wrists, arms, and shoulders may start to hurt. In contrast, newer computers and mobile phones allow you to perform many functions by simply touching a pad or the computer screen. These improvements reduce the strain on your joints and muscles; in other words, they make computers and mobile phones more ergonomic.

3   Ergonomic design is based on **two main principles**. The first principle is efficiency. Ergonomically designed products require less strength or fewer steps to use than non-ergonomically designed products. Better efficiency can lead to an increase in productivity. The second principle is human comfort: Ergonomic products will not cause pain and are comfortable to use. Products that are not designed with attention to these principles can cause pain or even serious injury. Better comfort can also increase productivity. If you are comfortable, you may do better work.

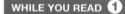

WHILE YOU READ ❶

Read ahead and highlight the two main principles.

WHILE YOU READ ❷

Highlight the context clues that help you understand the definition of *workstation*.

4   One place where workplace injuries often occur is at office **workstations** – a desk, chair, and computer. It may seem strange to think of a desk as a dangerous place, but in fact, people who sit at a computer all day can get hurt. There are two main causes of injury to people who use computers a lot: repeated movements and poor posture. Typing involves very small, repeated movements, which can cause a strain on joints and muscles. Over a long period of time, this strain can cause serious pain and injury. Poor posture is also usually the result of a badly designed workstation.

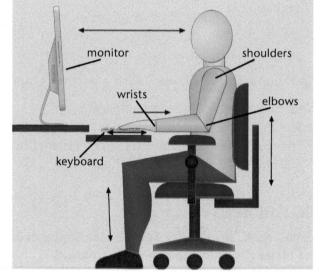

Figure 5.1 The Ergonomically Designed Workstation

5   **What** does an ergonomic workstation look like? Figure 5.1 is a good example. Many injuries at work are caused by poorly designed chairs. An ergonomic chair lets you use good posture when you sit. It is adjustable, so that you can change the height. The correct height allows you to look at the monitor with your head straight. It allows you to use the keyboard with your elbows at an open angle (more than 90 degrees). Your feet should be flat on the ground. An ergonomic chair also gives support for your back and arms. The chair back should not be straight, however. It is better for your back if you lean backward a little bit. Finally, your keyboard should be at an angle that allows you to relax your wrists and keep them straight.

WHILE YOU READ 3

Scan ahead to find what the position should be of: *elbows, feet, back,* and *wrists*. Highlight the information for each.

6   Doctors say laptop computers are increasing the chance of workplace injury. Laptops were originally designed for occasional use when a regular computer was not available. However, more and more people are using a laptop as their primary computer. Laptops do not have an ergonomic design. The monitor is too close to the keyboard, and the keys are very small. Both of these problems can cause strain on the back, neck, shoulders, and wrists. It is difficult to use good posture with a laptop. In addition, because laptops are so light and portable, many people use them in bed, in the car, or on a train, where it may be even more difficult to sit correctly. Doctors and other experts are especially worried that children and students, who are increasingly using laptops to play games and do their schoolwork, are risking **injury**.

Laptop users risk injury to their back, neck, and wrists.

WHILE YOU READ 4

What is the main idea of paragraph 6? Highlight it.

7   Ergonomic design is not just about comfort; there are also economic benefits. Repeated movement injuries in the United States cost $20 billion a year. More than one million American employees miss at least one workday every year because of a repeated movement injury. Consequently, businesses have become very interested in ergonomics. A healthy workforce is more productive than a workforce that misses work because of injury or pain. An investment in ergonomics can help a business save money.

8   The key principles of ergonomics are an understanding of both tasks and the users who perform those tasks. Ergonomics can significantly improve the comfort of our environment and the efficiency of our workplaces.

Main Idea Check

Match the main ideas below to five of the paragraphs in Reading 2. Write the number of the paragraph on the blank line.

_____ A A poorly designed workstation can cause pain and injury.

_____ B Ergonomic design follows two basic principles.

_____ C Ergonomic design has economic benefits.

_____ D The features of computers and phones have become more ergonomic.

_____ E Using a laptop can cause physical problems.

A Closer Look

Look back at Reading 2 to answer the following questions.

1 According to paragraph 2, why are the features on newer computers and phones more ergonomic than the controls on older ones?
   a They are easier to see.
   b They do not require as many small movements.
   c They cause less strain on the neck and back.
   d They use more high technology.

2 According to paragraph 4, what are two main causes of injury to people who use a computer a lot?
   a Laptop computers
   b Back strain
   c Repeated movements
   d Poor posture

3 According to paragraph 5, why is an adjustable chair so important? Circle all that apply.
   a It allows you keep your feet flat and your head straight.
   b It reduces the number of small movements you make when you type.
   c It can move when you need to reach papers or the telephone.
   d It supports your arms and back.
   e It keeps your keyboard flat.

4 According to paragraph 6, why are doctors particularly worried about children who use laptops?
   a Their hands are too small to use laptops correctly.
   b They use their laptops on trains.
   c It causes more strain on their eyes.
   d They spend more and more time working and playing on their laptops.

5 According to paragraph 7, why are businesses investing in ergonomic products?
   a Workers with injuries complain a lot.
   b Ergonomic products are becoming cheaper.
   c Businesses don't want to lose money when workers stay home with injuries.
   d Ergonomic products are more widely available than in the past.

Skill Review

In Skills and Strategies 4, you learned that writers use supporting details to help you understand the main idea. One way to practice finding supporting details is by writing an outline of a paragraph.

A Complete these outlines for paragraphs 6 and 7 of Reading 2. Find the main ideas and write the supporting details. The main idea for paragraph 6 has been done for you.

Paragraph 6:

Main idea: *Laptops are especially likely to cause injury.*

   Supporting detail: _____

   Supporting detail: _____

   Supporting detail: _____

Paragraph 7:

Main idea: _____

   Supporting detail: _____

   Supporting detail: _____

B Compare your outlines with a partner's.

Definitions

Find the words in Reading 2 that complete the following definitions. When a verb completes the definition, use the base form, although the verb in the reading may not be in the base form.

1 _____ is all of the items that are needed for a particular activity or purpose. (*n*) Par. 1

2 A/An _____ is a machine or object used for a particular purpose. (*n*) Par. 2

3 _____ is pain caused by using your body too much. (*n*) Par. 2

4 _____ are the places where two bones are connected. (*n pl*) Par. 2

5 _____ are the parts of the body that produce movement. (*n pl*) Par. 2

6 _____ is how you hold your body when you are standing or sitting. (*n*) Par. 4

7 To _____ means to include something in an activity. (*v*) Par. 4

8 _____ is the distance something is above a surface. (*n*) Par. 5

9 To _____ is to move the body either backward or forward. (*v*) Par. 5

10 To _____ something is to not do something that is expected or usual. (*v*) Par. 7

Word Families

A The words in bold in the chart are from Reading 2. The words next to them are from the same word family. Study and learn these words.

NOUN	VERB	ADJECTIVE
adjustment	*adjust*	*adjustable*
injury	*injure*	—
relaxation	*relax*	—
risk	*risk*	*risky*
selection	*select*	—

B Choose the correct form of the words from the chart to complete the following sentences. Use the correct verb tenses and subject-verb agreement. Use the correct singular and plural noun forms.

1 He seriously _____ his knee while he was playing football. The doctor was not sure if he would walk again.

2 The car seat is _____ so that both tall and short people can drive.

3 Her family lost a lot of money after they made some very _____ investments.

4 Many people suffer terrible _____ in motorcycle accidents.

5 You should _____ the mirrors in a car before you start to drive, especially if another person drove it before you.

6 He finally made his _____ after he did a lot of research about different computers.

7 The firefighter _____ his life to save the children in the burning house.

8 After a hard day of work, it is important to take time for some _____.

9 She _____ a special cake to bring to grandmother for her birthday.

10 Research suggests that if you stop working and _____ for 30 minutes before you go to bed, you will sleep better.

Academic Word List

The following are Academic Word List words from Readings 1 and 2 of this unit. Use these words to complete the sentences. (For more on the Academic Word List, see page 257.)

complex (*adv*)	devices (*n*)	injured (*v*)	principles (*n*)	symbol (*n*)
conflicts with (*v*)	identity (*n*)	involves (*v*)	relax (*v*)	visual (*adj*)

1 After a week of exams, the students had a few days to _____ and enjoy themselves.

2 Many soldiers died or were _____ during the war.

3 The _____ $ means dollars.

4 The problem was very _____, so it took a long time to solve it.

5 In the twenty-first century, people will use their mobile phones and other portable _____ for more tasks.

6 The loud music _____ the quiet and peaceful appearance of the park.

7 The clothes that people wear often express their personal _____.

8 Architects have to learn the basic _____ of physics before they begin to design buildings.

9 The images in the film made a strong _____ impact. Everyone in the audience remembered what they had seen.

10 Success often _____ hard work and a little luck.

Critical Thinking

Reading 2 discusses the importance of ergonomic design. Ergonomics may be especially important for specific populations, such as children, older people, and disabled people. For example, older people often have trouble opening jars and bottles because they do not have a lot of strength in their hands.

A **With a partner, think about the needs of one of the groups of people above, and complete the following activities.**

1   Make a list of the special challenges the group may face in using everyday objects.

2   Choose one everyday object and discuss how ergonomic design could help the people in this group use this object.

B **Share your ideas with the rest of your class.**

Research

Carefully examine workstations you have used at home, at school, or at work. Then find answers to the following questions.

- Are the furniture and computers ergonomically designed and arranged? Refer back to Figure 5.1.
- How and where do you use a computer? Are you risking injury?

Writing

Write two paragraphs. The first paragraph will describe some of the problems you found in your workstation. The second paragraph will explain how you could make your workstation more ergonomic.

Improving Your Reading Speed

Good readers read quickly and still understand most of what they read.

A Read the instructions and strategies for Improving Your Reading Speed in Appendix 3 on page 271.

B Choose either Reading 1 or Reading 2 in this unit. Read it without stopping. Time how long it takes you to finish the text in minutes and seconds. Enter the time in the chart on page 273. Then calculate your reading speed in number of words per minute.

Taking Notes from a Reading

If you need to understand a reading and remember the most important information – perhaps for a test – it is important to take notes. Many students take notes on the page next to the reading. This is called *annotating*. They also take notes in a separate notebook. When you write on the page, you can circle or highlight important ideas, words, and information. You can number supporting details and write definitions of key terms in the margin. When you take notes in a notebook, you can make an outline.

Examples & Explanations

More and more homeowners are thinking "green" as they design their homes. As a result, it is becoming easier to find environmentally smart home products that are attractive and can save money. Many products require less energy and therefore lead to lower energy bills. Energy-efficient appliances and florescent lights are examples. Another choice is the growing variety of natural floor products. Bamboo floors and cotton carpets are examples of these renewable resources. Finally, recycled materials, such as old stone and wood, can add interest to the design as well as help the environment. So homeowners can design homes that help the environment, look great, and save money.

doesn't hurt the environment

① ②

can replace them

③

The reader has circled the main idea and numbered the supporting details.

Important words are highlighted and the definitions are written in the margin.

In a notebook, the student made the following simple outline.

I. Products in home – good for environment + save money

  A. Reduce electricity
    1. Energy-efficient appliances
    2. Florescent lights

  B. Renewable floor products
    1. Bamboo
    2. Cotton

  C. Recycled materials
    1. Wood
    2. Stone

Strategies

These strategies will help you take notes from a reading.

- As you read, circle main ideas and number supporting details.
- Highlight important words and write definitions in the margin.
- Use your annotated text to help you make your outline.
- Begin your outline with the topic or main idea of the paragraph.
- Add the most important supporting details.
- Use a system of numbers and letters to show the difference between very important and less important details.
- Keep your outline simple. Don't write too much detail.

Skill Practice 1

Read the following paragraph. As you read, circle the main idea and number the supporting details. Highlight any important vocabulary words, and write the definitions in the margin. Compare your answers with a partner.

Before the invention of the sewing machine, clothes were made by hand one at a time. This took a long time. Technology, however, has completely changed the manufacturing of clothes. In the 1830s, the sewing machine was invented. This changed the way clothes were made. Military uniforms were the first items of clothing to be produced using this technology. Production increased as technology continued to change. In 1859, a foot pedal was added to the sewing machine. Now clothing could be made more quickly. Later, after the invention of the electric sewing machine, clothing could easily be mass-produced. More recently, computer technology has dramatically changed the design and manufacture of clothes. It now takes only 90 minutes for computers and automatic machines to make a man's suit. This is a huge savings in time and labor from the hard, slow work of sewing by hand.

Skill Practice 2

Read the following paragraph. The student has already taken notes on the page. Use these notes to help you complete the outline on the next page.

Of all items of clothing, (the skirt has had the longest history.) In ancient ①
times, both men and women wore skirts. Ancient cave paintings show men
wearing skirts made of animal fur. By the eighteenth century, however, men ②
in most European countries were no longer wearing skirts. Almost everywhere
men wore long pants. Women's skirts at this time were long and full,
sometimes two meters across. It wasn't until the 1920s that designer Coco ③

Chanel shocked the western world by raising skirt lengths to the knee. In the ④
1960s, designer Mary Quant raised the skirt even more to a very short mini
length, but this style did not last long. By the late 1970s, miniskirts were not in *very short skirts*
fashion anymore. Today, the skirt is still a basic item of women's clothing, and
it can be any length.

I.   Skirts – long history

   A.   Ancient times

      1.   Men and women wore skirts

      2.   _____

   B.   _____

      1.   _____

      2.   Women's skirts were long + full. 2 meters across

   C.   _____

      1.   _____

   D.   Modern times

      1.   _____

      2.   Late 1970s, miniskirts were no longer popular.

Skill Practice 3

**Read the following paragraph. As you read, circle the main idea and number the
supporting details. Highlight any important vocabulary words, and write the
definitions in the margin. Then create an outline.**

An interior designer is a person who designs the spaces where people work
and live. The demand for interior designers is growing in the United States;
however, students should think carefully before choosing this career. They
need to understand what skills they must have. First, an interior designer
needs to have advanced computer skills because many companies use
software programs for design. Second, they need to understand the basics
of engineering and art. Good communication skills are also very important.
Designers must clearly explain their ideas to their customers. Finally, designers
usually need a college degree. After they receive the degree, they will need to
work for about three years at a beginning level. During this time, the salary is
not very high. Students should also know that the number of interior designers
is expected to grow. As a result, it will soon be quite difficult to find design
work because so many people are choosing interior design as a career.

Connecting to the Topic

Discuss the following questions with a partner.

1 Think about a room where you spend a lot of time – a place where you sleep or study.

- Describe the room. What color are the walls? What furniture is in the room?
- Is the room well designed or poorly designed? Explain your answer.
- Is the design of the room functional – that is, can people use it for a specific activity? Is it attractive? Or is it both? Explain your answers.

2 If you could change the design of the room, what things would you change? Explain your answers.

- The color?
- The arrangement of the furniture?
- Something else?

Previewing and Predicting

> Reading the title and first sentence of each paragraph is a quick way to predict what a text will be about.

A Read the title and first sentence of each paragraph in Reading 3, and look at the photos on pages 195–196. Then put a check (✓) next to the topics that you think will be included in the reading.

_____ A The design of very small living spaces

_____ B How our living spaces express our personalities

_____ C Design programs on television

_____ D The color and design of different living spaces

_____ E Preparing for a career in design

B Compare your answer with a partner's.

While You Read

As you read, stop at the end of each sentence that contains words in bold. Follow the instructions in the box in the margin.

🔊 The Design of Living Spaces

1   Home. It is where we cook our meals, invite our friends to visit, and go to sleep. It is also a place that can reflect our personality. The process of taking a home or a room and giving it color, furniture, and style is called *interior design*. Think about where you live. What would a stranger know about you if he or she walked into your home or room? White walls, wooden floors, and a few pieces of modern furniture suggest that you are a **calm** and organized person. Colorful walls, books and pictures, and lots of furniture suggest you are a more energetic and active person. How you choose to design your home or room says something to the world about who you are. It tells the world about your interests and about your personal identity.

2   One important aspect of interior design is balance. This means there is a good combination of colors and furniture so that a room feels comfortable. How do people achieve balance in their homes? Some people use feng shui to help them with this aspect of design. *Feng shui* is an Eastern philosophy. It teaches that all parts of people's lives should balance two kinds of energy – yin and yang. *Yin* is the quiet, passive energy, whereas *yang* is the strong and active **energy**. According to this philosophy, a living space with a good balance of these two types of energy brings good luck, health, and happiness.

3   Feng shui provides guidelines about how to decorate a **room**. In a bedroom, for example, the head of the bed should point in the correct

WHILE YOU READ ❶

Use context clues to guess if *calm* means (a) nervous, (b) noisy, or (c) peaceful.

WHILE YOU READ ❷

Find a word that signals contrast in this sentence. Then highlight the word with a meaning that contrasts with *passive*.

WHILE YOU READ ❸

Find two supporting details for this idea. Highlight them.

Balance is an important element of interior design.

direction. It should point north for an older married couple. North is a quiet, peaceful direction. For a young adult, however, feng shui says the the head of the bed should point south. This direction has more energy and passion. The head of the bed must not point northeast because this direction causes nightmares. Also, a bedroom should not have any mirrors in it because mirrors make it difficult to remove negative energy.

4   Color is another important aspect of interior design. **Different colors** have different emotional and physical effects on people. For example, people usually feel that red is the most exciting and stimulating color. For this reason, it is not a good color for a bedroom. Many people say they have nightmares if they sleep in a red room. In contrast, green is a more peaceful color. In some cultures green means health and good luck, so it is a popular color. Blue is also a good color in most cultures. It represents peace and stability. According to some studies, it is a masculine color; men often choose it for their living spaces. White, however, is used more than any other color in interior design. White is the combination of all colors, so it is a color of balance. It is often used in small rooms because it reflects light and therefore makes a small room look bigger. In addition, it does not conflict with other colors in the room.

WHILE YOU READ 4

Read ahead to highlight the different colors and their effects on people.

5   Small homes and rooms create special challenges for architects and interior designers. Some architects and designers are specialists in small living spaces. They try to make them both functional and attractive. In Japan, these small living spaces are called *kyosho jutaku*. For example, windows appear anywhere across a wall or in the ceiling, to allow as much light as possible into narrow spaces. Furniture folds into the wall, which allows one room to be used in many different ways. A bed may have a desk, chair, and dresser underneath it. Traditional designers think of horizontal, or floor space. **In contrast**, designers of small living spaces say that they try to use three-dimensional space. For example, they may put storage space, such as closets or bookshelves, high on walls, above other furniture.

WHILE YOU READ 5

Highlight the two ideas that contrast.

6   Whether we live in a large home, a small apartment, or one room, we spend the majority of our time at home. Our homes need to meet our basic needs of sleeping, eating, and washing. However, for most of us, our living spaces do a lot more than that. By using a combination of balance, color, and arrangement, our homes can be functional, and attractive, and they reflect our personalities.

Main Idea Check

Here are the main ideas of paragraphs 1–5 in Reading 3. Match each paragraph to its main idea. Write the number of the paragraph on the blank line.

_____ A Small living spaces need careful design.

_____ B Feng shui designers believe it is important to arrange furniture in a specific way.

_____ C The design of our home or room reflects who we are.

_____ D Colors can have an emotional and physical effect on people.

_____ E Feng shui teaches that balance is an important part of design.

A Closer Look

Look back at Reading 3 to answer the following questions.

1 According to paragraph 1, what kind of person is probably living in a room that is painted yellow and orange and is full of furniture and books?

a A disorganized and artistic person

b A quiet person who prefers staying at home alone

c A busy person who enjoys an exciting life

d An organized and very intelligent person

2 Yin is strong active energy. **True or False?**

3 A husband and wife, who are both 65 years old, are designing a peaceful bedroom. According to paragraphs 3 and 4, what three principles of Feng shui can guide them in their design?

a The door should point north to remove negative energy.

b The head of the bed should point north.

c There should not be any mirrors in the room.

d The colors should be soft.

e The walls should be blue.

4 Match the colors below to the emotions they often bring out in people.

_____ 1 blue   a balance

_____ 2 red   b stability

_____ 3 green   c peace

_____ 4 white   d excitement

5 Why do most people paint their rooms white, according to paragraph 4?

a It makes rooms appear larger than they are.

b It is the most popular color.

c It helps people to sleep better.

d It is a very functional color so designers like to use it.

6 Which of the following are some ways to solve the problem of small living spaces, according to paragraph 5? Circle all that apply.

   a Use three-dimensional space.

   b Fold furniture into the walls.

   c Paint the walls a bright color.

   d Put bookshelves high up on the walls.

   e Don't use windows.

7 Which of the following is *not* stated in Reading 3?

   a Blue, green, and white are good colors for a bedroom.

   b The head of a bed should not face northeast.

   c Red is a very masculine color.

   d Some people believe that rooms have energy.

   e People often design their living space as an expression of their personality.

Skill Review

In Skills and Strategies 10, you learned that taking notes can help you understand and remember what is in a text. Annotating a text by highlighting words and making notes in the margins is an effective way to prepare for a test.

A **Annotate Reading 3. Highlight important information and makes notes on things you need to remember. Then create an outline.**

B **Compare your outline with a partner's.**

Definitions

Find the words in Reading 3 that complete the following definitions. When a verb completes the definition, use the base form, although the verb in the reading may not be in the base form.

1 To _____ something is to show an idea or feeling. (*v*) Par. 1

2 A / An _____ is a person you don't know. (*n*) Par. 1

3 If you are _____, you are able to plan well and keep things neat. (*adj*) Par. 1

4 A / An _____ is two or more things that are put together. (*n*) Par. 2

5 _____ is a very strong emotion. (*n*) Par. 3

6 Something that is _____ creates interest and excitement. (*adj*) Par. 4

7 To _____ something is to describe it or act as a symbol for it. (*v*) Par. 4

8 Something that is _____ is related to men. (*adj*) Par. 4

9 A / An _____ is a piece of furniture where you keep folded clothes. (*n*) Par. 5

10 Something that is _____ can be measured in three ways: height, length, and width. (*adj-2 words*) Par. 5

Words in Context

Complete the following passages with words from Reading 3 in the box below.

achieve	calm	interior	stability
balance	guidelines	personalities	styles

1   People often express their _____ in the clothes they choose. People
        a
who are quiet and _____ may not like bright colors and the newest
                                  b
_____. They like _____, so they prefer to wear the same kinds
            c   d
of clothes every year.

2   Feng shui gives us _____ for the _____ design of homes
                                    e   f
and offices. It shows how you can _____ a / an _____
                                                    g   h
between different kinds of energy in the room.

Critical Thinking

Reading 3 discusses ideas about interior design and how it is related to other ideas such as personal identity or eastern philosophy. According to feng shui, for example, a living space with a good balance of yin and yang energy brings good luck, health, and happiness.

A **With a partner, discuss the following questions.**

1 Do you think that rooms can have a positive or negative energy?
2 Do you think the arrangement of a room can affect how people feel in that room?
3 Do you think colors affect how people feel?
4 Do you think colors can affect health or luck?

B **Compare your answers with the rest of your class.**

Research

Survey a few of your classmates. Find answers to the following questions.

- What color or colors do you like to use in your room or home?
- How does the design of your room or home reflect your personality?

Writing

Write two paragraphs. The first paragraph will describe a room that reflects your personality. The second paragraph will describe a room of one of your classmates. Choose a room that contrasts with yours.

Connecting to the Topic

Discuss the following questions with a partner.

1 When you buy new clothes, what is important to you? The price? The color? The style? How do the clothes make you look? Explain your answers.

2 What does a person's choice of clothing say about him or her? Explain your answers.

3 Does anyone you know have a tattoo (words or images on the skin)? What kinds of people get tattoos? Explain your answers.

Previewing and Predicting

Looking at photos and reading titles, headings, and first sentences of paragraphs can help you predict what topics might be in a text.

A Look at the photos, the section headings, the first sentence of each paragraph, and the title of Reading 4. What do you think sections II–IV will be about? Check (✓) the topics that you think might be included in each section.

SECTION	HEADING	TOPICS	✓
II	Fashion and Identity	A history of fashion Fashion and self-expression How clothes are made Changes in women's fashions Top designers in women's fashions	____ ____ ____ ____ ____
III	How Fashion Moves through Society	Factors in fashion trends Tattoos as fashion Where to study about fashion The role of designers in fashion trends Fashion trends in Asia	____ ____ ____ ____ ____
IV	Why Fashions Change	What is coming next in fashion How young people affect fashion The business of fashion The science of fashion How to start a clothing business	____ ____ ____ ____ ____

B Compare your answers with a partner's.

While You Read

As you read, stop at the end of each sentence that contains words in **bold**. Follow the instructions in the box in the margin.

◀) Fashion

I. Introduction

1   Think about the clothes you are wearing right now. Why did you choose to buy these clothes? And why did you choose to wear them today? Like most people, you probably chose them for several reasons. Perhaps you bought them because of their price. Perhaps you are wearing them because they are comfortable. However, it is also likely that there was another important reason for your choices – fashion – the styles that are popular now.

II. Fashion and Identity

2   Fashion influences the choices we make in shoes, jewelry, hairstyles, and especially clothes. Clothes are more than a way to cover our bodies or to stay warm and dry. They help us to express our personal identities, that is, they tell other people how we want them to see us. One well-known writer argues that clothes are a kind of language; they always send a message. She expresses it this way, "To choose clothing either in a store or at home is to define and describe ourselves."[1]

3   Clothing design has described and defined us throughout history. In earlier times, clothing provided a lot of **information** about the people who wore them. It showed where they were from, their job, their class, and sometimes even their religion. Until the end of the nineteenth century, clothing continued to signal differences, especially class. The working class wore clothes that were easy to move in; they were designed for physical labor. In contrast, the clothes of the upper class often restricted movement; they were designed for leisure. Their clothes sent a very clear message that the people wearing them did not do any physical labor.

4   The history of women's clothing is another good example of the powerful messages that clothing can send. Traditionally, women's fashions were often designed to prevent them from doing physical work. This message was not limited to clothing. Long, painted fingernails sent a similar message of leisure. In China, until the early twentieth century, it was the fashion for wealthy women to bind their feet so that the feet would stay very small. This process also made it difficult for them to walk, so it clearly showed that they did not need to **work**.

5   Slowly women's fashion began to change. During World War I, women in many countries had to go to work for the first time because men were fighting in the war. Women worked in offices, in factories, and on farms. In order to work safely, they needed a style of clothes that was different from the long, full dresses that were common at that time, so many of them began to wear pants. Many women still choose to wear pants.

WHILE YOU READ 1
Scan ahead to find four kinds of information. Highlight them.

WHILE YOU READ 2
What is the main idea of paragraph 4? Highlight it.

---
[1] Lurie, A. (1981). *The Language of Clothes*

III. How Fashion Moves Through Society

6   What determines fashion? This is a complicated question, and the answer has changed throughout history. Until the twentieth century, the middle class usually copied the fashions of the rich. In Europe, designers in Paris created fashions, and rich people all over Europe wore them. This "top-down" trend in fashion can still be seen today. In Milan, New York, Paris, and Tokyo, great design houses such as Giorgio Armani, Christian Dior, Ralph Lauren, and Kenzo design unique fashions for the rich and famous. Celebrities, such as movie and music stars, contribute to fashion trends. When they wear these designer clothes, demand for the clothes increases. Consumers who are not as wealthy want these designs, too. So this **top-down** trend continues when less famous designers produce similar, but cheaper clothes. The fashions that began as very expensive designs eventually appear in shopping malls. People who are not rich can afford to buy these clothes.

WHILE YOU READ 3

Scan the paragraph to find an explanation of *top-down*. Highlight it.

7   The top-down fashion trend was dominant for many years. Today, however, there is another important fashion trend that moves in the opposite direction; it moves in a "**bottom-up**" direction. This happens when groups of people – usually young people – develop their own style of clothes. This is often called "street fashion." When famous designers become aware of this street fashion, they use it in their clothes. Hip-hop design is a good example of street fashion that moved from the street into the general fashion world. Hip-hop music and fashion developed on the streets of New York City in the African-American community, but it spread from urban to suburban, from black to white, and from New York to the rest of the world.

WHILE YOU READ 4

Scan ahead to find an example of *bottom-up*. Highlight it.

Some fashion moves in a bottom-up direction.

8   Top designers quickly noticed a demand for this style. Versace, Tommy Hilfiger, and Ralph Lauren began to design hip-hop clothing based on street styles. Celebrities have also contributed to bottom-up fashion trends. In 1994, a well-known rapper, Snoop Dog, appeared on television. He wore Hilfiger clothes, and by the end of that year, Hilfiger clothing sales had increased by 90 million U.S. dollars. Young people all over the world began wearing sweatshirts, very large pants, and expensive sports shoes, just like famous hip-hop artists. (See the photo on page 203.) Soon, the hip-hop artists began to design and sell their own clothing. Designers want to be sure they are part of new bottom-up trends. Therefore, many clothing and shoe companies employ young people to find out what is popular on the **street**.

WHILE YOU READ ⑤

Paragraph 8 has many noun + noun collocations. Look back in the paragraph and find four of them. Highlight them.

9   Another good example of a bottom-up fashion trend is not about clothing at all. Tattoos were not always part of traditional fashion. (See the photo on the right.) They began in the military and in prisons. People with tattoos sent a message that they were tough and strong. Many athletes adopted this identity; they wanted to look tough and strong, too. People with tattoos also sent the message that they were outsiders, and they were not part of the fashion world. This message appealed to many other celebrities, such as musicians and actors. Tattoos soon became part of the general fashion world, so they no longer send the original message. They have become especially popular among young women. A recent survey showed that almost 25 percent of all U.S. adults under 50 have a tattoo. Even a special edition *Barbie*, the famous American doll, has a tattoo!

IV. Why Fashions Change

10   Today's fashions move from the top down and from the bottom up. Celebrities and the media play a significant role in the popularity of new fashions and in how rapidly these fashions are adopted by the public. Consumers see new fashions on television and on the Internet, and soon they can find these fashions at their local mall. Everything they want is available very quickly. They can change the message they want to send about themselves by making changes in their clothes, shoes, and hairstyle. This consumer need for choice encourages constant change in fashion.

Tattoos are popular even among the general population.

11   Young people play an especially important role in how fashion changes. Young people often want to show that they are different from their parents' generation. Many of them reject their parents' world, including their fashion choices. Young people can send this message very clearly with their own fashion choices. For example, in the 1970s, some young people rejected the current fashion by wearing clothes that were torn and dirty.

Because bottom-up fashion trends move rapidly, soon torn jeans became fashionable. Anyone could buy clothes like this at their local shopping mall. Although young people wanted to reject the world of fashion, the world of fashion adopted and promoted these new designs. This is a typical fashion cycle. Fashions that shocked the public yesterday are normal today and boring **tomorrow**.

12   Finally, it is important to acknowledge the role of business in fashion trends. Most consumers get rid of their clothes even when the clothes are still usable. They buy new clothes because they want them, not because they really need them. If people only bought the clothes they really needed, many clothing businesses would fail. These businesses need to persuade consumers that they should buy new and different clothes every year. One way to do this is to constantly change fashions. For example, skirts become shorter and then longer, and then shorter again. Shoes have high heels and then low heels. New colors and styles become popular. If fashions constantly change, people will always want and buy new clothes. As a result, the fashion business will continue to be successful.

WHILE YOU READ 6

What is the main idea of paragraph 11? Highlight it.

Main Idea Check

Match the main ideas below to five of the paragraphs in Reading 4. Write the number of the paragraph on the blank line.

_____ A Young people often want fashions that are different from their parents' fashions.

_____ B Tattoos are a good example of bottom-up fashion trends.

_____ C Historically, women's clothing prevented them from doing physical work.

_____ D The media are important in promoting new fashion.

_____ E In the past, clothing identified people's jobs and origins.

A Closer Look

Look back at Reading 4 to answer the following questions.

1 According to paragraph 3, in the past, people's clothing told a lot of things about them. Which one of the following was *not* one of those things?

  a The person's job
  b The person's class
  c The person's age
  d The person's religion

2 Which fashions in paragraphs 3 and 4 send a message of leisure? Circle all that apply.

  a Clothing that restricts movement
  b Long fingernails
  c Pants
  d Bound feet
  e Full dresses

3 Why did women's fashion change during World War I?

  a Women needed different clothes to fight in the war.
  b Women needed a new style of clothes to work in factories and on farms.
  c Women wanted to be equal with men.
  d The government designed a new uniform for women.

4 Reread paragraphs 7 and 8. Then complete the diagram. Put sentences A–E in the correct order. Write the correct letter in each box.

  A Designers started to copy hip-hop style in their own clothes.
  B The sales of designer hip-hop fashion skyrocketed.
  C Young African Americans developed hip-hop music and fashion as their own style.
  D Other young people around the world adopted hip-hop style clothing.
  E Famous artists started to wear designer hip-hop clothes.

5 Tattoos are a good example of a top-down fashion trend. **True or False?**

6 Reread paragraph 11. Then complete the diagram. Put sentences A–D in the correct order. Write the correct letter in each box.

A Fashion designers noticed torn clothes as a fashion trend and copied it.
B Young people rejected fashion by wearing torn clothes.
C Torn clothes were not shocking anymore because they had become a fashion for average people.
D Torn clothing arrived in shopping malls.

Skill Review

In Making Connections on page 127, you learned that writers use words and phrases to signal cause and affect or to give reasons for why something has happened. Identifying and understanding these words and phrases will help you better understand academic reading.

A Reread paragraphs 1 and 5 below from Reading 4.

1 Paragraph 1 discusses clothing choices. Highlight the words that signal the *reasons* for these choices.

Think about the clothes you are wearing right now. Why did you choose to buy these clothes? And why did you choose to wear them today? Like most people, you probably chose them for several reasons. Perhaps you bought them because of their price. Perhaps you are wearing them because they are comfortable. However, it is also likely that there was another important reason for your choices – fashion – the styles that are popular now.

2 Paragraph 5 shows causes and effects in women's fashion. Highlight the words that signal *cause* and *effects* and label the causes (C) and the effects (E).

Slowly women's fashion began to change. During World War I, women in many countries had to go to work for the first time because men were fighting in the war. Women worked in offices, in factories, and on farms. In order to work safely, they needed a style of clothes that was different from the long, full dresses that were common at that time, so many of them began to wear pants. Many women still choose to wear pants.

B Compare your paragraphs with a partner's.

Definitions

Find the words in Reading 4 that complete the following definitions. When a verb completes the definition, use the base form, although the verb in the reading may not be in the base form.

1 Decorative items worn on clothes or the body, such as rings or necklaces are examples of _____ . (n) Par. 2

2 A/An _____ is an idea or information that someone is trying to communicate. (n) Par. 2

3 A/An _____ is a group of people with a similar economic position. (n) Par. 3

4 To _____ is to tie very tightly. (v) Par. 4

5 To become _____ of something is to know about it. (adj) Par. 7

6 The _____ is a group of people who fight for their country, often in wars. (n) Par. 9

7 To _____ something is to begin to use it. (v) Par. 9

8 _____ are people who are not part of the group. (n pl) Par. 9

9 The _____ means people in general. (n) Par. 11

10 The _____ is the back part of a shoe. (n) Par. 12

Synonyms

Complete the sentences with words from Reading 4 in the box below. These words replace the words or phrases in parentheses, which are similar in meaning.

acknowledge	dominant	normal	survey
appeal	leisure	prison	tough

1 For most people (free time) _____ activities happen on the weekends. (n) Par. 3

2 A few countries are (very influential) _____ in world politics. (adj) Par. 7

3 If you break the law, you may go to (jail) _____ . (n) Par. 9

4 He acted (very strong) _____ , so many people were afraid of him. (adj) Par. 9

5 Fashions that are new and shocking often (are attractive) _____ to young people. (v) Par. 9

6 The government did a (study) _____ to find out about public opinion. (n) Par. 9

7 Her behavior was (as expected) _____. She didn't do anything unusual. (*adj*) Par. 11

8 It is important to _____ (recognize) the work of others and to thank them for it. (*v*) Par. 11

Academic Word List

The following are Academic Word List words from Readings 3 and 4 of this unit. Use these words to complete the sentences. (For more on the Academic Word List, see page 257.)

achieve (*v*)	aware (*adj*)	guidelines (*n*)	normal (*adj*)	styles (*n*)
acknowledged (*v*)	dominant (*adj*)	military (*adj*)	stability (*n*)	surveys (*n*)

1 The president met with the country's _____ leaders about the war.

2 I speak several languages, but English is my _____ language.

3 Political leaders often do _____ of voters to find out about their opinions.

4 He _____ that he had made a mistake and said he would try to do better.

5 The manager distributed _____ for the project so that everyone would know what to do.

6 The streets were quiet, and everything seemed _____, just like any other day.

7 The new students were not _____ of the school rules, so they got into trouble.

8 If you work hard, you are likely to _____ success.

9 The architects were concerned about the _____ of the building. They were worried it might fall.

10 Young people are often fashion leaders. They adopt new _____ in clothing and jewelry.

Critical Thinking

Reading 4 defines and discusses two fashion trends: *bottom-up* and *top-down*. According to the writer, the bottom-up trend in fashion is recent. Until the late twentieth century, fashion trends were top-down.

A With a group, discuss the following questions.

1 What do bottom-up fashion and top-down fashion mean? Use your own words to explain the meanings.

2 Why do you think bottom-up fashion became popular in the late twentieth century? What was happening in the world that might explain it?

3 What are some bottom-up fashions trends that you are familiar with? Explain how they began.

4 Which kinds of fashions are you more likely to buy? Bottom-up or top-down? Explain why you think you have this preference.

B Compare your answers with the rest of your class.

Research

Look through a fashion magazine, or look at some fashion websites on the Internet.

- Find an example of a bottom-up or top-down fashion.
- Find some examples of clothes that you would want to wear. Think about the origin of the fashion. Did it begin as a street fashion or a luxury item?

Writing

Write two paragraphs. The first paragraph will describe the fashion you found in your research. The second paragraph will discuss the origin of the fashion.

Improving Your Reading Speed

Good readers read quickly and still understand most of what they read.

A Read the instructions and strategies for Improving Your Reading Speed in Appendix 3 on page 271.

B Choose either Reading 3 or Reading 4 in this unit. Read it without stopping. Time how long it takes you to finish the text in minutes and seconds. Enter the time in the chart on page 273. Then calculate your reading speed in number of words per minute.

REVIEW OF CONNECTORS

In Units 1–4, you learned that writers have several ways to make connections. To do this, they connect words and ideas in their writing using:

- repetition of words and phrases. (See page 41.)
- pronouns to refer to previous ideas. (See page 85.)
- words or phrases to show cause and effect. (See page 127.)
- words or phrases to contrast one idea with another. (See page 169.)

Exercise 1

In the following paragraphs, underline repeated key words, circle pronouns and their antecedents, and highlight any transition words.

1   Objects are often redesigned in order to improve their usability. One example of this is wheeled luggage. People no longer strain joints and muscles because they don't have to lift heavy luggage. This results in fewer injuries.

2   The Museum of Modern Art in New York has a collection of everyday objects. A paper clip, a bottle opener, and a plastic top on a cup are examples of objects in the museum. These objects all provide simple solutions to everyday problems. Because they are functional and easy to use, these objects have become a part of everyday life.

3   Interior designers work in many different types of spaces. Some focus on one aspect of design, such as preventing repeated injuries with computers. Others, however, design homes and create spaces that reflect the owners' personalities. A third group may design specific spaces, such as hotel rooms.

4   It is important to be comfortable when you are driving for a long time. Before you drive, you should adjust the seat to correspond to your height. You should also adjust your seat to lean backward a little bit. Finally, make sure the safety belt is flat over your shoulder.

5   Musicians have always influenced fashion design. For example, Elvis Presley dominated rock music in the late 1950s and early 1960s. His music and fashion reflected new ideas at that time and were very popular. Because of his popularity, young people adopted his style and wore "Elvis clothes."

Exercise 2

Make a clear paragraph by putting sentences A, B, and C into the best order after the numbered sentence. Look for transition words, pronouns, and repeated key words to help you. Write the letters in the correct order on the blank lines.

1 The interior of a car is designed for average-sized people. ___ ___ ___

| **A** As a result, these car seats can be comfortable for drivers of all shapes and sizes. | **B** Ergonomically designed car seats therefore allow vertical and horizontal adjustments. | **C** However, not everyone is the same height and weight. |

2 A 1997 report found that it was difficult for a majority of older drivers to read road signs. ___ ___ ___

| **A** These new signs are simple and have less information on them. | **B** As a result, many road signs were redesigned. | **C** The information is clearly written in a contrasting color. |

3 Life expectancy is longer today than it was in the past. ___ ___ ___

| **A** Car door handles, for example, are larger and simpler today than they were 20 years ago. | **B** Therefore, we are now seeing people who are driving cars in their eighties or nineties. | **C** Designers are paying attention to this as they design car interiors for older drivers. |

4 Injuries from repeated movements do not only occur at work. ___ ___ ___

| **A** People who play video games are also at risk of injury. | **B** Because of this, video game companies have designed ergonomic controls to reduce muscle and joint strain. | **C** Playing video games for hours, for example, puts a significant strain on the wrists and thumbs. |

5 The Hong Kong Disneyland shows that culture plays an important role in design.

___ ___ ___

| **A** Although four is unlucky, the color red represents luck. | **B** For example, in Chinese culture, the number four is unlucky, so there is no fourth floor in any Hong Kong Disneyland building. | **C** Therefore, many of the Disneyland rooms are decorated in red. |

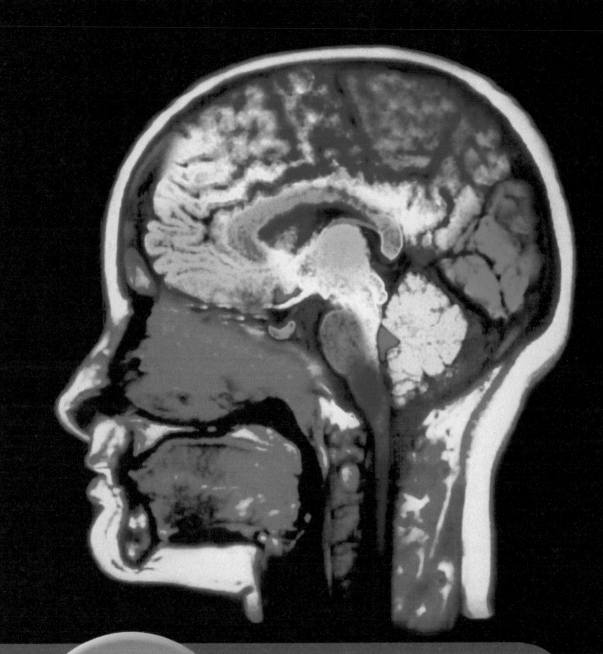

6

THE BRAIN AND BEHAVIOR

SKILLS AND STRATEGIES

- Collocations
- Preparing for a Reading Test

Collocations

In Skills and Strategies 7 on page 130, you learned about collocations. You learned that certain nouns, and certain adjectives and nouns, often appear together. There are also other kinds of collocations, including verbs + nouns. For example, when you read the noun *crime*, it often appears with the verb *commit*. *Commit a crime* is a collocation. Other collocations include adjectives + prepositions and verbs + prepositions. Remember that it is important for you to notice and learn collocations because it helps you see groups of words and read more quickly.

Examples & Explanations

As we **engage in** communication, we hear lots of words.

Verbs often appear with a specific preposition. When this happens, you should use the verb + preposition combination. For example, the words *engage* + *in* should be learned as a collocation because the verb *engage* alone means something different.

Language learners **face** many **challenges**, but learning new vocabulary is one of the most important challenges.

Verbs also can be followed by a variety of nouns to form collocations. For example, the verb *face* is frequently followed by *challenges*, *problems*, and *difficulties*.

Scientists are **interested in** learning how young children learn a language.

Adjectives often appear with a specific preposition. When this happens, you should learn the adjective + preposition combination. For example, the words *interested in* should be learned as a collocation.

The Language of Collocation

Many different combinations of words form collocations. The following are some common collocations.

VERB + NOUN	ADJECTIVE + PREPOSITION	VERB + PREPOSITION
commit a crime	angry at	depend on
face • problems • difficulties • challenges	based on good at interested in	engage in escape from hope for
spend • time • money	unhappy with	invest in

Strategies

These strategies will help you notice and learn collocations.

- When you are reading, try to notice which words often come together. These are likely to be useful collocations.

- If you want to check to see if you found a collocation, you can look in a dictionary. Look up one of the words. Many learner dictionaries contain example sentences that include collocations, and some dictionaries actually list collocations with the word.

- In Skills and Strategies 9 on page 172, you learned to write down new vocabulary on vocabulary cards. If your example sentence contains a collocation, underline it.

- Try to use collocations when you write and speak.

Side 1

> crime
>
> When a celebrity <u>commits a crime</u>, everyone wants to read about it.

Side 2

> Does an <u>illegal activity</u>

Skill Practice 1

Read the following paragraph. Look at the context of the words in bold. What other words appear near them? Look for combinations of verb + noun, adjective + preposition, and verb + preposition. Complete the collocations by filling in the blank lines below. If you can't figure out the meaning of a word, look it up in a dictionary.

The Ancient Egyptians were the first to write about the brain. However, they didn't pay **attention** to the brain because they did not think the brain was very important. They certainly did not think it was **connected** to thinking or making **decisions**. They believed that the center of life was the heart. An early Greek doctor was the first to suggest that the brain plays a **role** in human thought. However, a more famous Greek, Aristotle, disagreed. Like the ancient Egyptians, he believed that the heart was the center of thought. He also believed that the brain was **responsible** for cooling the heart and blood.

1 _____ attention _____

2 connected _____

3 _____ decisions

4 _____ role _____

5 responsible _____

Skill Practice 2

Read the following paragraph. Then look back in the paragraph, and find collocations to fill in the blank lines below. If you can't figure out the meaning of a word, look it up in a dictionary.

Does playing video games help your brain? Ask a parent or teacher, and the answer will probably be no. However, recent research suggests that this answer may not be correct. One university professor believes that video games can exercise the mind and help us develop skills. The professor argues that these games are successful because they follow one of the most important principles of learning: Learning is most effective when a task pushes the limit of learners' abilities. When learners become good at something, their success makes them feel happy, and they want to continue. However, if they get too good at it, they will become bored. This is why video games are so effective. When learners become good at one level, the game gets harder. So they always face a challenge. Our brains work best when there is a challenge. Perhaps parents and teachers should also take advantage of this opportunity to increase their brain power!

1 play _____ (n)

2 _____ (v) skills

3 _____ (v) principles

4 _____ (v) the limit

5 good _____ (prep)

6 face _____ (n)

7 _____ (v) advantage _____ (prep)

Skill Practice 3

Read the following paragraph. When you find a collocation, highlight it. The sentences below contain blank lines with collocations from the paragraph. Complete the sentences by filling in the blank lines. Two letters of each collocation have been done for you.

    Dr. Alan Hirsch thinks he can predict personality from which snack foods a person prefers. Hirsch, a scientist from the Smell and Taste Treatment and Research Foundation, has spent more than 20 years studying this issue. He has asked more than 18,000 Americans about their favorite salty snack. He found that people who like tortilla chips (a Mexican-style snack) want everything to be perfect. If you want someone you can depend on, you need to find someone who prefers peanuts. They are never late for appointments. Hirsch can also predict personalities based on ice-cream flavor preferences. Do you like vanilla? You are probably a private person, but you like to take risks. Are you a chocolate lover? You like to be the center of attention, and you get bored easily. Strawberry? You should avoid stress. People who like strawberries worry about everything!

1 Scientists have _sp_____ many _____ trying to find a cure for cancer.

2 It is important for children to have friends that they can _de_____ _____ and trust.

3 She could not wake up so she was _la_____ _____ her math test.

4 In the early twentieth century, the value of the American dollar was _ba_____ _____ the price of gold.

5 Young people often like to _ta_____ _____. Many of them choose dangerous sports like skiing and skydiving.

6 You should try to _av_____ _____ because it can have negative effects on your health.

7 Parents always _wo_____ _____ their children. They don't want them to get into trouble.

Connecting to the Topic

Discuss the following questions with a partner.

1 Do you think that adults can learn new skills as easily as children? Why or why not?

2 If you play Mozart and Beethoven to babies, do you think that you can increase their intelligence? Why or why not?

3 Athletes train by exercising. Do you think people can train their brains, for example, by learning a new language or reading a challenging book? Why or why not?

4 What do you think happens to the brain as adults become older? Can elderly people learn new skills, for example?

Previewing and Predicting

Reading the first sentence of each paragraph and thinking of a question the paragraph might answer is a quick way to predict what a text will be about.

A Read the first sentence of paragraphs 2–7 in Reading 1, and think of a question that you expect the paragraph to answer. Then choose the question below that is most like your question. Write the number of the paragraph (2–7) next to that question. The first paragraph has been done for you.

PARAGRAPH	QUESTION
	Do we know everything about the brain?
	How has technology helped us to learn about the brain?
	Does the brain change as we grow?
	What happens to the brain in old age?
2	What are the parts of the brain?
	How do humans understand information?

B Compare your answers with a partner's.

While You Read

As you read, stop at the end of each sentence that contains words in **bold**. Follow the instructions in the box in the margin.

Brain Development and Function

1   The brain is our most amazing organ. It allows us to think, dream, speak, and make decisions. It is one of the things that makes us human. It controls everything we do, such as breathing, enjoying a bowl of ice cream, or deciding which cell phone to buy. Scientists have been studying the brain for thousands of years. They are only now beginning to understand its structure, function, and development.

2   The brain is part of the nervous system, which consists of billions of special cells, called *neurons*. These neurons constantly send information back and forth at very high speeds from different parts of the body to different parts of the brain. Scientists now understand that these different parts of the brain have separate functions:

- **The brain stem**. This part of the brain resembles the brains of many animals. It controls functions like respiration and heart rate. In other words, it controls the essential functions automatically.
- **The cerebellum**. This part of the brain controls muscles and movement. New research suggests it is also involved in thinking.
- **The thalamus**. This part of the brain helps the brain stem, but it also plays an important role in memory and emotional responses.
- **The cerebral cortex**. This is what we usually think of as the human brain. It is the center of cognition, that is, where thinking and

Figure 6.1 Major Parts of the Brain

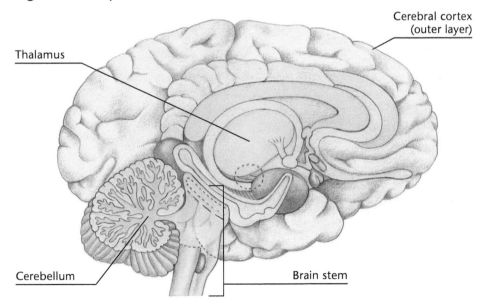

Thalamus

Cerebral cortex (outer layer)

Cerebellum

Brain stem

decision making takes place. It is divided into four parts, or *lobes*. Each lobe is responsible for different functions, including vision, hearing, speech, movement, and memory. Together, they allow humans to process information, and to respond **to it**.

3   New technologies have allowed us to learn a great deal about the structure of the brain. Technology such as CT scans and MRIs provide **images**, or pictures, of areas deep within the brain. For example, in the 1980s, scientists were able to use MRIs to study the *amygdala*, the brain's center for emotion. This important but tiny structure had been invisible on images prior to MRIs. This technology plays a very important role in helping doctors understand the brain and diagnose serious diseases such as brain cancer.

4   Technology can also show how the brain processes information. It shows the area where activity is occurring. It works like this: A doctor places a patient in an MRI machine. The doctor then asks the patient to solve a math problem, for example. As the patient thinks about this task, blood flows to the part of the brain responsible for solving mathematical problems. This area then lights up on an MRI image and indicates activity. The MRI machine makes images of the blood flow so the doctor can assess if the brain is working normally. The development of this technology has allowed scientists to understand more about which parts of the brain are responsible for different functions.

WHILE YOU READ ❶

Look back through the list of the different parts of the brain and their functions. Highlight the collocations that include the words *involve*, *role*, and *responsible*.

WHILE YOU READ ❷

Use context clues to figure out the meaning of *image*. Highlight its meaning.

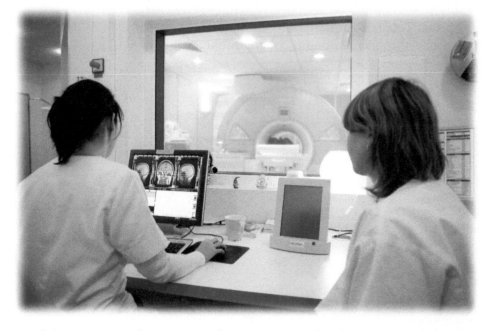

MRIs can provide important information about brain function.

5   **Scientists** are also interested in cognitive development, or how the brain grows and ages. They have found that the brain does not develop at a consistent rate. Before a child is two years old, there is a surge in brain growth and development. During these early years, billions of new

WHILE YOU READ ❸

As you read paragraph 5, look for the word that signals cause and effect. Highlight it.

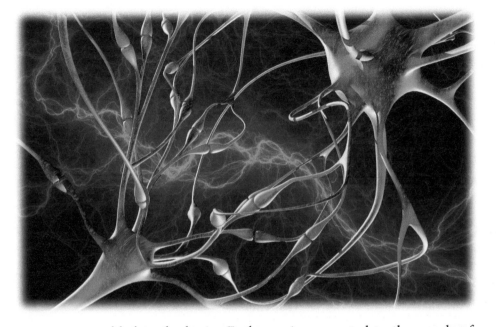

Connections between
neurons are crucial for
cognitive development.

neurons are added to the brain. Each one is connected to thousands of
other neurons, making trillions of connections. These connections are
very important because all information to and from the brain must pass
through these connections. Scientists have found that babies start out with
more neural connections than adults. These extra connections allow a
baby to learn new skills, such as language. However, after the age of three,
a new process begins. At this age, the brain begins to keep track of the
connections that it uses the most. Neural connections that are used a lot
remain strong and survive. Connections that are not used a lot become
weak and are lost. For example, a child who has books to read at an early
age may learn to read more easily than a child who has no access to books.

6   Understanding more about neural connections has also changed beliefs
about **old age**. Experts used to think that the brain reached its peak at
about age 40, and after that, began to decline. Now scientists believe that
older people who stay physically and mentally active continue to make and
keep neural connections. This means that even at an older age, adults can
still learn new skills. However, it often takes older adults longer to learn a
new skill because the rate at which the brain processes new information
slows down as an adult ages. At the same time, however, the different
parts of the brain begin to work together more efficiently as it ages. This
helps to compensate, or make up for, the loss of processing speed. As life
expectancy continues to lengthen, doctors are becoming more interested in
understanding how the brain ages.

7   There is still a great deal that we do not know about the brain, but
twenty-first century technology is allowing scientists to research the brain
in new and exciting ways. This technology will help us understand more
about how the brain works and help doctors better diagnose and treat
brain diseases and injuries.

WHILE YOU READ 4

What claim does
Paragraph 6 make?
Highlight it.

Main Idea Check

Here are the main ideas of paragraphs 2–6 in Reading 1. Match each paragraph to its main idea. Write the number of the paragraph on the blank line.

_____ A The brain does not develop at a consistent rate.

_____ B Older adults can continue to develop neural connections.

_____ C New technology has added to our understanding of the brain.

_____ D Different parts of the brain are responsible for different functions.

_____ E Scientists understand more about how the brain processes information.

A Closer Look

Look back at Reading 1 to answer the following questions.

1 Match the brain part to its function. Some parts match more than one function.

Part of Brain	Function
_____ 1 Stem	a Speech; hearing
_____ 2 Cerebellum	b Muscles; movement
_____ 3 Thalamus	c Breathing
_____ 4 Cerebral cortex	d Vision
	e Heart rate
	f Memory

2 The cortex is the only part of the brain involved in mental processes. **True or False?**

3 Which statements are correct according to paragraphs 3 and 4? Circle all that apply.
   a New technology like MRIs can help doctors diagnose serious brain illnesses.
   b Imaging technology provides information about the structure and the function of different parts of the brain.
   c An MRI machine makes blood flow to one part of the brain, and then makes an image of this.
   d Scientists were not able to see the amygdala until the twenty-first century.

4 A child's brain is fully developed by the age of two. **True or False?**

5 According to paragraph 5, which of the following statements correctly tells whether neural connections in a child's brain will remain strong?
   a They will remain if the child's brain is large.
   b They will remain if they are used frequently.
   c They will remain if the child's brain cannot keep track of them.
   d They will remain if the child is intelligent.

6 Learning new skills is difficult for older adults because the brain loses its ability to make new neural connections. **True or False?**

Skill Review

In Skills and Strategies 11, you learned that English has many collocations. These include combinations of verb + noun, adjective + preposition, and verb + preposition. Noticing these collocations will help you read more quickly and with a better understanding.

A Quickly scan Reading 1 to find collocations that begin with the following words, and highlight them. Then fill in the blanks below to complete each collocation. The words are listed in the order that they appear in the reading.

1 make _____

2 send _____

3 plays _____

4 divided _____

5 responsible _____

6 flows _____

7 lights _____

8 interested _____

9 connected _____

10 access _____

B Complete the following sentences using collocations from the list above.

1 Scientists are _____ _____ studying the effects of playing video games on the brain.

2 Doctors in developing countries often do not have the same _____ _____ technology as doctors in more developed countries.

3 In many educational computer games, the screen _____ _____ and music plays when the child finds the correct answer.

4 Technology _____ an important _____ in all areas of medicine.

5 Technology has helped scientists understand how neural connectors _____ _____ from one part of the brain to another.

6 It is important to have all the information before you _____ _____ related to your health.

7 Textbooks are _____ _____ separate chapters or units, each with its own topic.

8 Blood _____ _____ the lungs from the heart.

9 Nurses are _____ _____ the day-to-day care of their patients.

10 Scientists have found that brain development in older adults is _____ _____ mental and physical exercise.

C Compare your answers with a partner's.

Definitions

Find the words in Reading 1 that complete the following definitions. When a verb completes the definition, use the base form, although the verb in the reading may not be in the base form.

1 A/An _____ is the way in which a system is arranged or organized. (n) Par. 1

2 The purpose or way something works is a/an _____. (n) Par. 1

3 Nerve or brain cells are called _____. (n pl) Par. 2

4 To _____ means to be similar to someone or something. (v) Par. 2

5 To _____ means to name a disease or a medical problem. (v) Par. 3

6 A person who is receiving medical treatment is called a/an _____. (n) Par. 4

7 When something always happens or behaves in the same way, it is
_____. (adj) Par. 5

8 A sudden increase is called a/an _____. (n) Par. 5

9 To stay in the same place or in the same condition is to _____. (v) Par. 5

10 To _____ a patient means to find ways to improve the condition of that
person. (v) Par. 7

Words in Context

Complete the sentences with words or phrases from Reading 1 in the box below.

| back and forth | indicate | keep track of | prior to |
| consists of | involved in | nervous system | process |

1 The human brain can _____ many different ideas at the same time.

2 Green lights on an MRI _____ strong and normal blood flow in that part
of the brain.

3 Information travels _____ between neurons.

4 It is important to _____ your medical records so you can bring them with
you if you change doctors.

5 The brain and all the nerves are part of the body's _____.

6 Students are often _____ many different activities, such as sports, music,
and theater.

7 _____ modern technology, doctors had to cut into a brain in order to
study it. Now they use imaging technology.

8 A computer _____ three main parts: a processor, a monitor, and
a keyboard.

Critical Thinking

Reading 1 introduces the term *cognition* and discusses cognitive development in young children and older adults. It also explains how cognition develops at certain ages.

A **Discuss the following questions with a partner.**

1 What does the term *cognition* mean?

2 What does the writer mean by *cognitive development*?

3 Which of the following activities do you think use cognition?
   a Reading a book
   b Smelling the flowers in your garden
   c Reading a map
   d Sneezing
   e Learning a new language
   f Deciding that you are driving too fast

B **Refer back to the reading to complete the chart by filling in important changes that occur at these ages. The first one has been completed for you.**

AGES	COGNITIVE CHANGES
Under two years old	*Surge in brain growth and development*
Three years old	
Older adults	

Research

Because more people are living longer today, scientists are very interested in studying ways to maintain and improve cognition in the elderly. Research on this topic is still at an early stage. However, scientists have suggested several activities that may improve cognition in old age. Go online and find several of these suggested activities. Make a list.

Writing

Write two paragraphs. The first paragraph will explain the term *cognition* and describe the cognitive development of young children. The second paragraph will explain what happens to cognitive development in older adults and offer suggestions as to how these adults can maintain or improve their cognition. Use some of the examples you found in your research.

Connecting to the Topic

Discuss the following questions with a partner.

1 In what ways do you think teenagers behave differently than adults do?

2 People often criticize teenagers for their negative behavior. Do you think this is fair? Why or why not?

3 Do you think you are or were a typical teenager? Why or why not?

Previewing and Predicting

> Sometimes just looking at an illustration can help you predict what a text will be about.

A Look at the cartoon on page 227. Based on the ideas that the teenager expresses in the cartoon, how do you think he is likely to behave? Put a check (✓) next to the things you think he might do.

HOW IS THE TEENAGER LIKELY TO BEHAVE?	✓
Stay out late at a party the night before a big test	
Pack his clothes a week before he goes on a trip	
Leave his car windows open on a day when rain is predicted	
Forget to bring his homework to school	
Begin studying for his university admission test a year before the test	

B Compare your answers with a partner's.

While You Read

As you read, stop at the end of each sentence that contains words in **bold**. Follow the instructions in the box in the margin.

◄)) The Teenage Brain

1   Humans have a very long period of adolescence. During this time, as we go from childhood to adulthood, the human brain continues to develop. Parents, teachers, and scientists have all noticed that adolescents, that is, teenagers, often respond differently to situations than adults do. Teenagers may be more emotional, and sometimes they use poor judgment. Until recently, scientists believed that dramatic changes in hormones caused this teenage behavior. However, new research suggests that hormones are not the only cause. New technology can give us clearer images of the brain and its activity. These images show that a teenage brain is different from an adult brain. This difference may help explain why adults and teenagers behave differently.

2   Recently, scientists have discovered that the brain is only about 80 per-cent developed at adolescence. There is another surge of growth in neurons in early adolescence. However, this growth begins in the back of the brain in areas that control language and vision. Throughout adolescence, the brain continues to develop. The last part to develop is the frontal area. This is the part of the brain that controls planning, judgment, and emotion. This pattern of development helps explain why many teenagers make poor decisions and take risks. They do not always think about what will happen as a result of their actions. This is especially true in stressful situations. Scientists believe that the frontal area of the brain does not mature until the age of 25 to 30 – much later than they previously **believed.**

3   Studies of the brain suggest that teenagers are not very good at under-standing the emotions of others. Researchers believe this is connected to their brain development. One study asked adults and teenagers to respond

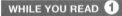

WHILE YOU READ ❶

What was the main idea of paragraph 2? Highlight it.

to a group of faces. They had to decide if the people were happy, angry, sad, or upset. The scientists examined the MRI images of the brains of the adults and teenagers in the study. They found that the teenagers performed badly on these tests compared to adults. The images showed that the two groups were using different parts of their brains to make their decisions. The teenagers were using a part of the brain related to emotion. **In contrast**, the adults were using a part of the brain related to judgment and planning. Scientists believe this may be why teenagers sometimes misunderstand other people's behavior. They may say, "My teacher hates me" or "My boyfriend is angry at me" even if these things are not really **true**.

WHILE YOU READ 2

Which statements in paragraphs 2 and 3 are in contrast? Highlight them.

WHILE YOU READ 3

Look back at paragraph 3. Highlight the collocations that include prepositions and the words *good*, *respond*, *compared*, *related*, and *angry*.

4   As children become adults, it is important for them to become independent, to explore unfamiliar situations, and to have new experiences. Sometimes, however, this leads teenagers to take part in risky behavior. Parents all over the world will tell you that their teenage children do not always use good judgment. Parents often ask them, "What were you thinking when you did that?" One reason why teenagers do not use good judgment is because of their incomplete brain development. Another reason is that during adolescence, there is a significant increase in hormones that affect adolescent behavior. Scientists believe that the high level of these hormones can sometimes lead teenagers into risky or dangerous situations. In these difficult and unfamiliar situations, the ability to plan and to use good judgment is crucial. Unfortunately, this ability has not fully developed in the teenage brain.

Teenagers often take risks.

5   Another factor that makes it hard for teenagers to use good judgment is lack of sleep. Doctors believe that teenagers need more sleep than adults because their brains are developing rapidly. They need 9 hours of sleep every day in order to function well. However, a recent study found that 90 percent of teenagers get less than 9 hours of sleep a night, and that 10 percent get less than 6 hours. They stay up late at night, and as a result, they cannot wake up the next morning. Parents used to think this was a behavioral problem. However, scientists have discovered that teenagers and adults have different "biological clocks." Every night our brains release a chemical that makes us sleepy. The chemical is released later at night in teenagers, so they do not become sleepy when children or adults do. Instead, at about 11:00 p.m., they are often wide awake. Most of them must get up early to go to school the next morning, which makes the problem worse. Because many teenagers do not get enough sleep, they are always tired. It is not clear how this shortage

of sleep affects memory, judgment, and learning, but scientists are certain that its effects are not **positive**.

6   While scientists continue to study the effects of lack of sleep on teenagers, they are also becoming interested in the effect of multitasking on the **teenage brain**. Students often video chat, check Facebook, text their friends, and listen to music, all while they are doing their homework. To older adults, this multitasking is a sign of lack of focus, but to teenagers, it is normal. Some evidence suggests that multitasking improves some skills. Hand-eye coordination, for example, improves by playing video games. However, scientists have also found that there are negative effects. Research suggests that students can learn facts while multitasking, but may not understand the information very well. It also takes longer to learn information while multitasking. This research is quite new, so scientists are still trying to understand both the positive and negative effects of multitasking.

7   The differences between adult and adolescent brains have raised questions and brought about changes in education and the legal system. For example, schools in several countries have decided to start the school day later so that students can stay up later at night and sleep later in the morning. Other schools offer more difficult classes later in the day. There are also legal questions. If teenagers' brains are still developing, are they completely responsible for their actions? What if they commit a crime? If they cannot fully control their emotions or predict consequences, should they receive the same penalty as adults? In the United States, some officials are taking this new research into account when they write laws and decide on penalties. New brain research is likely to result in more changes in education and the legal system that will **affect teenagers**.

WHILE YOU READ 4

What was the main idea of paragraph 5? Highlight it.

WHILE YOU READ 5

As you read the next sentence, highlight the examples that explain *multitasking*.

WHILE YOU READ 6

Look back at paragraph 7. Highlight the collocations that include the words *crime*, *account*, and *result*.

Scientists are studying the effects of multitasking.

Main Idea Check

Here are the main ideas of paragraphs 2–6 in Reading 2. Match each paragraph to its main idea. Write the number of the paragraph on the blank line.

_____ A Teenagers sometimes cannot judge other people's emotions.

_____ B Some areas of a teenager's brain are still growing.

_____ C There are two reasons why many teenagers take risks and use poor judgment.

_____ D Scientists are studying the effects of multitasking on the teenage brain.

_____ E Many teenagers do not sleep enough.

A Closer Look

Look back at Reading 2 to answer the following questions.

1 Reread paragraph 1. Which factors influence teenage behavior? Circle all that apply.

  a Parents

  b Changes in hormones

  c Developing brain

  d New technology

  e Teachers

2 Some parts of the brain have not fully developed by adolescence. How does this affect the behavior of teenagers? Circle all that apply.

  a They sometimes use poor judgment.

  b They feel a lot of stress.

  c They don't always think about the consequences of their behavior.

  d They often do not plan well.

  e They are angry, sad, and upset.

3 According to paragraphs 3 and 4, why are teenagers sometimes not good at judging other people's emotions?

  a They don't look closely at other people's faces.

  b They don't fully use the part of the brain related to judgment and planning.

  c They think other people hate them.

  d A high level of certain hormones makes it hard for them to think clearly.

4 Risky behavior may be related to the level of hormones. **True or False?**

5 Which of the following is stated in paragraph 5?

  a Adults and teenagers need the same amount of sleep.

  b Most teenagers become sleepy later in the evening than adults.

  c Many adults do not get enough sleep.

  d Lack of sleep for a teenager does not usually have negative effects.

6 Which statement is *not* correct according to paragraph 6?

 a Parents are concerned that new technology has negative effects on their children.
 b Teenagers find it normal to do several activities at the same time.
 c Scientists are studying the effects of multitasking on the adolescent brain.
 d So far, scientists have found that playing video games has no positive effects on teenage development.

7 What changes have occurred as a result of our new knowledge of the adolescent brain? Circle all that apply.

 a Some schools allow teenagers to start their classes later in the day.
 b Difficult classes such as science and mathematics are offered online.
 c If teenagers commit a crime in the United States, they get the same penalty as adults.
 d New research is changing the way some experts are writing laws in the United States.

Skill Review

In Making Connections on page 169, you learned that writers use special words and phrases to signal contrast. Knowing these words and phrases will help you connect ideas as you read.

A One very frequent marker of contrast is *however*. **Review Reading 2 and for each of the following paragraphs, find this marker. Then write what two ideas are in contrast.**

Paragraph 1

_____   _____

Paragraph 2

_____   _____

Paragraph 4

_____   _____

Paragraph 5

_____   _____

Paragraph 6

_____   _____

B Compare your answers with a partner's.

Definitions

Find the words in Reading 2 that complete the following definitions. When a verb completes the definition, use the base form, although the verb in the reading may not be in the base form.

1 _____ is the period of time between the ages of 13 to 19. (*n*) Par. 1

2 The period of time after adolescence is called _____. (*n*) Par. 1

3 _____ are natural chemicals produced by the body. (*n pl*) Par. 1

4 To _____ is to look at something very carefully. (*v*) Par. 3

5 If something is _____, it is connected to something else. (*adj*) Par. 3

6 If something is _____, it is essential or very important. (*adj*) Par. 4

7 A/An _____ of something means there is a shortage, or an absence. (*n*) Par. 5

8 When you _____, you remain awake. (*v – 2 words*) Par. 5

9 If you are _____ about something, you are sure, and you know it is true. (*adj*) Par. 5

10 _____ is the ability to make separate things work well together. (*n*) Par. 6

Word Families

A The words in bold in the chart are from Reading 2. The words next to them are from the same word family. Study and learn these words.

B Choose the correct form of the words from the chart to complete the following sentences. Use the correct verb tenses and subject-verb agreement. Use the correct singular and plural noun forms.

NOUN	VERB	ADJECTIVE
maturity	**mature**	*mature*
independence	—	**independent**
judgment	*judge*	—
response	**respond**	*responsive*
stress	*stress*	**stressful**

1 Lack of _____ is one reason why some teenagers make bad decisions.

2 People with _____ jobs often don't eat or sleep enough.

3 The teacher got no _____ when she asked the student to explain his behavior. The student didn't say a word.

4 Adolescence is a time of increasing _____, when young people start to do things without adults.

5 Teenagers sometimes do not use good _____ in unfamiliar situations.

6 When teenagers take part in risky behavior, parents often experience a lot of

_____.

7 My daughter is very _____. She always wants to do things by herself without help from other people.

8 Studies have found that girls often _____ earlier than boys do.

9 Because the teenage brain is not fully developed, teenagers often _____ to difficult situations differently than adults do.

10 Adolescents sometimes find it difficult to _____ the emotions of others.

Academic Word List

The following are Academic Word List words from Readings 1 and 2 of this unit. Use these words to complete the sentences. (For more on the Academic Word List, see page 257.)

adulthood (*n*)	consists of (*v*)	functions (*n*)	prior to (*adj*)	responds (*v*)
consistent (*adj*)	crucial (*adj*)	mature (*v*)	process (*v*)	stressful (*adj*)

1 Preparing for university entrance exams is often a very _____ experience.

2 When teenagers enter _____, they usually become more responsible.

3 The brain is divided into lobes, and each lobe controls different _____.

4 Some scientists believe it is difficult to _____ information while multitasking.

5 Very young children can learn an enormous amount very quickly, so it is

_____ to engage them in activities such as reading.

6 _____ the invention of technology such as MRIs, doctors found it more difficult to diagnose serious illnesses and injuries.

7 The cerebral cortex _____ four parts, or lobes.

8 Marie's school record is very _____. She always gets very good grades.

9 Researchers now believe that the human brain may not _____ until a person is 25 or 30 years old.

10 Doctors looked at MRI images to understand how the human brain _____ to emotions such as happiness and fear.

Critical Thinking

Reading 2 discusses biological reasons for teenage behavior.

A **With a partner, talk about behaviors that are typical of teenagers. Look back at Reading 2 for ideas. In addition, think of behaviors that the writer did not discuss.**

B **Make a list of these behaviors, and provide reasons to explain them. One example has been done for you.**

- *Teenagers often argue with their parents. They are trying to become more independent.*
- _____
- _____
- _____

C **Share your answers with a group.**

> **ANALYZING INFORMATION**
>
> Critical thinking involves thinking carefully about important topics that the writer has not completely explained.

Research

Interview five teenagers. Find out about their sleep habits. Find answers to the following questions. Then share your answers with your class.

- What time do they go to sleep on school nights? What about the weekend?
- How many hours a night do they sleep on school nights? The weekend?
- Do they feel they get enough sleep?
- Do they find it difficult to focus in school in the mornings?

Writing

Write two paragraphs. The first paragraph will describe the results of your research. The second paragraph will explain why many teenagers have a sleep problem.

Improving Your Reading Speed

Good readers read quickly and still understand most of what they read.

A Read the instructions and strategies for Improving Your Reading Speed in Appendix 3 on page 271.

B Choose either Reading 1 or Reading 2 in this unit. Read it without stopping. Time how long it takes you to finish the text in minutes and seconds. Enter the time in the chart on page 273. Then calculate your reading speed in number of words per minute.

Preparing for a Reading Test

Academic courses require a lot of reading. Instructors give tests to find out if students have learned, remembered, and understood the reading. Preparing for a test will increase your chances of passing the test and of showing the instructor what you have learned. Many of the strategies that you have learned so far in this book will help you prepare for tests: finding main ideas and supporting details, highlighting key words, taking notes, and outlining. Another important strategy is predicting questions. This means thinking about questions that might be on a test and answering those questions before taking the test.

Examples & Explanations

Scientists at the University of Southern California have discovered that damage to a specific part of the brain – the *insula* –actually helps people stop smoking. [Researchers studied 32 smokers who had damage to the insula.] ① This part of the brain is connected to feelings of hunger, pain, and desire to do things like smoke. [They found that when the insula was damaged, the smokers no longer felt the desire to smoke.] ② [In fact, 50 percent of this group immediately stopped smoking after brain damage occurred.] ③ Furthermore, the patients reported that stopping smoking was easy, although many had tried and failed before. [This is important information for scientists who are studying different treatments to help people stop smoking.] ④ It is possible that one day, scientists will find a treatment that breaks the connection between the insula and the desire to smoke.

This student has circled the main idea, numbered supporting details, and highlighted a key word.

Then, the student predicted some questions. She wrote each question on the front of a note card and the answer on the back. Here are the four questions and answers that she chose for this paragraph.

What is the insula?

It is the area of the brain connected to feelings of hunger, pain, and the desire to smoke.

How did scientists discover the connection between smoking and the insula?

Scientists studied 32 smokers with damaged insulas. After brain damage occurred, 50 percent easily stopped smoking.

How is the insula connected to smoking?

It is connected to the desire to smoke.

Why is research on the insula important?

It might help scientists find a treatment to help smokers stop smoking.

Strategies

These strategies will help you prepare for a reading test.

- Think of questions that focus on main ideas and supporting details. Use question words, such as *what*, *where*, *when*, *why*, *how*, and *who* to write your questions.
- Also, write questions that focus on definitions of key vocabulary and key terms.
- Write your questions on one side of a note card. Write your answers on the other side of the card.
- Test yourself. Mix up the cards in a different order each time you study them.

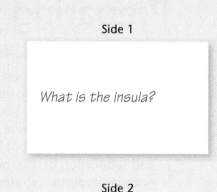

Side 1

What is the insula?

Side 2

It is the area of the brain connected to feelings of hunger, pain, and the desire to smoke.

Skill Practice 1

Read the following paragraph that a student has annotated. Then read the questions that the student predicted might be on a test. Write answers to the questions on the blank lines below.

Neurologists – scientists who study the brain – are trying to discover which part of the brain is connected to specific activities. This is known as brain mapping. Neurologists take images of brain activity while people are speaking, eating, sleeping, reading, or crying. These images identify which parts of the brain are responsible for which activity. Neurologists have even discovered the part of the brain connected to emotions, such as feeling worried. The images indicate that this feeling is created in the frontal lobes – the region of the brain behind the forehead. Mapping the brain has led to better understanding of this very complex organ.

showing which part of the brain is connected to which activity

① *feelings*

②

area of brain behind the forehead

③ *forehead*

Predicted test questions:

1 What is a neurologist?
2 How do we know that certain parts of the brain are connected to certain activities?
3 Which part of the brain do scientists believe is responsible for creating emotions?

Answers:

1 _____

2 _____

3 _____

Skill Practice 2

Read the following paragraph that a student has annotated. Then read the answers to three questions that the student predicted might be on a test. On the blank lines below, write three questions that match the three answers.

The brain is divided into two halves: the *left hemisphere* and the *right hemisphere.* Some research seems to suggest that each side controls a different way of thinking. Left-brain thinking is very analytical. It is scientific and focuses on details. Right-brain thinking, however, is more artistic and creative. Most people seem to use one side of their brain more than the other. This influences the way they think and learn. A left-brain thinker, for example, prefers to learn things in order, in a step-by-step approach. This person plans carefully and is very organized. A right-brain thinker prefers to first see the whole picture and then learn the details. This person is more interested in ideas and tends to be less organized. Some people use both sides of the brain equally. These people are usually good learners.

one half of the brain

① *uses logic and order*
②
③ *imaginative*
④
⑤
⑥

Predicted test questions:

1 _____

2 _____

3 _____

Answers:

1 The two halves are called the left and right hemispheres.

2 The left hemisphere is connected to analytical thinking.

3 They prefer to first see the whole picture and then learn the details.

Skill Practice 3

Read and annotate the following paragraph. Then write three questions that you think could be on a test. Write each question on one side of a note card. Write the answer to the question on the other side of the card. Work with a partner. Test each other by looking at the questions only.

The brain is the most complex machine in existence. It weighs only about 1.5 kilograms, but it is much more complicated than the most powerful computer. It has over 100 billion neurons. These neurons send messages across synapses, which are like wires connecting two battery cells. Each neuron has as many as 10,000 synapses. If every person in the world made a phone call at the same time, it would equal the same number of connections that a single brain makes in a day. Neurons send messages at speeds of over 300 kilometers per hour. If these brain cells become damaged by disease or by an accident, they may not grow back again. Today's scientists know a great deal about the human brain, but they also know that they still have much to learn about this very complex organ.

Connecting to the Topic

Discuss the following questions with a partner.

1 Which of these statements do you agree with? Which statements do you disagree with? Explain your answers.

   a Boys like to fight more than girls.
   b Boys are better at math and science than girls.
   c Girls are better at learning languages than boys.
   d Women talk more than men.
   e Women talk about their feelings more than men do.

Previewing and Predicting

> Reading the first sentence of several paragraphs and thinking of questions the paragraphs might answer is a quick way to predict what a text will be about.

A Read the first sentence of paragraphs 3–7 in Reading 3, and think of a question that you expect the paragraph to answer. Then choose the question below that is most like your question. Write the number of the paragraph (3–7) next to that question. The first paragraph has been done for you.

PARAGRAPH	QUESTION
	What is female intuition?
3	How do differences in the male and female brain change as girls and boys grow older?
	What are some differences between the adult male brain and the adult female brain?
	Why did men's and women's brains develop differently?
	How do male and female brains process information?

B With a partner, discuss what you think the whole reading will be about.

While You Read

As you read, stop at the end of each sentence that contains words in **bold**. Follow the instructions in the box in the margin.

The Male and Female Brain

1   A hundred years ago, if you asked if male and female brains were different, most people would answer, "Of course!" Today, however, most people believe that although men and women are physically different, their brains are the same. They believe that differences between men and women are a result of culture and experience rather than physical differences. However, recent research on the brain suggests that maybe people were correct 100 years ago. Male and female brains do work differently, and this results in clearly distinct or separate abilities. Culture and experience have an important influence on male and female abilities, but biology also plays a significant and possibly more important role.

2   Differences between men and women become clear very early in life. Girls seem to develop verbal abilities more quickly than boys do. Girls learn to talk sooner than boys do, and they develop a more extensive vocabulary. Scientists believe that the brain is responsible for this difference. The brain is divided into two parts, called *hemispheres*. The left hemisphere is dominant for language; the right hemisphere is dominant in receiving and thinking about information from the outside world. These two parts of the brain are connected by the *corpus callosum*, a major neural connector with millions of nerves. Scientists have found two possible differences in how males and females process language. First, when men talk, they use mainly the left hemisphere. However, when women talk, they seem to use both hemispheres. Second, some research shows that a part of the corpus callosum is wider in the female brain. These differences may allow women to understand and respond verbally more **quickly than men do**.

> **WHILE YOU READ** 1
>
> Look back at paragraph 2. Highlight the collocations that include the words *responsible*, *divided*, and *connected*.

Figure 6.2 The Two Hemispheres of the Brain

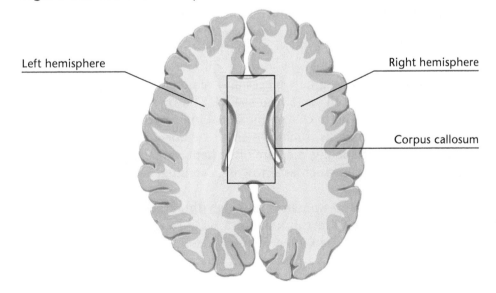

Left hemisphere

Right hemisphere

Corpus callosum

There are differences
in how boys and
girls play.

3   As children grow, these differences **continue**. Researchers conducted an experiment – they showed pictures of people and objects to children. Later they asked the children to recall the pictures. The girls remembered people more than objects. The boys remembered objects more than people. When they are between three and five years old, boys are more likely to be interested in toys such as trucks, machines, and building blocks. Girls are more likely to be interested in toys that are like people, such as dolls. Boys tend to play and fight physically. Girls usually play more quietly and solve their problems with words. It is true that these patterns also reflect cultural and social influences, but researchers believe that many reasons for these differences come from the brain.

4   These differences continue when children become adults. Men are better than women at tasks that require spatial ability. In other words, men can see objects in their mind; they can imagine a shape without actually touching it. For example, they can build a three-dimensional object by looking at a two-dimensional **plan**. Women have more difficulty with these tasks. Men are also better at finding new places and remembering routes. Their memory of the route is both visual and spatial. They see the whole route in their minds. Women tend to change the visual information into language. They remember landmarks, such as a small tree or a tall building, rather than the route itself. Finally, men are often better at tasks that require good physical coordination such as throwing, catching, and hitting a ball.

5   Another difference between men and women is how they think about information. Women have the capacity to think about a wide range of information at the same time, whereas men often focus on details. Brain images show that when women are solving a problem, for example, more

WHILE YOU READ ➋

As you read this paragraph, highlight the differences between boys and girls.

WHILE YOU READ ➌

Look back. What does this example about building an object refer to? Highlight the answer.

areas of their brains are active. Brain images also show that female brains have 15 to 20 percent more neurons and neural connections than male brains. This gives females more power to process information.

6   A women's ability to focus on the whole situation rather than on the details may explain female intuition. In many cultures, there is a belief that women sense things that men do not. For example, women may know a person is worried or unhappy before that person expresses those feelings. Scientific research is now explaining this intuition. Women do not just focus on one part of communication, such as words – they consider the whole person. They interpret people's faces and voices, and they use this information to guess what people are feeling.

7   How did these differences in male and female brains **develop**? Researchers believe this was connected to human survival. Thousands of years ago, men and women had different responsibilities for every day survival. Therefore, different parts of their brains developed to perform these responsibilities. For example, some experts believe that differences in spatial abilities developed when men were hunters. Men went to new and unfamiliar places to hunt. In order to find their way home, they had to remember routes. Their superior physical coordination was also an advantage in hunting. Women, on the other hand, stayed nearer to the home, often collecting food. They remembered places to find food by remembering nearby landmarks. Women were also responsible for raising the children, and understanding feelings was an important part of this activity.

WHILE YOU READ 4

Highlight the main idea of paragraph 7.

Men may have developed spatial skills as hunters.

8   It is important to emphasize that these differences between males and females are group differences. Of course some males have abilities that are more typical of females, and some females have abilities that are more typical of males. However, as researchers learn more about the human brain, it is becoming much clearer that there are biological differences between a male and a female brain. We cannot say, for example, that males are more or less intelligent than females. However, what we can say is that male and female brains are different.

Main Idea Check

Here are the main ideas of paragraphs 2–7 in Reading 3. Match each paragraph to its main idea. Write the number of the paragraph on the blank line.

_____ A Women appear to have stronger verbal abilities than men.

_____ B Female intuition can be explained by biology.

_____ C Male and female adults have different abilities.

_____ D As male and female children grow, their brains continue to be different.

_____ E Survival explains biological differences in the male and female brain.

_____ F Women think about information differently than men.

A Closer Look

Look back at Reading 3 to answer the following questions.

1 Most scientists today think that male and female brains are the same. **True or False?**

2 Which statements are correct according to paragraph 2? Circle all that apply.
   a The corpus callosum prevents neural connection between the left and right hemispheres.
   b The left and right hemispheres of the brain are responsible for different functions.
   c Research shows that the corpus callosum is wider in males than in females.
   d Biological differences explain why young girls tend to have better communication skills than boys.

3 Which statements are _not_ correct according to Paragraph 3? Circle all that apply.
   a Research shows that boys and girls remember people and objects differently.
   b Girls always prefer to play with toys like dolls, whereas boys always prefer to play with toys like trucks and machines.
   c Boys respond to problems more physically than girls.
   d The differences between boys and girls can be completely explained by biology.
   e How parents raise their children can explain some differences between boys and girls.

4 Reread paragraph 4. Which one of the following activities requires spatial ability?
   a Imagining a three-dimensional shape
   b Planning how to get from one place to another
   c Using a landmark to remember a place
   d Playing ball games

5 According to paragraph 5, what are some of the ways that women process information? Circle all that apply.

  a They focus on the details.
  b When solving a problem, many areas of their brain are active.
  c They sense things about other people.
  d They focus on the words only.
  e They can interpret people's faces.

6 Why does the writer use the example of hunting in paragraph 7?

  a It shows that men had different responsibilities than women.
  b It explains why women preferred to stay closer to the home than men.
  c It shows the connection between different responsibilities and brain development.
  d It explains why men are more physically coordinated than women.

7 Science can explain why men tend to be better at performing some tasks than women. **True or False?**

Skill Review

In Skills and Strategies 12, you learned that preparing for a test increases your chances of passing the test. Predicting questions is a good strategy as part of this preparation.

A Read paragraph 2 of Reading 3 again. Then read the questions that a student predicted might be on a test. Write answers to these questions on the blank lines.

1 Which hemisphere plays the most important role in language?

_____

2 What part of the brain connects the two hemispheres?

_____

3 How do men and women process language differently?

_____

B Choose another paragraph from Reading 3. Write three questions you predict might be on a test. Write each question on one side of a note card. Write the answer on the other side. Work with a partner. Test each other by looking at the questions only.

Definitions

Find the words in Reading 3 that complete the following definitions. When a verb completes the definition, use the base form, although the verb in the reading may not be in the base form.

1 To _____ a study is to organize and direct it. (*v*) Par. 3

2 A/An _____ is a scientific study. (*n*) Par. 3

3 To _____ means to be likely to do something. (*v – 2 words*) Par. 3

4 _____ means related to space. (*adj*) Par. 4

5 If you _____ something, you have a picture or idea of it in your mind. (*v*) Par. 4

6 _____ is knowing something based on feelings. (*n*) Par. 6

7 To _____ means to feel or be aware of something. (*v*) Par. 6

8 To _____ means to describe or understand the meaning of something. (*v*) Par. 6

9 People who search for and kill animals for food are known as _____. (*n pl*) Par. 7

10 If someone is _____, he or she is smart and can learn easily. (*adj*) Par. 8

Synonyms

Complete the sentences with words from Reading 3 in the box below. These words replace the words or phrases in parentheses, which are similar in meaning.

biology	collected	extensive	route
capacity	distinct	recall	superior

1 I remember his address but I cannot (remember) _____ his phone number.

2 He wanted to be a doctor so he studied (life science) _____ in college.

3 Each part of the brain has a (separate and different) _____ function.

4 Some people have the (ability) _____ to do several things at the same time.

5 Engineers usually have (wide) _____ knowledge of math and physics.

6 Adults and children can both learn new languages, but children's ability is (better) _____ .

7 The parents (gathered together) _____ all the information from the doctor and then discussed the best way to treat their son.

8 An accident closed the freeway, so we had to find a different (way) _____ to school.

Critical Thinking

Reading 3 claims that there are distinct differences between men and women. It discusses typical male skills and abilities and typical female skills and abilities.

A Think about yourself. Complete the following chart. Read each skill and ability. Then decide if you are very good at it, okay at it, or not at all good at it. Put a check (✓) in the appropriate column.

SKILLS AND ABILITIES	NOT GOOD	OKAY	VERY GOOD
Following directions from a map			
Learning a foreign language			
Writing in my native language			
Understanding mathematics			
Understanding sciences			
Talking about my feelings			
Fixing something mechanical when it is broken			
Installing new software			

B Go around the room and collect responses from each of your classmates. Consider whether the ability to do a particular skill well is typically male or typically female.

Research

Work in a group. Ask your group members if they agree or disagree with the following generalizations.

- Males are better at math and science than females.
- Females are better at history and languages than males.
- Males are better at sports than females.
- Females are more emotional than males.

Writing

Write two paragraphs. The first paragraph will describe the activities and skills we often think men and women are good at. The second paragraph will discuss whether you think these generalizations are true. Include examples from your chart and your research.

Connecting to the Topic

Read the definition of *addiction*, and then discuss the following questions with a partner.

addiction (*n*) the need or strong desire to do or have something, or a very strong liking for something

1 Which of the following activities do you think are addictions?

- Shopping for clothes
- Smoking cigarettes
- Talking on the phone
- Drinking wine
- Eating chocolate
- Studying for long periods of time
- Playing video games

2 What are some other addictions? Is there something that you do and can't stop doing? Explain your answers.

Previewing and Predicting

Reading titles, sections headings, and first sentences of each paragraph is a quick way to help you predict what a text will be about.

A **Read the title of Reading 4, the section headings, and the first sentence of each paragraph. Then put a check (✓) next to the topics you think will be included in the reading.**

_____ A Why people drink alcohol

_____ B Supply and demand of video games

_____ C Stopping an addiction

_____ D Why some people become addicts and others don't

_____ E Changes that occur in the brain as a result of addiction

_____ F How you can help an addict

B **Compare your answers with a partner's.**

While You Read

As you read, stop at the end of each sentence that contains words in bold. Follow the instructions in the box in the margin.

Addiction and the Brain

I. Introduction

1   There are many kinds of addiction. The most common are alcohol, cigarette, and drug addiction. However, some people can also be addicted to activities such as shopping or playing video games. These people repeat this behavior even though they know it is harmful. Many years ago, people thought that addicts were weak. They thought people could stop their addiction if they really wanted to. Now doctors think that addiction is a mental illness and that addicts cannot control their behavior. One reason for this change in attitude is a new understanding of the role of the brain in addiction.

II. The Role of Pleasure in Addiction

2   Scientists have increased our knowledge of addiction and the brain. They made an important breakthrough when they discovered a chemical in the brain called *dopamine*. Dopamine is a **neurotransmitter**. Neurotransmitters send messages from one neuron to another. Dopamine sends messages of pleasure to the brain during enjoyable experiences. These experiences could be eating a delicious meal, getting a good grade on a test, or falling in love.

3   How is dopamine connected to addiction? Drugs like nicotine in cigarettes cause a release of dopamine in the brain. As this chemical floods the brain, the person feels happy. Normally, when the body produces too much dopamine, the brain is able to control and reduce the amount of dopamine. However, drugs like nicotine in cigarettes interrupt this process, and the brain is unable to control the amount of dopamine. So the good feelings continue. The body quickly becomes used to the drug. People then need more nicotine to experience the same level of pleasure as before. Therefore, the person needs another cigarette. Addiction develops and the only way to experience pleasure is to keep smoking. At this point, the brain can no longer control how much dopamine it **really needs**.

4   Scientists are trying to learn more about why people become addicted to activities such as playing video games. Scientists have taken images of people's brains while the people were playing video games. These images

---

WHILE YOU READ ❶

Highlight the words that help you understand the meaning of *neurotransmitter*.

WHILE YOU READ ❷

Look back in paragraph 3. Highlight the collocations beginning with the words *reduce, interrupt,* and *keep*.

showed that dopamine levels sharply increased during the game but quickly decreased when the game ended; the feeling of excitement and pleasure disappeared. The desire to play more video games then increased. In order to experience the same level of excitement, the players returned to the video games and played for hours or days.

5   Researchers also studied changes in brain activity when people shop. They have discovered two biological explanations. First, they found that dopamine floods the brain as shoppers look at an item and think about buying it. However, the chemical balance in the brain quickly returns to normal after the person buys the item. At this point, the shopper often feels worried or anxious about the purchase. In order to experience excitement and pleasure again, the "shopaholic" searches for another item to buy. Second, MRIs show that people who are addicted to shopping have less activity in the area of the brain that predicts consequences. Some people are so addicted that they have lost their homes because they cannot stop spending money.

III. Stopping an Addiction

6   It is sometimes hard to understand why drug addicts cannot just stop their negative behavior. Again, science explains why it is so **difficult**. Dopamine is connected to survival. For example, when you eat, the brain releases dopamine and there is a feeling of pleasure. The brain remembers this pleasure and connects it to the activity of eating. In this way, the brain teaches us to continue eating in order to survive. Drugs imitate the same process. The brain interprets the drug as pleasure and wants to continue the activity. It remembers the pleasure connected to the drug. This is how drug addiction begins.

WHILE YOU READ ③

Read ahead to find the supporting details for this claim. Highlight them.

7   Science provides another reason why addictions are so difficult to stop. The brain remembers things that are important, such as threats and dangers. Think about a time when you were very frightened. Perhaps you felt like everything stopped for a few minutes. Afterwards, you could not remember anything except the threat. That was your brain at work. When a person experiences fear, specific areas of the brain shut down, so that the person can focus on fighting the threat. In other words, the brain is designed to help you in times of danger. However, brain images show that the area of the brain that shuts down during danger also controls judgment and decision-making. The brain responds to addictive drugs and activities in the same way it does to danger – parts of it shut down. So it is physically very difficult for addicts to make good decisions because the part of the brain controlling good judgment is no longer working **well**.

WHILE YOU READ ④

Look back at paragraph 7. Highlight the collocations that include the words *work, shut, focus, controls,* and *responds*.

8   Why do some people become addicts while others do not? Scientists believe that some people have genetic, that is, biological characteristics that make addiction more likely. These characteristics are passed from one generation to the next generation. For example, more than 60 percent of people who are addicted to alcohol have parents who were also addicted

to alcohol. Scientists have also found that people with other mental health problems are more likely to become addicts. More research will help clarify the connection between biological characteristics and addiction.

9   Researchers do know that the environment plays an important role in **addiction**. In particular, stress increases the chance that people will become addicts. One scientist showed this idea with two groups of rats in the 1970s. He built a small community for the first group of rats. These rats had lots of food, friends, and space to play. He called these the "happy rats." In contrast, each rat in the second group was left alone in a very small cage. These rats experienced a lot of stress. He called these the "stressed rats." The scientist offered two kinds of water to both groups. The first was only water. The second was water with an addictive drug. The happy rats did not take the addictive water, although it was available. The stressed rats repeatedly chose the water with the drug in it.

WHILE YOU READ 5

Highlight the main idea of paragraph 9.

IV. Treatment

10   Addicts usually need professional help to end an addiction. This is because ending a drug addiction is difficult and can be very painful. In one type of treatment, addicts take medicine that can help decrease their desire for the drug. For drug addictions, some doctors believe that the best answer is a vaccine. Vaccines prevent diseases by creating antibodies. The antibodies destroy the origin of the disease. Scientists are trying to create a vaccine with antibodies that would destroy drugs before they reach the brain. If scientists are successful, this will help solve the problem of addiction.

11   A second type of treatment tries to teach addicts to change their own **behavior**. In this case, the addicts must first admit they have a problem. Then they have to stay away from the people and places connected to the addiction because these may make the addict want to take the drug again. A sound or a smell may remind the addict of the drug. In serious cases, some addicts have to stay at special treatment centers where they learn to live a healthy life again.

WHILE YOU READ 6

Read ahead to find the supporting details for this claim. Highlight them.

12   Stopping an addiction to an activity, such as shopping or playing a video game, might not be physically painful. However, it can be just as difficult as stopping a drug or alcohol addiction. Doctors report that even young children who are addicted to video games will get very angry and upset if their parents take these games away from them. Experts, therefore, say that parents should slowly reduce the amount of time that children spend playing video games. This will help the children change their addictive behavior.

13   The human brain is designed to help humans survive. The complex processes within the brain allow humans to live a healthy life. However, addiction can imitate these healthy processes and lead to addiction. Addictions are complex and difficult to break. Scientists will continue to learn more about the brain as they try to both prevent and treat addiction in the future.

Main Idea Check

Match the main ideas below to five of the paragraphs in Reading 4. Write the number of the paragraph on the blank line.

_____ A The discovery of dopamine increased understanding of the brain and addiction.

_____ B Stress plays an important role in addiction.

_____ C Breaking an addiction is difficult because dopamine is connected to survival.

_____ D Science explains why some people are more likely to become addicts than others.

_____ E Dopamine plays a role in shopping addiction.

A Closer Look

Look back at Reading 4 to answer the following questions.

1 According to paragraph 1, what are doctors today more likely to think about drug addicts? Circle all that apply.

  a They are weak.

  b They choose to continue this negative behavior.

  c They have a mental illness.

  d They can stop their addiction if they want to.

  e They cannot stop their addiction.

2 Reread paragraph 3. Then complete the diagram. Put sentences A–E in the correct order. Write the correct letter in each box.

  A Nicotine prevents the brain from reducing the amount of dopamine.

  B The good feelings continue.

  C When a person smokes, nicotine in the cigarette causes the release of dopamine in the brain.

  D People need more nicotine to enjoy the pleasure, so they smoke another cigarette.

  E As dopamine floods the brain, the smoker feels happy.

3 Addiction to activities doesn't involve dopamine. **True or False?**

4 According to paragraph 7, why do parts of the brain sometimes shut down?

  a To help a person respond to a dangerous situation

  b To allow a person to focus on an addiction

  c To create a feeling of fear

  d To help a person forget a frightening situation

5 Children of alcoholic parents are more likely to become addicts. **True or False?**

6 Why does the writer use the example of the rat experiment in paragraph 9?

    a It shows that rats like to be alone.

    b It shows that stress increases the chance of addiction.

    c It shows that all rats will become addicted to drugs.

    d It shows that rats experience stress.

7 According to paragraph 10, why do some doctors believe that a vaccine will reduce addiction?

    a Vaccines are the only treatment for addiction.

    b Vaccines will destroy the drugs before they affect the brain.

    c Vaccines are used today to decrease the desire for drugs.

    d Vaccines can't produce antibodies.

8 Reread paragraphs 10 and 11. What should people do to break their addiction to alcohol? Circle all that apply.

    a They should ask their friends to stop drinking.

    b They should seek medical help.

    c They should slowly reduce the amount of alcohol they drink.

    d They should understand that they have a serious problem.

    e They should only drink in the evenings and at home.

Skill Review

In Skills and Strategies 12, you learned that preparing for a test increases your chances of passing the test. Predicting questions is a good strategy as part of this preparation.

A Read sections I and II of Reading 4 again. Then read the questions that a student predicted might be on a test. Write answers to these questions on the blank lines below.

1 What is dopamine?

_____

2 What is the effect of nicotine on dopamine?

_____

3 What changes occur in the brain when people play video games and go shopping?

_____

B Reread sections III and IV. Write three questions you predict might be on a test for each section. Write the question on one side of a note card. Write the answer on the other side. Work with a partner. Test each other by looking only at the questions.

Definitions

Find the words in Reading 4 that complete the following definitions. When a verb completes the definition, use the base form, although the verb in the reading may not be in the base form.

1 How you think or feel about something and how this makes you behave is a/an
_____ . (n) Par. 1

2 A/An _____ is an important discovery or new idea. (n) Par. 2

3 _____ is a dangerous chemical substance in cigarettes. (n) Par. 3

4 A strong hope or need to do something is a/an _____ . (n) Par. 4

5 A/An _____ is something you buy. (n) Par. 5

6 To _____ means to copy a behavior or an action. (v) Par. 6

7 _____ means related to the body. (adv) Par. 7

8 _____ refers to the biological process of passing things from parents to children. (adj) Par. 8

9 A medicine that stops people from getting a disease is called a/an _____ . (n) Par. 10

10 _____ are things the body produces to fight disease. (n pl) Par. 10

Words in Context

A Use context clues to match the first part of each sentence to its correct second part and to understand the meaning of the words in **bold**.

_____ 1 I couldn't find

_____ 2 Taking medicine is

_____ 3 The teacher asked

_____ 4 Even when they study hard, students

_____ 5 Although they know a lot more about the structure of the brain today, scientists

_____ 6 Researchers hope that new technology will help

_____ 7 My friend was badly hurt in the accident, but the doctors said there was

_____ 8 Researchers believe that playing video games is

a complain that they are so **anxious** about the entrance test that they can't sleep at night.

b a good **chance** she would fully recover.

c **clarify** why some people become addicts but others do not.

d one form of **treatment** to break a nicotine addiction.

e several **items** I needed at the store, so I ordered them online.

f the students not to **interrupt** until she was finished; she would then answer questions.

g addictive, so parents should limit the **amount** of time children spend doing this.

h **admit** they still need to learn a lot more about this organ.

B Compare your answers with a partner's. Discuss what clues helped you match the parts of the sentences and helped you understand what the words in **bold** mean.

Academic Word List

The following are Academic Word List words from Readings 3 and 4 of this unit. Use these words to complete the sentences. (For more on the Academic Word List, see page 257.)

attitude (*n*)	clarify (*v*)	distinct (*adj*)	interpret (*v*)	purchase (*n*)
capacity (*n*)	conduct (*v*)	intelligent (*adj*)	physically (*adv*)	route (*n*)

1 Scientists still use animals such as rats in order to _____ experiments.

2 Women can often _____ how people feel without asking them.

3 I didn't understand the connection between dopamine and addiction, so I asked the teacher to _____ this.

4 Even though shopaholics feel bad after they have made a big _____, they continue shopping.

5 The student had a very positive _____ toward school; he worked hard and asked questions when he didn't understand something.

6 Young boys are often more _____ active than young girls.

7 When scientists examined the MRIs, they found _____ differences in the way girls and boys process language.

8 The friends used their smart phones to plan the quickest _____ to the restaurant.

9 Research has shown that very young children have the _____ to learn a second language quickly and easily.

10 Parents often do not understand how their very _____ children can make such poor decisions.

Critical Thinking

Reading 4 talks about addictions to smoking, drinking alcohol, drugs, and shopping.

 Discuss the following questions with a partner.

1 What other addictions are there?

2 Addictions are usually connected to a negative behavior, such as smoking. Is it possible to be addicted to something positive? Can you be addicted to hard work, for example?

3 Do you think some addictions are more dangerous than other addictions? Explain your answer.

 Share your answers with the rest of the class.

Research

Do some online research about addictions. Choose an addiction that is not in the reading. Find answers to the following questions.

- Are there any treatments for this addiction?
- What are the treatments?
- Are the treatments easily accessible? For example, are they free?

Writing

Write two paragraphs. The first paragraph will explain the addiction. The second paragraph will explain current treatments for the addiction.

Improving Your Reading Speed

Good readers read quickly and still understand most of what they read.

A Read the instructions and strategies for Improving Your Reading Speed in Appendix 3 on page 271.

B Choose either Reading 3 or Reading 4 in this unit. Read it without stopping. Time how long it takes you to finish the text in minutes and seconds. Enter the time in the chart on page 273. Then calculate your reading speed in number of words per minute.

REVIEW OF CONNECTORS

In Units 1–4, you learned that writers have several ways to make connections. To do this, they connect words and ideas in their writing using:

- repetition of words and phrases. (See page 41.)
- pronouns to refer to previous ideas. (See page 85.)
- words or phrases to show cause and effect. (See page 127.)
- words or phrases to contrast one idea with another. (See page 169.)

Exercise 1

In the following paragraphs, underline repeated key words, circle pronouns and their antecedents, and highlight any words or phrases that show cause and effect or contrast.

1   Some people suffer from loss of memory as they get older. Normally, they lose their most recent memories first. Gradually, they forget other things, including even where they live. This can cause a lot of stress for the people who love them.

2   There are several distinct types of memory. One type is known as short-term memory. Researchers have conducted experiments to understand more about short-term memory. As a result of these experiments, they have found that short-term memory means that humans can remember things for only about 30 seconds.

3   Humans have very good vision compared to many other animals. Other animals do not have good vision, but their other senses are powerful. For example, cats have an excellent sense of smell and hearing. On the other hand, some insects cannot hear, but they are sensitive to very small movements.

4   An atlas is usually a book of maps, but scientists are working on a new kind of atlas – an atlas of the brain. This atlas consists of images of 7,000 healthy brains. The scientists plan to put these images on the Internet so that people can see them in three dimensions. Scientists hope that these images will lead to greater understanding of the brain.

5   Several studies have explored the idea that music can improve intelligence. One study claimed that music lessons could improve spatial processing. Another study tried to show that music lessons improve memory. However, no studies have been able to show a consistent beneficial effect of music on intelligence.

Exercise 2

Make a clear paragraph by putting sentences A, B, and C in the best order after the numbered sentence. Look for transition words, pronouns, and repeated key words to help you. Write the letters in the correct order on the blank lines.

1 Most medicines treat diseases. ____ ____ ____

| A It does this by stimulating the production of antibodies. | B However, a vaccine is different from most medicines because it is designed to prevent diseases, not treat them. | C These antibodies destroy the disease before it starts. |

2 There are many ways to reduce the level of stress in your life. ____ ____ ____

| A Either choice works well. The most important thing is to find a method of relaxation that is effective for you. | B Other people find that exercise helps them to manage stress and relax. | C Some people choose to get involved in activities in their community. |

3 You feel pain because your brain tells you to feel it. ____ ____ ____

| A Finally your brain sends out a message to do something, for example, to cry or hold your head. | B Then your brain senses the problem and where the problem is coming from. | C If you hit your head, neurons send a message through your nervous system to your brain. |

4 The cerebellum is an important part of your brain. ____ ____ ____

| A It controls movement and coordination. | B So if your cerebellum is damaged, it is difficult to do simple things like walking, because this involves coordination and balance. | C It also helps you control your balance. |

5 The brain has a specific response to threats. ____ ____ ____

| A Then neurotransmitters are released. | B As a result of these physical changes, the body is ready to respond to the threat. | C First, the heart and breathing rates increase. |

Key Vocabulary

The Academic Word List is a list of words that are particularly important to study. Research shows that these words frequently appear in many different types of academic texts. Words that are part of the Academic Word List are noted with an Ⓐ in this appendix.

UNIT 1 • READING 1

The News Media in the Past

afford *v* to have enough money to buy something • *Newspapers were expensive in the early 1800s, so many people could not **afford** to buy them.*

appetite *n* a desire or need for something, often food • *People have an **appetite** for news. They want to find out what is happening in the world.*

assassinate *v* to kill an important person for political reasons • *The country was shocked when the president was **assassinated**.*

average *adj* of a level considered to be typical or usual • *Our students are of **average** age for a program of this type.*

crime *n* an act that is against the law • *Reports indicate that the number of **crimes** in large cities is rising.*

dramatically Ⓐ *adv* suddenly and in a way that is clear to see • *The Internet has **dramatically** changed how many people get the news*

eager *adj* having or showing desire or interest • *The candidate's supporters were **eager** to hear the election results.*

erupt *v* to explode and throw out hot rock, gasses, and smoke • *When the volcano **erupted**, people had to leave their homes and move to a safer place*

focus on Ⓐ *v* to direct attention toward something or someone • *This television program **focuses on** business news.*

gather *v* to come together in a large group in one place • *The reporters **gathered** for the press conference.*

immigrant Ⓐ *n* a person who has come to a new country in order to live there • *In the nineteenth century, many **immigrants** came to the United States from Europe.*

local *adj* from or in a particular place, usually the place where you live • *Newspapers usually report **local** news as well as international news.*

natural disaster *n* an event that results in a lot of damage and is caused by something that exists in nature • *Every year, **natural disasters** – earthquakes, eruptions, floods, typhoons – happen in countries around the globe.*

publish Ⓐ *v* to make available to the public, usually by printing a book, magazine, or newspaper • *The author **published** his first book last year, and it was very successful.*

terrified *adj* the feeling of being very frightened • *The horror movie was so real that people in the audience were **terrified**.*

villager *n* a person who lives in a small town called a village • *In the past, **villagers** got their news from travelers who were passing through their villages.*

volcano *n* a mountain that may throw out ash, rocks, and burning lava • *Although it is dangerous, many people live near Mount Vesuvius, a famous **volcano** in Italy.*

wire *n* a long, thin piece of metal with a plastic covering that can carry electricity • *High winds during the storm blew down **wires**, and many people lost electricity.*

UNIT 1 • READING 2

The History of Electronic Media

accelerate *v* to increase speed • *Technology has **accelerated** the time it takes for news to travel from one country to another.* **acceleration** *n* the rate at which the speed of something changes and causes it to move faster or happen more quickly • *This car has good **acceleration**, which makes it easier to enter a busy highway.*

accessible Ⓐ *adj* possible to enter or use • *The Internet has made news more **accessible** to people all around the world.* **access (to)** *n* the opportunity to use or have something • *Many people in India do not have **access** to computers.* **access** Ⓐ *v* to be able to enter or use something • *I can **access** the Internet with my cell phone.*

available Ⓐ *adj* able to be used or obtained • *Twenty-four-hour news is now **available** in most countries.* **availability** *n* the state of being available • *I'll check on the **availability** of tickets.*

battery *n* a small object that provides electrical power • *I couldn't use my cell phone because I'd forgotten to recharge the **battery**.*

broadcasting *n* the sending out of sound or pictures that are carried over distances by radio waves • *All the television networks began **broadcasting** the election results early the next day.*

convenient *adj* easy to use; helpful • *Cell phones are very **convenient** because they are small and can be carried anywhere.*

global Ⓐ *adj* relating to the whole world • *The newspaper reported a **global** increase in the cost of food.*

impact Ⓐ *n* an effect that causes big changes • *Television had a huge **impact** on how people got their news.*

influence *n* the power to have an effect on people or things • *My teacher had a good influence on me. I've developed better study habits.* **influence** *v* to have a strong effect on someone or something • *Coverage of international events on television has influenced how people look at the world.* **influential** *adj* able to have a strong effect on someone or something • *The BBC's large, international audience makes it an influential news source.*

live *adj* seen or heard at the same time an event is happening • *The soccer match was seen live around the world.*

negative Ⓐ *adj* not happy or hopeful • *The news about the economy was very negative: the government expects more people to lose their jobs.*

pace *n* the speed at which something moves • *Technological change is moving at a faster pace than ever before.*

significant Ⓐ *adj* important • *The invention of the radio was a significant event in the history of communications technology.* **significance** Ⓐ *n* the importance someone or something has • *Political leaders quickly understood the significance of live broadcasts.*

traditional Ⓐ *adj* relating to people's beliefs, customs, or ways of doing things that have existed for a long time • *The newspaper had an interesting story about traditional Chinese food.* **tradition** Ⓐ *n* a belief or custom that has existed for a long time • *Last night's program reported on traditions in different communities around the world.*

transmit Ⓐ *v* to send or give something • *Information was transmitted by telegraph from place to place through wires on land and cables under the oceans.*

former *adj* of an earlier time; previous • *The new president invited the former president to discuss education plans .*

ignore Ⓐ *v* to pay no attention to • *The teacher ignored the students' request for less homework .*

last *v* to continue over a period of time • *The movie lasted two and a half hours.*

reject Ⓐ *v* to refuse to accept, use, or believe someone or something • *The editor rejected the story because the journalist used inaccurate information .*

research Ⓐ *v* to find information about something • *Reporters have to research their stories carefully before they write.*

solution *n* an answer to a problem • *There is no easy solution to the problem of poverty.*

survivor Ⓐ *n* a person who lives after experiencing a dangerous situation • *CNN reported there were several survivors of the airplane crash.*

transform Ⓐ *v* to completely change something or someone • *Online news has transformed traditional television newscasts.*

upload *v* to move electronic information from one computer system to another • *The reporter uploaded her photos from her smart phone to her computer, and then printed them.*

value *n* the amount of money something is worth • *The value of the company increased sharply because its products were very popular.*

worthwhile *adj* useful, important enough to do • *Most people consider nursing to be a worthwhile career.*

UNIT 1 • READING 3

Citizen Journalism

attack *v* to try to hurt or damage something or someone with violence • *The news reported that the army attacked an enemy base last night.*

audience *n* the group of people who are watching or listening to something • *The audience for television news programs is very large.*

concept Ⓐ *n* an idea, often for something different • *CNN introduced the concept of twenty-four-hour news.*

control *n* the power or ability to make someone or something do what you want • *Editors have control over the stories printed in their newspapers.*

devastation *n* very serious damage • *People used their cell phones to take pictures of the devastation caused by the storm.*

editor Ⓐ *n* a person who is in charge of something that will be printed or broadcast, such as a newspaper or a television show • *The editor carefully checked the reporter's story.*

execution *n* the act of killing someone as a punishment • *Many news organizations refused to print pictures of the execution.*

UNIT 1 • READING 4

Ethical Reporting

addict *n* a person who cannot stop doing something that causes harm, especially taking drugs • *Some doctors believe addicts need medical help before they can stop taking drugs.*

arrest *v* to use legal authority to catch someone and take them to be charged with a criminal act • *The police arrested three men and charged them with selling stolen computers.*

benefit Ⓐ *v* to have a good effect • *Good access to the news benefits society.*

celebrity *n* a famous person • *Magazines and newspapers are full of stories about celebrities.*

complain *v* to say that you are not happy or satisfied with someone or something • *The singer complained that the reporters were following her everywhere.*

confess *v* to say that you have done something bad or wrong • *The man confessed to stealing the money.*

document Ⓐ *n* an official written paper • *Before I started my job, I had to produce several documents, including my driver's license and my passport.*

fake *adj* not real • *He was arrested for having a fake passport.*

illegal Ⓐ *adj* against the law • *In most countries, it is illegal to print lies about people.* OPPOSITE: **legal** *adj*

mentally ill Ⓐ *adj phr* having problems related to your mind • *Research shows that many homeless people are* **mentally ill**.

poisonous *adj* containing a substance that will cause illness or death • *The reporter discovered that the factory was emptying* **poisonous** *chemicals into the river.*

pressure *n* the feeling of responsibility, stress, or worry • *There is a lot of* **pressure** *on reporters to make sure their stories are accurate.*

pretend *v* to behave as if something is real when it is not • *The journalist* **pretended** *that he was a doctor in order to get into the hospital.*

privacy *n* the right to keep personal matters secret • *People become upset when reporters don't respect their* **privacy**.

resign *v* to give up a job • *The company manager* **resigned** *because he got a better job in a different city.*

security Ⓐ *n* safety and protection • *The report showed that more* **security** *is needed in government buildings.*

sensational *adj* very exciting • *The* **sensational** *news about the celebrity was on the front page of several newspapers.*

shocked *adj* surprised by a sudden, unpleasant, or unexpected event • *People all around the world were* **shocked** *to hear about the huge earthquake in Japan.*

UNIT 2 • READING 1

Education Around the World

academic Ⓐ *adj* connected with education and learning by study and thought, not practical or technical training • *The program offers many* **academic** *subjects, such as math and physics.*

advantage *n* something that helps you have a greater chance of success • *Learning a second language is an* **advantage** *in today's global economy.* OPPOSITE: **disadvantage** *n*

compulsory *adj* necessary to do because of a rule or law • *In most countries, education is* **compulsory** *for children.*

contribute to Ⓐ *v* to give money, time, or help for something • *Each year, business leaders* **contribute** *a lot of money* **to** *education.*

curriculum *n* the subjects that are taught in a school or university or in a particular course of study • *The school's* **curriculum** *includes English and Chinese.*

development *n* growth; the process of becoming more modern and advanced • *Education plays an important role in a country's* **development**.

elsewhere *adv* in another place or in other places • *Schools in the capital city had computers, but* **elsewhere**, *children had no access to technology.*

emphasize Ⓐ *v* to state or show that something is especially important • *My parents* **emphasized** *the importance of studying.*

expand Ⓐ *v* to increase in size or amount • *Online education is* **expanding** *as more people are able to connect to the Internet.*

fee Ⓐ *n* the money you must pay for a service • *Many universities charge an extra* **fee** *to use computer labs.*

funding Ⓐ *n* money given by an organization or government to pay for a particular activity, such as research, building, or starting a new business • *The university had* **funding** *from the government to pay for its new library.*

individual Ⓐ *n* one person, or a particular person • *Most people believe that every* **individual** *has the right to a good education.*

industrialization *n* the process of building factories and producing goods in a city or country • **Industrialization** *is changing the way people live in India.*

meet the needs *v phr* to have or do enough of what is required • *Education today must* **meet the needs** *of the twenty-first century.*

opportunity *n* the possibility of doing something • *All children should have the* **opportunity** *to go to school.*

productivity *n* the rate at which a country or company makes things • *Research shows that national* **productivity** *increases when citizens are well educated.*

scores *n* the number of correct answers on a test • *The teacher told the students to check their* **scores**; *everyone who got 75 percent or above passed.*

vary Ⓐ *v* to change in some way or cause similar things to differ • *The cost of higher education* **varies** *from one country to another.*

UNIT 2 • READING 2

Testing in Education

argue *v* to strongly disagree in talking or discussing something • *The two students* **argued** *about who should pay for the meal.* **argument** *n* a strong verbal disagreement • *I had an argument with my friend.*

cheating *n* behaving in a dishonest way in order to win or gain something • **Cheating** *is not allowed in school.*

colony *n* a country that is ruled by another country • *Hong Kong used to be a* **colony** *of Great Britain.*

compare *v* to look for similarities in two or more things or people • *The teacher asked the students to* **compare** *the high school system of their country to that of another country.*

competition *n* an organized event in which people try to win something • *The school held a* **competition** *for the best singer.* **compete** *v* to try to get or win something • *Students who want to* **compete** *to get into the best schools need good test scores.* **competitive** *adj* having a strong desire to be better than others • *He will be successful because he is a very* **competitive** *person.*

consider *v* to spend time thinking about a decision • *It is important to* **consider** *students' interests as well as their test scores.*

efficient *adj* able to work well without wasting time or money • *The testing center was very **efficient**; it took only one hour to take the test and get the results.* **efficiency** *n* the ability to work well without wasting time, energy, or money • *Computers have improved the **efficiency** of businesses everywhere.*

enormous Ⓐ *adj* very large; huge • *A college education can have an **enormous** effect on a person's future.*

evaluate Ⓐ *v* to judge the quality of something • *Tests are one way to **evaluate** a student's progress.* **evaluation** *n* the act of judging something or someone • *At the end of the semester, students turn in **evaluations** of their teachers.*

factor Ⓐ *n* a fact or situation that influences a result • *Test results are an important **factor** in student admissions for most colleges and universities.*

measure *v* to evaluate or judge • *Tests are one way to **measure** how well students understand the information.*

obtain Ⓐ *v* to get something • *Students must **obtain** permission to leave school early.*

performance *n* the way you do something, especially how successful you are • *Her **performance** in class was not good enough to pass.* **perform** *v* to do a job or a piece of work • *She **performed** very well on the test.*

policy Ⓐ *n* guidelines; a set of rules • *The school has a strict attendance **policy**.*

profitable *adj* resulting in a benefit • *The restaurant was so **profitable** that the owner decided to open a second one.*

UNIT 2 • READING 3

Alternative Education

alternative Ⓐ *adj* not traditional; not the usual way of doing something • *Homeschooling is an example of **alternative** education.*

approach Ⓐ *n* a method or way of doing something • *People have different **approaches** to how to prepare for a test.*

approximate Ⓐ *adj* almost exact • *School officials reported that about 11 schools had cheated; the number was **approximate** as officials were still investigating the problem.*

concentrate on Ⓐ *v* to give a lot of attention to something; to give thought and effort to something • *At school I **concentrated on** science because I wanted to be a doctor.*

concerned *adj* worried • *My parents are **concerned** I will not get into the college I want to go to.*

criticize *v* to say someone or something is bad or wrong in some way • *The teacher **criticized** the student's writing.*

design Ⓐ *v* to make a plan for something; to make a drawing that shows how something will work • *Students **designed** a new building as part of their final exam.*

dissatisfied *adj* not pleased with something • *The teacher was **dissatisfied** with the test results.*

especially *adv* particularly; emphasizing the importance of something • *The teacher was **especially** happy with the students' scores because the exam was very difficult.*

estimate Ⓐ *v* to judge or calculate approximately how large something is • *Experts **estimate** that the number of students who want to go to university will increase by 50 percent in the next few years.*

hands-on *adj* learning by doing something rather than reading or studying about it • *The engineering course is very **hands-on**; students get to design and build their own projects.*

high-tech *adj* using a lot of modern equipment, especially computers • *The new library is very **high-tech**; students check out books online.*

likely *adv* expected to happen • *It is **likely** that more students in the future will take online classes.*

location Ⓐ *n* a specific place • *The map showed the **location** of the library.*

obsolete *adj* no longer used • *Technology changes so quickly that older computers can quickly become **obsolete**.*

shortage *n* a situation where there is not enough of something • *There is a **shortage** of math teachers in the United States.*

statistics Ⓐ *n* a collection of numerical facts • ***Statistics** show that in Hong Kong there is a lack of university places for high school graduates.*

workplace *n* a place where people do their jobs • *Employees are happier when their **workplace** is comfortable.*

UNIT 2 • READING 4

Skills for the Twenty-First Century

accurate Ⓐ *adj* correct; without any mistake • *The report was **accurate**; there were no mistakes.*

analyze Ⓐ *v* to study something very carefully • *The scientist **analyzed** the results of the experiment.*

collaborate *v* to work together with someone to achieve something • *The two scientists **collaborated** on the research.*

creative Ⓐ *adj* using original and unusual ideas; imaginative • *The students got high scores because their presentation was very **creative**.*

curiosity *n* a strong desire to know or learn about something • *Children have a natural **curiosity** about the world.*

current *adj* at the present time; now • *Under **current** law, a student must be eighteen to enter this school.*

effectively *adv* done well; producing the intended result • *The political leader spoke clearly and **effectively**, so most people agreed with her.*

encounter Ⓐ *v* to experience something, usually a problem, that you have to deal with • *We **encountered** several problems when we began to homeschool our children.*

encourage *v* to help someone feel confident and be able to do something • *Students liked the math teacher because he always **encouraged** them to do well.*

essential *adj* very important • *It is **essential** that all students prepare carefully for their university admission tests.*

expert Ⓐ *n* a person who knows a lot about a particular subject • *The university employed an **expert** to help find a solution to the problem of increasing tuition costs.*

incorporate Ⓐ *v* to include or bring together as part of something • *She **incorporated** several ideas into her final design.*

investor Ⓐ *n* a person who provides money to a business in order to help it grow and make a profit • *In order to make our business grow, we needed several **investors**.*

launch *v* to begin a new project or business • *We're planning to **launch** a new Internet service next month.*

lend *v* to give someone something that you expect will be returned soon • *The teacher **lent** the new student a textbook.*

range Ⓐ *n* a group of things that are different, but belong to the same general type • *The teacher had books on a wide **range** of subjects.*

region Ⓐ *n* a large geographical area • *There are still a few **regions** in the world that do not have Internet access.*

require Ⓐ *v* to need something • *If you **require** help with your homework, please ask.*

UNIT 3 • READING 1

Supply and Demand in the Global Economy

affect Ⓐ *v* to influence someone or something • *The price of oil **affects** everyone.*

approximately Ⓐ *adv* about; a little more or a little less • *The price of milk increased by **approximately** 30 percent.*

consumption Ⓐ *n* the act of eating or drinking, or the amount of something you eat or drink • ***Consumption** of tea has increased worldwide.*

crop *n* a plant that is grown in large amounts on a farm • *A storm destroyed this year's **crop** of corn.*

effect *n* a result; an impact • *The rising cost of gas had a negative **effect** on global business.*

energy Ⓐ *n* the power from fuel or electricity to make things work • *Oil fuels a lot of the world's **energy**.*

event *n* something that happens, especially something important • *Graduating college has been one of the most important **events** in my life.*

fuel *n* a substance such as gas or oil that produces heat or energy • ***Fuel** prices increased last month.*

illustrate Ⓐ *v* to explain something by providing examples or pictures • *The fact that the United States imports a lot of Japanese cars **illustrates** the popularity of these vehicles.*

ingredient *n* a part of something, usually food • *Wheat is an **ingredient** of many basic food items such as bread.*

major Ⓐ *adj* very important or very serious • *Traffic is a **major** problem in the city center.*

note *v* to pay careful attention to something • *It is important to **note** that the cost of corn is rising quickly.*

plant *n* a large industrial building or factory • *The **plant** produces electricity.*

previously Ⓐ *adv* before a particular time • *We now use technology that was not **previously** available.*

protest *v* to show that you strongly disagree with something • *People went into the streets to **protest** the high cost of food.*

skyrocket *v* to quickly increase by a large amount • *The cost of oil **skyrocketed** in 2008.*

surplus *n* an amount of something that is more than is needed or used • *The country produced a **surplus** of corn last year.*

survive Ⓐ *v* to continue to live, especially after an accident or illness; to exist • *People need clean drinking water in order to **survive**.*

UNIT 3 • READING 2

The Workforce of the Twenty-First Century

attract *v* to make someone interested in something • *The company **attracted** new employees by offering good salaries.* **attraction** *n* something that makes people interested in something or someone • *The company's location is a strong **attraction**.* **attractive** *adj* good enough to make people interested • *A skilled workforce made it **attractive** for the company to move to India.*

blame *v* to say that someone or something is responsible for something bad • *My supervisor **blamed** me for losing the documents.*

challenge Ⓐ *n* a task or activity that needs time and effort in order to do it successfully • *New immigrants to a country face many **challenges**; learning a new language is perhaps the greatest.*

create Ⓐ *v* to make something new • *You need a lot of different skills as well as hard work to successfully **create** a new business.*

developing *adj* becoming modern or more advanced • *Technology is helping the economies of **developing** countries to grow more quickly.*

employment *n* work for which you are paid • *Most students quickly found **employment** after they graduated.* **employ** *v* to pay someone to work for you • *A new company came to the city and **employed** over 100 workers.*

flexible Ⓐ *adj* 1. able to easily change to fit a new situation • *Students like working here because the hours are **flexible**.* **flexibility** *n* the ability to change according to a new situation • ***Flexibility** is an important skill in today's workplace.*

hire *v* to employ someone to work for you • *The company* **hired** *a new engineer.*

manufacturing *n* the process of making things in a factory • **Manufacturing** *has increased recently in many developing countries.* **manufacture** *v* to make something in a factory • *This company* **manufactures** *televisions.*

practice *n* something that is regularly done • *When it moved overseas, the company changed its business* **practices.**

precisely Ⓐ *adv* exactly; accurately • *Please explain* **precisely** *what happened.*

prevent *v* to stop something from happening or someone from doing something • *Heavy rain* **prevented** *the farmers from planting their crops.* **prevention** *n* the act of stopping something or someone from doing something • *The* **prevention** *of crime is an important part of police work.*

specialist *n* a person who has expert skill or knowledge in a particular subject • *The company hired a computer* **specialist** *to improve their website.*

willing *adj* eager and happy to do something • *I am* **willing** *to work hard in order to be successful at this job.*

workforce *n* the total number of people who work for a company or within a country • *India's* **workforce** *is growing as more jobs are created in that country.*

UNIT 3 • READING 3

Communication Technology in Business

constant Ⓐ *adj* continuous; without stopping • *CNN provides a* **constant** *stream of news.*

consumer Ⓐ *n* a person who buys goods and services to use • *Even though smart phones are expensive,* **consumers** *continue to buy them.*

distribute Ⓐ *v* to give something to each of the people in a large group • *The government* **distributed** *food and water after the hurricane.*

face-to-face *adj phr* being in the same place with someone; being able to look directly at someone • *Some of the class was online, but most of it was* **face-to-face** *so the students got to work together in the classroom.*

innovation Ⓐ *n* a new idea or a new method of doing something • *The university's engineering school is a center of* **innovation.**

interaction Ⓐ *n* the activity of communicating with other people • *The school encouraged* **interaction** *between teachers and parents.*

key *n* the most important thing • *Education is the* **key** *to success.*

member *n* a person who is part of a group or team • *How many* **members** *does your team have?*

mining *n* the process of digging substances such as coal and gold from the ground • **Mining** *expanded during the nineteenth century.*

participation Ⓐ *n* the act of taking part or being involved in something • *The company valued public* **participation** *in developing new products.*

promote Ⓐ *v* to help something become successful • *He designed an advertisement to* **promote** *the new movie.*

prosperity *n* the condition of having money and being successful • *An educated, trained workforce greatly contributes to a country's* **prosperity.**

reward *n* something given in exchange for good work • *The store gives a* **reward** *to the employee with the best sales record each week.*

role Ⓐ *n* the position or job that someone or something has in a particular situation • *Manufacturing can play an important* **role** *in a country's economy.*

share *v* to give or tell something to someone else • *The manager* **shared** *his knowledge of the company's history with the new employee.*

suggestion *n* an idea or a plan someone offers • *Does anyone have a* **suggestion** *for how to solve this problem?*

task Ⓐ *n* a particular thing or job you need to do • *The firefighter had the dangerous* **task** *of rescuing the child from a burning building.*

team Ⓐ *n* people who work or play together as a group • *A* **team** *of four worked on the project.*

UNIT 3 • READING 4

Business and Sustainability

climate *n* general weather conditions in a place or region • *Most scientists agree that global warming is changing the earth's* **climate.**

damage *v* to physically harm someone or something • *Some chemicals* **damage** *the environment when released into the air.*

drought *n* a long period of time with no rain • *The* **drought** *destroyed the rice crop.*

emit *v* to send out light, sound, heat, gas, or other substance • *Hybrid cars are better for the environment because they* **emit** *less carbon dioxide than regular cars.*

eventually Ⓐ *adv* in the end; finally • **Eventually** *there will be Internet access worldwide.*

flood *n* a large amount of water that takes over what is usually dry land • *The storm caused* **floods** *in several parts of the city.*

hybrid *n* something that is a mix of two things • *One of Toyota's best selling cars is a* **hybrid** – *it uses gas and electricity.*

image Ⓐ *n* an idea people have of someone or something • *I had a clear* **image** *of life in Hong Kong.*

level *n* the amount or position of something • *The water* **level** *in the river rose after the storm; people were worried about floods.*

pollute *v* to harm the environment • *Factories that burn fossil fuels **pollute** the environment.*

primarily Ⓐ *adv* mainly; mostly • *People who live on the island make their money **primarily** from visitors who spend money in hotels and restaurants.*

reduce *v* to make something smaller in size or amount • *The company **reduced** the price of their computers in order to encourage more people to buy them.*

renewable *adj* if something is renewable, it can be used and easily replaced • *Wind power is an example of **renewable** energy.*

resource Ⓐ *n* something such as land, water, or minerals that exists in a country and can be used to increase its wealth • *It is important to take care of natural **resources**, such as forests and rivers.*

run out (of) *v* to use all of something so there is nothing left • *The business closed because it **ran out of** money.*

solar *adj* from the sun • *More countries in the world are using **solar** power to provide energy to homes.*

tropical *adj* having the characteristics of the hottest places on earth; very hot and humid • *Thailand has a **tropical** climate and often experiences very heavy storms.*

use up *v* to finish the available supply of something • *We are **using up** the world's oil supply.*

UNIT 4 • READING 1

Population Trends

according to *prep phr* as shown by something or as said by someone • ***According to** city leaders, population growth is slowing.*

agriculture *n* farming • ***Agriculture** is an important part of the country's economy.*

demography *n* the study of human populations • ***Demography** helps us understand future needs of countries.*

existing *adj* current; present • *Under **existing** law, families in some areas of China are encouraged to have just one child.*

explosion *n* a large and sudden increase • *Better health care has led to an **explosion** in world population.*

figure *n* a number • *Population **figures** show that developing countries are growing faster than developed countries.*

financial Ⓐ *adj* relating to money • *The city had **financial** problems because it was growing so quickly.*

hygiene *n* the practice of keeping yourself and things around you clean in order to prevent disease • *We have seen less disease since people learned more about the importance of **hygiene**.*

penalty *n* a punishment for breaking a law or a rule • *The **penalty** for speeding is $100.*

population *n* the number of people in a city, country, or other area • *The world's **population** is growing.*

replace *v* to take the place of someone or something • *The city **replaced** the old school with a new one.*

restrict Ⓐ *v* to limit the size or number of something • *The university **restricted** the number of new students.*

retired *adj* no longer working, usually after reaching a certain age • *The number of **retired** people in the country is growing.*

single *adj* not married • *More women today choose to be **single** than they did in the past.*

specific Ⓐ *adj* detailed • *Good writers use **specific** examples in order to support more general main ideas.*

support *v* to provide money, food, and other things necessary for life • *The children had to work because their parents could not **support** them.*

take seriously *v phr* to believe someone is important and deserves attention • *You need to **take** her more **seriously**; she has a lot of very good ideas.*

trend Ⓐ *n* the way a situation is developing or changing • *There is a general **trend** of people moving into cities.*

UNIT 4 • READING 2

Global Migration

allow *v* to make it possible to do something • *New laws in Europe **allow** people to move easily between countries.*

border *n* a political line that divides one country from another • *You usually need a passport in order to cross a **border**.*

homeland *n* the country where you were born • *Juan left his **homeland** when he was a child.*

income Ⓐ *n* money you earn from doing work • *The average **income** in developed countries is higher than in developing countries.*

intend (to) *v* to have as a plan to do • *I **intend to** graduate and then move to Canada.* **intention** *n* something you plan to do • *The government's **intention** was to encourage business growth by lowering taxes.*

issue Ⓐ *n* a serious problem which requires thought • *Pollution is a global **issue**.*

labor Ⓐ *n* workers, especially those who work with their hands • *When there is a **labor** shortage, a country tries to attract workers from other countries.*

migration Ⓐ *n* the movement of people from one area to another • *During the nineteenth century, there was a lot of **migration** to the cities.* **migrate** Ⓐ *v* to move from one area to another • *In the summer, farmworkers **migrate** to the north to find work.*

origin *n* the beginning or cause of something; the way something began • *The **origin** of this language is not known.* **original** *adj* in the first or earliest form • *My **original** plan to move to London changed when I got a better job offer.* **originate** *v* to come from, or to begin as • *Jazz music **originated** in North America and is now popular worldwide.*

permit *v* to allow something • *Most countries **permit** visitors to stay for several weeks.* **permission** *n* the act of allowing someone to do something • *I had **permission** to work in that country for one year.*

prosperous *adj* successful; making a lot of money • *As immigrants become more **prosperous**, other family members join them in the new country.*

resident Ⓐ *n* a person who lives in a specific place • *Mexico City **residents** complain about the traffic in that city.*

typical *adj* showing the normal or expected characteristics of a group • *In the nineteenth century, a **typical** Chinese immigrant in the United States was young, single, and male.*

wealthy *adj* rich • *People usually migrate from poor countries to **wealthy** countries.* **wealth** *n* all of the money and property something or someone has • *A country's **wealth** is connected to its natural resources.*

widespread Ⓐ *adj* happening or existing in many places • *The practice of moving to another country for work is **widespread** in Europe.*

UNIT 4 • READING 3

The Growth of Cities

community Ⓐ *n* all the people who live in a particular area • ***Communities** in the south part of the city worked together to reduce crime.*

critical *adj* very important • *In many growing cities, there is a **critical** need for clean water.*

evolve Ⓐ *v* to gradually develop over time • *Over the years, the small village **evolved** to become a large and busy city.*

harbor *n* a protected area of water next to land where ships can safely stay • *Hong Kong has one of the busiest **harbors** in the world.*

internal Ⓐ *adj* inside a person or a place • *When the bank found it had lost money, the manager started an **internal** investigation.*

model *n* a drawing or example of the way something is done or organized • *The author offered a **model** for developing older areas of the city.*

pattern *n* the particular way something is done or organized • *Many European cities follow the **pattern** of the rich people living close to the business district.*

rural *adj* relating to the countryside rather than the city • *Life in **rural** areas is generally more peaceful than life in the city.*

sector Ⓐ *n* one part of an area • *The industrial **sector** is several miles away from the city center.*

series Ⓐ *n* a group of similar things, one following another • *The city includes a **series** of small communities.*

services *n* things people need in order to live comfortably such as water, electricity, and transportation • *The city tried to provide **services** to all its residents.*

settlement *n* an area where a number of people move to and stay • *The first **settlements** developed near the river.*

sociologist *n* a person who studies how people live in a society • *The **sociologist** studied the effects of growing up in the city.*

suburb *n* an area of towns with homes and small businesses near a large city • *Houses are usually bigger in the **suburbs** than in the city.*

surround *v* to be all around something • *Apartments **surrounded** the park.*

trade *v* to buy, sell, or exchange things • *Cities began as centers where people **traded** things.*

urban *adj* relating to cities • *People migrate to **urban** areas for work.*

vibrant *adj* full of life; exciting • *The restaurants, clubs, and theaters make downtown a **vibrant** area.*

UNIT 4 • READING 4

Challenges Facing the World's Cities

bury *v* to put a dead body into the ground • *My father was **buried** in London.*

cemetery *n* an area of land where dead people are buried • *The **cemetery** was a quiet, peaceful place.*

consequences Ⓐ *n* results or effects of something that has happened • *Losing a job can have serious **consequences** for the whole family including the children.*

cycle Ⓐ *n* a series of events that keep repeating themselves • *It is difficult to break the poverty **cycle**; children who grow up in poverty often remain poor as adults.*

face *v* to deal with a difficult situation or problem • *Immigrants **face** many challenges when they move to a new country.*

generation Ⓐ *n* all the people about the same age in a family or society • *Three **generations** lived in the house: grandparents, parents, and children.*

huge *adj* very big; enormous • *In many cities, there is a **huge** difference between the rich and the poor.*

inequality *n* a condition of being different and not equal, often in ways that are not fair • *The differences in school funding result in **inequality** in educational opportunities.*

nutrition *n* the body's process of taking in and using food needed for good health • *Good **nutrition** is very important for young children.*

persist Ⓐ *v* to continue to exist or try to do something in spite of difficulties • *Poor nutrition and lack of education **persists** in some areas of the world.*

poverty *n* the state of being very poor • *Many people in the squatter settlements live in terrible **poverty**.*

provide *v* to make something available • *The city **provided** clean water for all its residents.*

rate *n* the speed or number of times at which something happens • *We need to lower the crime **rate** in the city center.*

respiratory *adj* related to breathing • *The patient had a **respiratory** illness.*

similar Ⓐ *adj* almost the same • *Immigrants in different countries face **similar** problems.*

tomb *n* a small building where someone is buried • *He was buried in the family **tomb** at the local cemetery.*

unique Ⓐ *adj* very special; the only one of its type • *The Eiffel Tower in Paris is a **unique** structure.*

victim *n* a person who is hurt or killed by something or someone • *Sadly, thousands of people each year become **victims** of crime.*

The Design of Everyday Objects

basic *adj* simple; most important • *What is the most **basic** rule of design?*

carve *v* to cut something into a particular shape, especially wood or stone • *He **carved** a beautiful bird from a piece of wood.*

complex Ⓐ *adj* having many parts, and therefore usually difficult to understand • *Designing comfortable furniture is a **complex** process.*

conflict (with) Ⓐ *v* to oppose or be difficult for two things to work together • *The design of the room **conflicted with** its use; it looked more like a living room than an office.*

confusing *adj* difficult to understand • *The instructions for setting the watch were so **confusing**, I couldn't use it.*

decorated *adj* made to look attractive • *My sister gave me a beautiful, **decorated** lamp.*

identity Ⓐ *n* who someone is • *The **identity** of this designer is not known.*

leather *n* the skin of an animal used as a material to make things • *The car seats were made of soft **leather**.*

luxury *adj* very comfortable and expensive • *The **luxury** version of the car had an amazing sound system, but I couldn't afford it.*

owner *n* a person who legally has something • *Who is the **owner** of that car?*

pay attention to *v phr* to do something carefully • *Clothes designers need to **pay attention to** the colors they choose.*

persuade *v* to make someone do something by giving good reasons • *The salesperson **persuaded** me to buy a new phone.*

pleasure *n* enjoyment; happiness • *My new painting gave me great **pleasure**.*

prefer *v* to choose or want one thing rather than another • *I **prefer** watching movies on my computer rather than on television.*

principle Ⓐ *n* a rule that influences how something is made or designed • *Steve Jobs believed appearance was an essential **principle** of design.*

store *v* to keep something for use at a later date • *A computer **stores** a huge amount of information.*

symbol Ⓐ *n* something that is used to represent something else • *The letter x is the mathematical **symbol** for multiplication.*

visual Ⓐ *adj* related to seeing • *Photography is a **visual** art.*

Ergonomics

adjustable *adj* able to be changed by small amounts • *The car seat is **adjustable**.* **adjust** Ⓐ *v* to make a small change to something • *I **adjusted** the chair in order to make it more comfortable.* **adjustment** Ⓐ *n* a small change you make to something • *The designer made a small **adjustment** to the model.*

device Ⓐ *n* an object or machine designed for a particular purpose • *New cars are designed with many safety **devices**.*

equipment Ⓐ *n* the set of tools or things that are needed for a particular activity • *Do you have all the **equipment** you need to fix the computer?*

height *n* a measure of how high or tall someone or something is • *The **height** of a desk is important.*

injury Ⓐ *n* the physical harm or damage done to a person or animal • *Workplace **injuries** happen every day.* **injure** Ⓐ *v* to harm someone or something • *He **injured** himself while playing soccer.* **injured** Ⓐ *adj* physically harmed • *The **injured** people were taken to the hospital.*

involve Ⓐ *v* to include someone or something in an activity • *Ergonomics **involves** thinking about how the body works.*

joint *n* a place in the body where two bones meet • *My hip **joints** hurt when I sit too long at my desk.*

lean *v* to bend forward, back, or to the side • *I had to **lean** forward to be able to see the computer screen.*

miss *v* to not be present at an activity or an event • *Each year, thousands of people **miss** work because they have hurt their backs.*

muscle *n* the tissue attached to bones in your body that makes you move • *I hurt a **muscle** in my leg.*

posture *n* the way in which a person holds their body when standing or sitting • *Poor **posture** may result in aches and pains.*

relax Ⓐ *v* to become calm and comfortable • *I **relax** by listening to music.* **relaxation** Ⓐ *n* the state of being calm, comfortable and not worried • *A vacation is a good opportunity for **relaxation**.*

risk *v* to do something where there is the possibility of being hurt • *He **risked** his life helping another man escape from the fire.* **risk** *n* the possibility of danger • *The firefighter took a huge **risk** when she went into the burning building.* **risky** *adj* • *This might be a **risky** business investment.*

select Ⓐ *v* to choose something or someone • *He **selected** the more expensive computer desk because it was well-designed.* **selection** Ⓐ *n* the activity of choosing something or someone • *The **selection** of a new company president is a long process.*

strain *n* something that causes worry or an injury • *Working too hard puts a **strain** on your health..*

The Design of Living Space

achieve Ⓐ *v* to gain something by effort or skill • *I have worked hard and **achieved** a lot during my career.*

balance *n* the state in which opposite qualities are of equal importance • *It's difficult to achieve **balance** in your life when you have to work and study.*

calm *adj* relaxed; not anxious • *The white walls and soft music made me feel very **calm**.*

combination *n* two or more things put together • *The apartment was decorated in a **combination** of interesting colors.*

dresser *n* a piece of furniture with drawers used for storing clothes • *I placed the **dresser** next to my bed.*

guidelines Ⓐ *n* rules or instructions about how to do something • *The designer gave me some general **guidelines** about how to decorate my home.*

interior *n* the inside of something • *The **interior** of the house was warm and inviting.*

masculine *adj* having qualities traditionally associated with men • *Blue is usually considered to be a **masculine** color.*

organized *adj* planned and arranged carefully • *The student's notes were very **organized**.*

passion *n* very strong emotion or feeling about something • *I have a **passion** for dance.*

personality *n* your qualities and character, especially the way they behave with others • *Consuelo has a friendly **personality**.*

reflect *v* to show or represent something • *The brightly painted walls **reflected** John's happy personality.*

represent *v* to be a sign of something • *In Chinese culture, red **represents** good luck.*

stability Ⓐ *n* the state of remaining the same; not moving or changing • *People who value **stability** often choose the same color and style of clothes.*

stimulating *adj* causing excitement and interest • *I took a very **stimulating** interior design class.*

stranger *n* a person you don't know or have never met • *Don't allow a **stranger** into your home.*

style Ⓐ *n* a way of doing something that is typical of a person • *His fashion **style** was unusual; he only wore black leather clothes.*

three-dimensional Ⓐ *adj* related to height, depth, and width • *The movie was **three-dimensional** so it was very real and exciting to watch.*

Fashion

acknowledge Ⓐ *v* to recognize the existence or the work done by someone • *The speaker **acknowledged** the committee's hard work.*

adopt *v* to begin using or to take something as your own • *Designers **adopted** hip-hop fashion and began to mass-produce it.*

appeal *v* to seem attractive or interesting • *The designer's fashions **appealed** to my sense of style.*

aware (of) Ⓐ *v* to know about something • *We were **aware** of the problem.*

bind *v* to tie very tightly • *Please use the brown string to **bind** that stack of newspapers.*

class *n* a group of people within society who have the same social and economic position • *Most people I know think of themselves as middle **class**.*

dominant Ⓐ *adj* strongest; most important • *Tommy Hilfiger is a **dominant** fashion designer today.*

heel *n* the back part of a shoe • *Some celebrities like to wear very high **heels**.*

jewelry *n* decorative items worn on the body, such as rings or necklaces • ***Jewelry** has been an important part of fashion for thousands of years.*

leisure *n* the time when you do not have to work • *People today do not have much **leisure** – they work too hard.*

message *n* information or an idea that someone is trying to communicate • *The clothes you wear send a **message** about who you are.*

military Ⓐ *n* an official, organized group that protects a country, such as an army or a navy • *Special uniforms are mass-produced for the **military**.*

normal Ⓐ *adj* ordinary; usual • *It was an **normal** Monday morning; I got up and went to class..*

outsider *n* a person who is not part of a group • *I was a lonely **outsider** in high school.*

prison *n* a place where criminals are kept • *More **prisons** are built every year.*

public *n* people in general • *The **public** likes to read about new fashions.*

survey Ⓐ *n* a set of questions people are asked in order to gather information • *A recent **survey** claims that most people expect they will work until their seventies.*

tough *adj* strong and difficult to defeat • *Some people choose clothes they think will make them look **tough**.*

Brain Development and Function

back and forth *adv phr* moving in one direction and then in the opposite direction • *She moved **back and forth** to the music.*

consist of Ⓐ *v* to be made of various things • *The brain **consists of** several parts, including the brain stem and the cerebral cortex.*

consistent Ⓐ *adj* always happening or behaving in the same way • *Progress is not always **consistent** in the field of medicine.*

diagnose *v* to identify and name the disease or medical problem • *The doctor **diagnosed** the illness as cancer.*

function Ⓐ *n* the purpose of something or the way it works • *The **function** of this x-ray machine is to help the doctor diagnose brain injuries.*

indicate Ⓐ *v* to show • *Tests **indicated** that his behavior was the result of a brain injury.*

involved in Ⓐ *adj* included in an activity • *The doctor is **involved in** a research study to find out more about the brain.*

keep track of *v phr* to follow the progress of something; to be aware of something • *It's important to **keep track of** your grades.*

nervous system *n* the brain and all the nerves in the body that make movement and feeling possible • *Cells called neurons communicate information throughout the **nervous system**.*

neuron *n* a nerve or brain cell • *The brain contains millions of **neurons**.*

patient *n* a person who is receiving medical treatment • ***Patients** with brain injuries require a lot of care.*

prior to Ⓐ *adv phr* before • *It was much more difficult to understand brain function **prior to** the development of x-ray technology.*

process Ⓐ *v* to deal with something using a specific set of actions • *Computers can **process** an enormous amount of information in less than a second.*

remain *v* to stay the same • *The doctor said I should **remain** in bed for another two days.*

resemble *v* to be similar to someone or something • *The two sides of the brain **resemble** each other in size.*

structure Ⓐ *n* the way in which a system is arranged or organized • *The human body is a complicated **structure**.*

surge *n* a sudden increase • *Babies experience a growth **surge** at three months.*

treat *v* to find ways to improve the condition of a sick or injured person • *Different doctors **treat** the same illness in different ways.*

The Teenage Brain

adolescence *n* the period of time when a young person changes from a child to an adult • ***Adolescence** can be a difficult time, as the body is going through many changes.*

adulthood Ⓐ *n* the period of time when a person is fully grown and mature • ***Adulthood** is less stressful than adolescence, but it brings many new responsibilities.*

certain *adj* sure of something; know something is true • *The parents were **certain** that something was wrong with their daughter.*

coordination Ⓐ *n* the ability to make separate parts work together well • *You need very good physical **coordination** in order to play tennis.*

crucial Ⓐ *adj* essential; very important • *It is **crucial** for teenagers to eat well and get enough sleep.*

examine *v* to look at something very carefully • *The doctor **examined** his patient carefully.*

hormone *n* one of several chemicals in the blood that control processes in the body, such as growth • ***Hormones** affect the way you feel.*

independent *adj* not needing to ask other people for help • *I am very **independent**. **independence** n the freedom and ability to make decisions and take care of yourself • *Teenagers want to have more **independence** from their parents.*

judgment *n* a decision that you form after thinking about something • *Sometimes she does not show good **judgment**. **judge** v to decide about something after thinking carefully • *After losing the sight in one eye, he was less able to accurately **judge** distances.*

lack of *n* a shortage; absence of something • *Teenagers who suffer from a **lack of** sleep do not perform well in school.*

mature Ⓐ *v* to develop physically and mentally • *Boys and girls tend to **mature** at different ages. **maturity** Ⓐ n physical and mental development • *It takes **maturity** to be a good leader. **mature** Ⓐ adj sensible; mentally developed • *Although he was only fourteen, he was very **mature**.*

related (to) *adj* connected to something • *Poor study skills is often **related to** lack of sleep.*

respond Ⓐ *v* to say or do something as a reaction to something else • *The young girl **responded** very well to the medicine. **response** Ⓐ n something said or done in reaction to something else • *I applied to university, and I am now waiting for a **response**.*

stay up *v* to remain awake • *He **stayed up** late the night before the test.*

stressful Ⓐ *adj* making you worry a lot • *Taking tests can be very **stressful**. **stress** n continuous feelings of worry caused by difficulties in life • *Stress can lead to health problems. **stress** Ⓐ v to worry about something • *I'm **stressing** about the final exam tomorrow.*

The Male and Female Brain

biology *n* the study of living things • *Biology can help us understand differences in how individuals think.*

capacity Ⓐ *n* the ability to do something • *Her capacity to remember huge amounts of information is amazing.*

collect *v* to bring together from a variety of places • *The researchers have collected the data and will soon publish the results.*

conduct Ⓐ *v* to organize and direct a particular activity • *The scientists conducted an experiment using rats.*

distinct Ⓐ *adj* clearly separate and different • *There are distinct differences between the teenage brain and the adult brain.*

experiment *n* a scientific study • *Scientists used mice in an experiment to see how the brain responds to stress.*

extensive *adj* a lot of; wide-ranging • *Extensive research shows that male and female brains are different.*

hunter *n* a person who kills or captures animals • *Traditionally, men rather than women were the hunters.*

imagine *v* to have a picture or idea of something in your mind • *Can you imagine life in the next century?*

intelligent Ⓐ *adj* having the ability to learn and understand something well • *The teacher was obviously very intelligent.*

interpret Ⓐ *v* to describe or understand the meaning of something • *Men and women interpret information differently.*

intuition *n* an ability to know something based on feelings • *My intuition told me something was wrong.*

recall *v* to remember • *As people grow older, it becomes harder to recall specific information.*

route Ⓐ *n* the way from one place to another • *Men are usually good at remembering routes.*

sense *v* to feel or be aware of something • *Mothers can often sense when something is wrong with their children.*

spatial *adj* related to space • *Engineers often have very strong spatial skills; they can see objects in their minds.*

superior *adj* better • *Private universities are not always superior to public ones.*

tend to *v* to be more likely to do something • *Boys tend to play video games more than girls do.*

Addiction and the Brain

admit *v* to recognize and accept something as true • *The boy admitted he had left school early that day.*

amount *n* how much something is; often related to time and money • *Many parents spend a huge amount of time helping their children with homework.*

antibody *n* a chemical the body produces to fight disease • *Antibodies from their mother's milk protect babies from disease-causing bacteria.*

anxious *adj* nervous; worried • *I felt anxious as I waited for the doctor to see me.*

attitude Ⓐ *n* an opinion or feeling about something • *The public attitude toward mental health is changing.*

breakthrough *n* an important discovery or new idea • *There have been several medical breakthroughs recently.*

chance *n* the possibility or opportunity to do something • *There is a good chance that you will recover completely.*

clarify Ⓐ *v* to make something clear and easy to understand • *Could you please clarify what you just said?*

desire *n* a strong hope or need to do something • *It is hard to quit smoking because the desire for a cigarette is very strong.*

genetic *adj* the biological process of passing things from parents to children • *Scientists disagree about which behaviors are genetic and which are learned as we grow up.*

imitate *v* to copy • *Some drugs imitate natural chemicals found in the brain.*

interrupt *v* to stop something before it finishes • *The teacher interrupted me while I was explaining why I was late.*

item Ⓐ *n* one thing that is part of a list • *I needed several items at the pharmacy .*

nicotine *n* a dangerous chemical in tobacco • *Smokers quickly become addicted to nicotine.*

physically Ⓐ *adv* related to the body • *Men are usually physically stronger than women.*

purchase *n* something you buy • *I felt I shouldn't have made so many purchases.*

treatment *n* the medicines and other things used to cure an illness or injury • *Addicts often need to go to a special center for treatment.*

vaccine *n* a substance used to stop people from getting a particular disease • *Children get several vaccines when they are young.*

Index to Key Vocabulary

Words that are part of the Academic Word List are noted with an Ⓐ in this appendix.

Improving Your Reading Speed

Good readers read quickly and understand most of what they read. However, like other skills, reading faster is a skill that requires good technique and practice. One way to practice is to read frequently. Read about topics you are interested in, not just topics from your academic courses. Reading for pleasure will improve your reading speed and understanding.

Another way to practice is to choose a text you have already read and read it again without stopping. Time yourself, record the time, and keep a record of how your reading speed is increasing.

These strategies will help you improve your reading speed:

- Before you read a text, look at the title and any illustrations. Ask yourself, *What is this reading about?* This will help you figure out the general topic of the reading.
- Read words in groups instead of reading every single word. Focus on the most important words in a sentence – usually the nouns, verbs, adjectives, and adverbs.
- Don't pronounce each word as you read. Pronouncing words will slow you down and does not help you to understand the text.
- Don't use a pencil or your finger to point to the words as you read. This will also slow you down.
- Continue reading even if you come to an unfamiliar word. Good readers know that they can skip unfamiliar words as long as they understand the general meaning of the text.

Calculating Your Reading Speed

After you have completed a unit in this book, reread one of the readings. Use your cellphone or your watch to time how long it takes you to complete the reading. Write down the number of minutes and seconds it took you in the chart on the following pages.

You can figure out your reading speed; that is your words per minute (wpm) rate by doing the following calculation:

First, convert the seconds of your reading time to decimals using the table to the right.

Next, divide the number of words per reading by the time it took you to complete the reading. For example, if the reading is 525 words, and it took you 5 minutes 50 seconds, your reading speed is about 90 words per minute (525 ÷ 5.83 = 90).

Record your wpm rate in the chart on the following pages.

Seconds	Decimal
:05	.08
:10	.17
:15	.25
:20	.33
:25	.42
:30	.50
:35	.58
:40	.67
:45	.75
:50	.83
:55	.92

UNIT	READING TITLE	NUMBER OF WORDS IN READING	YOUR READING TIME minutes:seconds 00:00	READING SPEED (WPM)
Unit 1 The News Media	The News Media in the Past	687	_____ : _____	
	The History of Electronic Media	621	_____ : _____	
	Citizen Journalism	924	_____ : _____	
	Ethical Reporting	1,263	_____ : _____	
Unit 2 Education	Education Around the World	706	_____ : _____	
	Testing in Education	975	_____ : _____	
	Alternative Education	802	_____ : _____	
	Skills for the Twenty-First Century	1,152	_____ : _____	
Unit 3 The World of Business	Supply and Demand in the Global Economy	723	_____ : _____	
	The Workforce of the Twenty-First Century	745	_____ : _____	
	Communication Technology in Business	900	_____ : _____	
	Business and Sustainability	1,092	_____ : _____	

UNIT	READING TITLE	NUMBER OF WORDS IN READING	YOUR READING TIME minutes:seconds 00:00	READING SPEED (WPM)
Unit 4 Population Change and Its Impact	Population Trends	908	_____ : _____	
	Global Migration	703	_____ : _____	
	The Growth of Cities	633	_____ : _____	
	Challenges Facing the World's Cities	1,380	_____ : _____	
Unit 5 Design in Everyday Life	The Design of Everyday Objects	986	_____ : _____	
	Ergonomics	746	_____ : _____	
	The Design of Living Space	701	_____ : _____	
	Fashion	1,343	_____ : _____	
Unit 6 The Brain and Behavior	Brain Development and Function	848	_____ : _____	
	The Teenage Brain	1,027	_____ : _____	
	The Male and Female Brain	916	_____ : _____	
	Addiction and the Brain	1,323	_____ : _____	

UNIT 1, READING 1

McLean, A. 2004. This Month in History. *Smithsonian*, May.

UNIT 1, READING 3

Kahney, L. 2003. Citizen Reporters Make the News. *Wired*, May 17. http://www.wired.com/culture/ lifestyle/news/ 2003/05/58856.

Stelter, B. and Cohen, N. 2008. Citizen Journalists Provided Glimpses of Mumbai Attacks. *New York Times*, November 29. http://www.nytimes.com/2008/11/30/world/asia/ 30twitter.html

UNIT 1, READING 4

Banville, L. 2006. Background Report: The Janet Cooke Case. *The Online NewsHour, PBS*. http://www.pbs.org/ newshour/bradlee/background_cooke.html (accessed Aug. 12, 2008).

Paper Exposes Palace Security. 2003. *BBC*, November 19. http://news.bbc.co.uk/2/hi/uk_news/3282625.stm.

Sandoval, G. and McCullagh, D. 2011. How Gizmodo Escaped Indictment in iPhone Prototype Deal. *CNET*, October 12. http://news.cnet.com/8301-13579_3-20118994-37/how-gizmodo-escaped-indictment-in-iphone-prototype-deal/

UNIT 2, READING 1

Carey, K. 2004. The Funding Gap. *The Education Trust*. http://www2.edtrust.org/EdTrust/Product+Catalog/main. htm#ff.

Siegel, B. 2007. Stressful Times for Chinese Students. *Time*, June 12. http://www.time.com/time/printout/ 0,8816,1631854,00.html

United Nations Educational, Scientific and Cultural Organization. 2005. Global Education Digest. Montreal: UNESCO Institute for Statistics.

UNIT 2, READING 2

Arenson, K. 2007. World Briefing. *New York Times*, March 13.

Bureau of labor statistics – www.bls.gov/emp/ep_chart_ 001.htm

Economist. 2006. Back to School. March 23.

Ihlwan, M. 2000. South Koreans Are Crazy for Cramming. *BusinessWeek*, October 30.

Moore, L. 2007. The Secret to Smarter Schools. *U.S. News & World Report*, 142:11, March 26.

Organisation for Economic Co-operation and Development, Programme for International Student OECD, PISA 2009 Database http://www.oecd.org/pisa/

Rowley, I., and H. Tashiro. 2005. Japan: Crazy for Cramming. *BusinessWeek*, April 18.

Vencat, E. 2006. The Perfect Score. *Newsweek International*, March 27.

UNIT 2, READING 3

Associated Press. 2005. Summit Told U.S. High Schools "Obsolete." February 26. http://www.msnbc.msn.com/ id/7033821/.

Going the Distance: Online Education in the United States. 2011, *Sloan Consortium*. http://sloanconsortium.org/ publications/survey/going_distance_2011

National Center for Education Statistics. 2005. Participation in Education: Homeschooled Students. *The Condition of Education*. Table. http://nces.ed.gov/programs/coe/2005/ section1/table.asp?tableID=227.

UNIT 2, READING 4

Economist. 2007. Capturing Talent. August 16.

Internet World Stats. Internet Usage Statistics. http:// internetworldstats.com/

UNIT 3, READING 1

Economist. 2007. Cheap No More. December 6.

Economist. 2007. The End of Cheap Food. December 6.

Grillo, I. 2007. 75,000 Protest Tortilla Prices in Mexico. *Washington Post*, February 1. http://www.washingtonpost. com.

UNIT 3, READING 2

CIO Update. 2010. It's Not Just Developer Jobs Going Overseas. December 2. http://cioupdate.com/career/ article.php/3915431/Its-Not-Just-Developer-Jobs-Going-Overseas.htm

World Bank, Development Prospects Group, Migration and Remittances Team. 2006. *Remittance Trends 2006*. Migration and Development Brief 2. http://siteresources. worldbank.org/INTPROSPECTS/Resources/334934-1110315015165/MigrationDevelopmentBriefingNov2006. pdf.

UNIT 3, SKILLS AND STRATEGIES 6

Internet World Stats. Internet Usage Statistics. http:// internetworldstats.com/

UNIT 3, READING 3

CAAM. 2011. Chinese Motorcycle Production Increase. December 14. http://www.caam.org.cn/MotorCycle Statistics/20111214/1005065619.html

Howe, J. 2006. The Rise of Crowdsourcing. *Wired*, June 14.

The Wall. 2011. Five ways brands are using crowdsourcing in 2011. May 18. http://wallblog.co.uk/2011/05/18/five-ways-brands-are-using-crowdsourcing-in-2011/

Weingarten, M. 2007. Designed to grow. *Fortune Small Business*, July/August, 17:6.

World Bank, Data & Statistics. 2007. *World Development Indicators 2007*. July. http://web.worldbank.org/WBSITE/ EXTERNAL/DATASTATISTICS/0,,contentMDK:20399244 ~menuPK:1504474~pagePK: 64133150~piPK:64133175~ theSitePK:239419,00.html.

UNIT 3, READING 4

Fishman, C. 2006. How Many Lightbulbs Does It Take to Change the World? One. And You're Looking at It. *Fast Company*, September.

Fishman, C. 2007. How Green is Wal-Mart? *Fast Company*, September.

Gunther, M. 2007. Green Is Good. *Fortune*, April 2, 155:6.

Martin, A. 2007. In Eco-Friendly Factory, Low-Guilt Potato Chips. *New York Times*, November 15. McGregor, J. 2005. Green Thumbs. *Fast Company*, December.

Raupach, M., et al. 2007. Anthropogenic C Emissions: Fossil Fuel. In Recent Carbon Trends and the Global Carbon Budget, by P. Canasell, et al, fig. *Global Carbon Project*, November 15. http://www.globalcarbonproject.org/products/reports.htm.

Revkin, A., and M. Wald. 2007. Solar Power Wins Enthusiasts but Not Money. *New York Times*, July 16.

Seeking Alpha. 2011. The Real Issue with Solar Energy Isn't its Cost. November 9. http://seekingalpha.com/article/306468-the-real-issue-with-solar-energy-isn-t-its-cost

Worldwatch Institute. 2007. World Annual Photovoltaic Production, 1975–2007.

UNIT 4, READING 1

Allen, J. D. 2006. Population Growth over Human History. Lecture, University of Michigan, January 4. http://www.globalchange.umich.edu/globalchange2/current/lectures/human_pop/human_pop.html.

Economist, 2007. How to Deal with a Falling Population. July 26.

Krock, L. 2004. World in Balance. *Nova*, *PBS*, April. http://www.pbs.org/wgbh/nova/worldbalance/campaigns.html.

Population Reference Bureau. 2007. World Population Highlights. *Population Bulletin*, September, 62:3. http://www.prb.org/Publications/Datasheets/2007/2007WorldPopulationDataSheet.aspx.

UNIT 4, READING 2

BBC News. 2004. Factfile: Global Migration. Special Report: Migrant World. BBC, March 19. http://news.bbc.co.uk/2/shared/spl/hi/world/04/migration/html/migration_boom.stm.

DeParle, J. 2007. A Global Trek to Poor Nations, from Poorer Ones. *New York Times*, December 27.

DeParle, J. 2007. Rising Breed of Migrant Worker: Skilled, Salaried and Welcome. *New York Times*, August 20.

Schrover, M. 2004. Migration: A Historical Perspective. *BBC News*, March 23.

UNIT 4, READING 3

Klenieski, N. 2002. *Cities, Change and Conflict: A Political Economy of Urban Life*. Belmont, CA: Wadsworth.

Rubenstein, J. 2004. *The Cultural Landscape: An Introduction to Human Geography*. Upper Saddle River, NJ: Prentice Hall.

United Nations Department of Economic and Social Affairs, Population Division. 2006. *World Urbanization Prospects: The 2005 Revision*. New York, United Nations Publication, October. http://www.un.org/esa/population/publications/WUP2005/2005wup.htm.

UNIT 4, READING 4

About.com. Top 10 Cities of the Year 1950. From *Four Thousand Years of Urban Growth: A Historical Census*, by T. Chandler (Lewiston, NY: St. David's University Press, 1987). Table. http://geography.about.com/library/weekly/aa011201g.htm.

Kraas, F. 2007. Megacities and Global Change: Key Priorities. *Geographical Journal*, March.

Levinson, H. 2008. Tomb with a View. *BBC News*, March 6. http://news.bbc.co.uk/.

Naim, M. 2007. The Hidden Pandemic. *Foreign Policy*, July/August.

Rubenstein, J. 2004. *The Cultural Landscape: An Introduction to Human Geography*. Upper Saddle River, NJ: Prentice Hall.

State of the World's Cities 2010/2011: Bridging the Urban Divide UN-Habitat UN Human Settlements Programme

United Nations. 2007. World Urbanization Prospects. *2007 Revision*. http://www.un.org/esa/population/publications/wup2007/2007WUP_ExecSum_web.pdf

United Nations Human Settlements Programme. 2007. Crime and Violence: Facts and Figures. In *Enhancing Urban Safety and Security – Global Report on Human Settlements 2007*. London and Sterling, VA: UN-Habitat / Earthscan.

United Nations Office for the Coordination of Humanitarian Affairs and UN-HABITAT. 2007. Tomorrow's Crises Today: The Humanitarian Impact of Urbanization – Overview. IRIN News Service, September. http://www.irinnews.org/InDepthMain.aspx?InDepthId=63&ReportId=73996.

UNIT 5, SKILLS AND STRATEGIES 9

Browne, A. 2008. Profile in Style: Philippe Starck. *New York Times Style Magazine*, March 16.

UNIT 5, READING 1

Jordan, P. 2000. *Designing Pleasurable Products*. London: Taylor and Francis.

Marcus, G. 2002. *What Is Design Today?* New York: Abrams.

Norman, D. 2002. *The Design of Everyday Things*. New York: Basic Books.

Norman, D. 2004. *Emotional Design*. New York: Basic Books.

UNIT 5, READING 2

Ehrenfeld, T. 2007. Five Reasons Your Office Is Bad for You. *Newsweek*, December 14.

Friess, S. 2005. Laptop Design Can Be a Pain in the Posture. *USA Today*, April 12.

Health Canada. Adjusting and Adapting Your Workstation. http://www.hc-sc.gc.ca/ewh-semt/occup-travail/checklist-aidememoire_e.html.

Van, J. 2006. Lean Back Study Finds 135-Degree Body-Thigh Angle Is Better than Straight Up for Long Periods of Sitting. *Chicago Tribune*, December 6.

UNIT 5, READING 4

Bay, O. 1997. Life, Young Street. *Toronto Star*, September 30.

Berfield, S. 2003. The CEO of Hip-Hop. *BusinessWeek*, October 27.

Lurie, A. 1981. *The Language of Clothes*. New York: Random House.

Patton, P. 2008. Urban Outfitters. *Fast Company*, February.

Survey Shows 24 Percent of Americans Ages 18-50 Are Tattooed, *Fox News*, June 12, 2006. http://www.foxnews.com/story/0,2933,199143,00.html

UNIT 6, SKILLS AND STRATEGIES 11

Carey, B. 2007. Brain Injury Said to Affect Moral Choices. *New York Times*, March 22.

CBS. 2000. Do "Munchies" Mirror Our Inner Selves? *CBS Worldwide*, August 29. http://www.cbsnews.com/stories/2000/08/29/national/main228848.shtml.

Pinker, S. 2008. The Moral Instinct. *New York Times Sunday Magazine*, January 13.

UNIT 6, READING 1

Freudenrich, C. 2001. How Your Brain Works. June 6. http://www.howstuffworks.com/brain.htm.

Guttman, M. 2001. The Aging Brain. *USC Health Magazine Online*, Spring. http://www.usc.edu/hsc/info/pr/hmm/01spring/brain.html.

Moffett, S. 2006. *The Three-Pound Enigma*. Chapel Hill, NC: Algonquin Books.

UNIT 6, READING 2

Frontline. 2002. Inside the Teenage Brain. *Frontline, PBS*. http://www.pbs.org/wgbh/pages/frontline/shows/teenbrain/.

Goudarzi, A. 2006. Teenage Brain Lacks Empathy. *Msnbc.com Live Science*, September 8. http://www.msnbc.msn.com/id/14738243&csid=0.

National Institute of Mental Health. 2008. Teenage Brain: A Work in Progress. National Institutes of Health, June 26. http://www.nimh.nih.gov/health/publications/teenage-brain-a-work-in-progress.shtml.

Wallis, C. 2004. What Makes Teens Tick? *Time*, May 10.

Wendel, T. 2003. The Teen Brain. *USA Weekend*, May 18.

UNIT 6, READING 3

BBC Science and Nature. 2005. Secrets of the Sexes: Brainsex. Programme 1. BBC, July. http://www.bbc.co.uk/sn/tvradio/programmes/sexsecrets/.

Kimura, D. 2002. Sex Differences in the Brain. *Scientific American*, May 13.

Marano, H. 2003. The New Sex Scorecard. *Psychology Today*, July–August.

Moir, A., and D. Jessel. 1992. *Brain Sex*. New York: Dell.

Onion, A. 2005. Scientists Find Sex Differences in Brain. *ABC News*, January 19. http://abcnews.go.com/Technology/Health/story?id=424260&page=1.

Wolinsky, H. 2008. Why Are Girls Better At Language Than Boys? *Chicago Tribune*, April 1.

UNIT 6, READING 4

Cate, B. 2003. Cocaine and Your Brain. *Scholastic Choice* 19:2, October.

D'Angelo, L. 2004. Brain Change: Two Very Different Ways. *Science World* 60:14, April 26.

Dell, K. 2005. Paths to Pleasure. *Time*, January 9.

Denizet-Lewis, B. 2006. An Anti-addiction Pill? *New York Times Sunday Magazine*, June 25.

Interlandi, J. 2008. Are Vaccines the Answer to Addiction? *Newsweek*, January 14.

Interlandi, J. 2008. What Addicts Need. *Newsweek*, March 3.

Johnson, S. 2005. Your Brain on Video Games. *Discover*, July 24.

Lemonick, M. 2007. The Science of Addiction. *Time*, July 16.

Nash, J. 1997. Addicted. *Time*, May 5.